Songwriting

Andrew West is Professor and Head of Postgraduate Studies at Leeds College of Music. Previously a professional songwriter in London and Nashville, he designed and ran the world's first MA Songwriting at Bath Spa University, where he was made a fellow in 2009.

The Art of Songwriting

Andrew West

Bloomsbury Methuen Drama

An imprint of Bloomsbury Publishing Plc

B L O O M S B U R Y

LONDON · OXFORD · NEW YORK · NEW DELHI · SYDNEY

Bloomsbury Methuen Drama

An imprint of Bloomsbury Publishing Plc

Imprint previously known as Methuen Drama

50 Bedford Square	1385 Broadway
London	New York
WC1B 3DP	NY 10018
UK	USA

www.bloomsbury.com

BLOOMSBURY, METHUEN DRAMA and the Diana logo are trademarks of Bloomsbury Publishing Plc

First published 2016

British Library Cataloguing-in-Publication Data
A catalogue record for this book is available from the British Library.

ISBN: PB: 978-1-4725-2781-3
ePDF: 978-1-4725-2811-7
ePub: 978-1-4725-2440-9

Library of Congress Cataloging-in-Publication Data
A catalog record for this book is available from the Library of Congress

Cover design by Alice Marwick

Typeset by Fakenham Prepress Solutions, Fakenham, Norfolk NR21 8NN
Printed and bound in India

CONTENTS

ACKNOWLEDGEMENTS

I would like to thank Rachelle and Ethan for the eye of the tiger, my mum for singing along to the radio, Roger Cook for the sentimental education, Stephen Ward for the real education, the British Library for the archive, Paul Rutter for the critical eye, Nick Lowe for the postcard, John Prine for the map, and Anna Brewer for the invaluable guidance. Thanks also to my students, past and present. I could have written it without you, but it would have been short.

INTRODUCTION

A number of highly valuable books exist to help the beginner songwriter write better songs; in this field *The Craft and Business of Songwriting* by John Braheny and *Tunesmith* by Jimmy Webb are unsurpassed. By exploring the mechanisms of song to identify and contextualize the elements that convey emotion and communicate meaning, this book shares that aim. Cognizant that those who listen to songs don't tend to write them, it is equally intended for those who are not songwriters, but would like to know more about why, among the arts, song is considered both universal and mysterious in character.

I come to the writing of this book as a songwriter and as a critical listener, a combination that inclines me to consider not only how songs are made, but also how they are perceived. By examining the processes that go into their making and exploring the types of effect they can have upon audiences, *The Art of Songwriting* seeks to move the reader closer to an understanding of what songs are, and what they do. Reflecting Elliott's criticism that music texts tend to be linear and propositional, moving the reader quickly from concept to concept (1995: 246), his fellow author Schafer views the experience of music as more of a mosaic than a linear progression (1995: 94). Since much of what we know about song comes to us courtesy of innate capacities for music and language already developed at birth, in a sense we are all experts in the field. This natural expertise is, however, continually refracted through the lens of our unique individual experience, and with the comments of Elliott and Schafer in mind, I have tried to write this book using the lightest of prescriptive frameworks.

Our cultural narrative continues to imbue the worlds of literature, film and art with sumptuous layers of context, yet historically song has received relatively scant critical attention. While the seminal works of Proust, Malevich and Woody Allen can be absorbed as commentary and artefact on a balanced footing, with very few exceptions the equally durable – and often more popular – song has to sing for its own supper. Yet our lasting obsession with popular song can't just be a matter of call and response; as John Prine (1995) sings, 'Fifty million Elvis Presley fans can't be all wrong'. By deconstructing, analysing and rationalizing song in its myriad forms, I have set out to do my best to demystify the art. Dissenting or suspicious voices exist; as Keith Richards (1977) and Leonard Cohen (cited in Zollo 2003: 335) warn, nobody – not even the songwriter – knows where songs come from. I disagree with these honourable gentlemen on remarkably few things, but on this one issue I would beg to differ.

Hiding in a relative's loft one dimly lit evening in the late seventies, I chanced upon a dusty rack of sepia-tinted Buddy Holly Extended Plays. Schooled in the theatrical pretence of leather-jacketed pop stars with names like Marc and Suzi, I wasn't expecting all that much from the wholesome, bespectacled individual whose smiling face beamed from the sleeve, or from cardboard titles like 'Everyday', 'That'll be the day' or 'Wishing'. As a spark for the imagination, they paled into insignificance alongside 'King of the rumbling spires' and 'Metal guru'. Nevertheless, with time to burn and the naturally inquisitive mind of a ten-year-old, I read through the short biography written on each of the back sleeves: the humble boy from the rural heartland; the whirlwind rise to fame; the great promise; the tragic end. Eyeing the Roberts turntable in the corner, I emptied out the long-neglected vinyl and surveyed the surface scratches, wondering what sort of metamorphosis could possibly bring all of this bleak, monochromatic information to life. As I introduced each side, one by one, to the needle, I felt my impressionable young soul entering the world of Buddy Holly, sinking in to the music, never to return. It wasn't just the brightness of sound or the compositional economy that drew me in with such unquestioning force; it was the authenticity of expression. It was *real*.

A few years later, I formed a band of my own and we rode around in a van, occasionally alighting to play our own tunes to a variety of either captive or disinterested audiences. Uncomplicated fun was the currency, and in that sense we did very well. Then, in 1990 Hugh Cornwell invited me to join a band that became known as Cornwell, Cook and West. While at first I knew very little about the other member of the trio, Roger Cook, I had for a long time been a fan of Hugh's band The Stranglers. While back in the late seventies and early eighties The Sex Pistols, Joy Division, and later New Order were bands I related to on an emotional level, Hugh's band were intriguingly distant, full of intellectual ideas that most folk would never contemplate. In songs like 'Genetix' and 'The man they love to hate' they used strange time signatures, almost impossibly thick bass textures and virtuosic synthesizer lines to create a sound that made them difficult to categorize or trace. The lyrics tended to be about birds, historical figures or unidentified flying objects; in essence The Stranglers were elusive and as they moved from album to album, their sound kept evolving. They didn't have any love songs and I could never even begin to imagine where their songs came from or how they wrote them. Much as I enjoyed working with Hugh, three decades later I still don't.

Soon after joining CCW, as we tuned ukuleles and sipped rough cider backstage at London's Bloomsbury Theatre, I asked Roger if he had written any songs I might have heard. Quite casually he ran through a few random verses and choruses of 'Something's got a hold of my heart', 'Here comes that rainy day feeling' and 'You've got your troubles (I've got mine)'. In those off-the-cuff performances, for a fleeting moment I glimpsed the immensity of the journey from notoriety to recognition. Like Hugh, Roger was someone from the land of jukebox music, an artist and above all a *communicator* whose songs people *understood*. These were not just songwriters who wrote great songs, they were also performers who made great records.

Over the next few years, as CCW veered unpredictably and blissfully unconcerned between Van Morrison's Wool Hall recording studio, our local pub Tuckers Grave, the London Palladium and a variety of other venues large and small, I would watch Roger from my position at stage left, and try to figure out why I had to work so hard to captivate an audience, yet he seemed to find it so easy. Then, one night it struck me that the songs he was singing had been written by someone who had opened their mind to song *entirely*, who at the moment of writing was free of inhibition or limitation, and whose creative process had allowed him to create songs capable of fearlessly drifting out there into the world of sound.

As anyone who knows Roger or Hugh will testify, in casual conversation, neither would choose to discuss the intellectual merits of songwriting. Any discussion about Marvin Gaye, The Inkspots, Captain Beefheart or Frank Zappa would inevitably be about how great certain records were, never any kind of critical appreciation. As songwriters, there were distinct differences between the two though. While almost every song Hugh wrote ended up on one of his records, of the 3,000 that Roger has written, the wider world is familiar with around fifty. Over time, I began to sense that their respective writing methods were quite different; while Hugh would absorb people, places and ideas that interested him and then convey his impressions of the experience to his audience, Roger would strum away, delving into his subconscious to see what, if anything, might come out.

What continues to make both great at what they do, the defining element that the millions who love their work connect with, is an unmistakeable authenticity in the song crafting and performance that comes from ownership, from self-knowledge. Neither sets out to impress, and neither relies upon guesswork. In 1990, as a young songwriter searching for my own voice and struggling to get to grips with the artistic enormity of The Beatles and Bob Dylan, it was a revelation to discover that there was more than one way to write songs. In the years to follow, I have come to realize there are, in fact, an infinite number of ways to go about writing a song, and that it is up to the individual to find his or her own method. Back then all I had to do was figure out which one was mine.

After CCW, I spent a few years rewriting US chart hits for use in film and television. As a library writer for Carlin in London, my role was to analyse and reinterpret existing songs, a discipline that got me deep into the psyche of the serial hit writer. This work was fruitful enough to propel me back and forth to Nashville for a couple of years, and before too long I had co-written about eighty songs with Nashville-based songwriters including Jennifer Kimball, Will Kimbrough, Robert Ellis Orrall, Kim Richey and my old mate, recently relocated to Tennessee, Roger Cook.

While each co-write inevitably led to a finished song, the process involved was always different. With Jennifer, we would discuss our separate lists of song titles, eventually agreeing on one that meant something to both of us. Using our voices as the focal point, the remainder of the song would be written without instruments; guitars, pianos, bass and drums would be added later. Co-writing with Tom Littlefield would be like completing a compositional crossword puzzle, with each syllable examined in forensic detail for sound and meaning. At her old place on Highway 96, Kim Richey would start the process by strumming a chord or two, casting the collaborative net. While most songs took a day to complete, each of the half-dozen songs I wrote with my West End Avenue neighbour Bill DeMain were co-written in under an hour. Sometimes Bill would write almost the entire song, and sometimes the shoe was on the other foot.

Helpfully, the process of adapting to each of these collabo-rative paradigms gradually sharpened my understanding of how I wrote best as a solo songwriter. By trying some methods and leaving others behind, I developed my own methodology, and eventually, one afternoon in 1998, I wrote a song called 'Someone up there' that, as far as I could tell, didn't sound like anyone else. The song captured the essence of what I wanted to convey, and in that sense it was a significant breakthrough for me as a songwriter.

During the six years I lived and wrote in the United States, Roger Cook and I eventually wrote around thirty songs together. In his writing room at Island Bound or in mine across the road at Warner Chappell, we would convene at 10.00 in the morning and write until 1.00. Somehow completing an unlikely route of musical time travel, two of our collaborations 'Sliding down the razor blade of love' and 'Too late now' were recorded by Stackridge and Joe Brown, artists who had influenced bands who had influenced me. The more Roger and I wrote together, the more I realized that, like him, I was inclined to write *anything* that instinctively felt like a good idea and to later review it and see if it was actually any good. As if lost in the sound, for large parts of the creative process my critical facility was virtually non-existent. The more I co-wrote, however, the more I found myself developing the strange and heightened ability, as Ivor Novello award-winning songwriter Iain Archer (2014) puts it, to work in a simultaneously cerebral and intuitive way; to create *and* be critical at the same time. This facility connected me to ideas in my subconscious mind: images and phrases hitherto lost in the jumble of a lifetime of listening and music making. Maybe that's what Keith Richards and Leonard Cohen are talking about when they say they don't know where songs come from, in which case our perspectives are happily reconciled.

Three hundred songs later I found myself back in England, being invited to design and oversee the world's first Master's degree in Songwriting. Within four years, Jez Ashurst, Paul Statham and I were told we had the second most successful Postgraduate course in the history of Bath Spa University, and along the way I would like to think we helped some extremely nice people become better songwriters. Central to our philosophy was the notion of encouraging students to discover the method of songwriting that allowed them, as individuals, to create songs that reflected and in some way succeeded in communicating what they intended to say. Once they had found a method that worked for them, that allowed them to draw from the well of their own being, the productivity and quality of the songwriting invariably went up. The songwriters were no longer waiting for inspiration to strike, but were instead using self-understanding to generate songs as they wished them to be heard. This notion of creative control, that songwriters can use critical and metacognitive networks to develop an original and communicative voice, is a thread in Chapter 3 of this book.

The Art of Songwriting is divided into three chapters: 'Song', 'Songwriters' and 'Songwriting'. Following an exploration of what songs are said to be, Chapter 1 surveys what is known about what I would argue to be the constituent elements of song: Music; Words; Structure; Creativity; and Communication. In doing so, the chapter aims to develop a granular image of song.

Using a series of sketches of modern songwriters, Chapter 2 moves from what song *is* to what songwriters *do*. To convey a sense of creative breadth, it uses a range of analytical methods to show how greatness is in part characterized by individuality – the unique fingerprint of each songwriter. Drawn from the era of popular recorded music, the songwriters included are a selection of those active during the past one hundred years, 1915–2015.

Adopting a more pedagogical tone, Chapter 3 explores how a songwriter might develop an effective methodology and acquire an individual voice. Finally, the chapter draws upon contemporary industrial and sociological thought and research to speculate upon how the songwriter, and the wider critical community, might collaborate to develop the art.

1

Song

1.1 Definition

As brief as 'You suffer' by Napalm Death, which is one second long, or as meditative as Television's 'Marquee moon', which is a few hundred times longer – as the twenty-first century unravels, songs in their myriad shapes and forms have become increasingly difficult to define. With the continued global expansion of genre and subgenre, and the increasing diversification of local, national and international markets, the listener is faced with an ever-expanding number of options. More than ever, there seems to be music for all occasions. For us listeners, it is perhaps this unpredictability, this sense of not knowing what combination of sounds might be coming next, that keeps us tuned in. For, as the emergence of playlists and the rise of prime time song-based television shows would indicate, after a century of popular recorded song our collective appetite for separating the songs we love from the songs we can live without is perhaps stronger than ever.

While there are some song structures we encounter more than others, and within some traditional and commercial fields there are instrumental textures we have become conditioned to anticipate, inside the compositional signature lies the authentic and individual, the interplay of real and metaphorical voices that resonate with and reflect the joy and tragedy of our existence; expressive bursts of organized sound waiting to be heard and felt. When we hear a great song, the sounds we absorb and relate to mirror and sometimes animate our lives. Almost unnoticed, the pleasures we take in identifying the expressive intention and deciphering the subtext feel as natural as breathing. The armchair critic in us can't wait to pass judgement. But what are songs? If, as Hallam (2001) claims, we all inherently understand music and language, why can't we all write a song that others can relate to? Why is one version of a song so much better than another? Why does our mind wander during one song and remain focused during the next? Why do some songs linger long in the memory while others disappear like smoke?

By definition, songs are a combination of things. In skeletal form they are the words and melodies we sing unaccompanied. As the philosopher Suzanne Langer observes (1953: 25, 26), songs are often spontaneous expressions of feeling that leap forth untamed. Making an important distinction between what might be considered expression and what might be classified as art, Langer adds that while *expression* refers solely to the condition of the songwriter, *art* occurs when expressions are given clearly for contemplation. To develop a performance, then, to qualify the actual existence of song, we need not only to tune our memory into a sound we take pleasure in rehearsing, we need also to shape our sound for an audience.

To illustrate this transition, a street performer has passed the rehearsal phase and is ready for us to engage and interpret her performance. The song she plans to sing, with voice and guitar, is 'Hey Jude' by The Beatles. Moving past what Toynbee (2000: 63) would view as an intentional effort to avoid musical expressionism, an action he would consider 'anti-creative' in the sense that it seeks to deny the existence of social relations between the musician and listeners in general, in doing so she will make the leap from solipsism to communication, from catharsis to expression.

Unfortunately, our busker is nervous and sings 'Hey Jude' at double speed. Our relationship with the original recording, made known to us by its yearning vocal, warm ensemble playing and oceanic coda somehow leads us to make a snap decision that this interpretation is 'wrong'; that our received understanding of the text is not being observed. In the absence of other textures, perhaps a banjo or ukulele, to give us a further clue, all we have to go on is a briskly delivered voice and guitar. By compromising the melody and diminishing the breadth of expression to which we have become accustomed, the busker seems to be missing the point.

The next day, however, our busker returns and is joined by a mandolin player and a fiddler. Now, moderated by the influence of the ensemble, the song is being played with gentle swing, at a tempo that allows the melody to be heard and the words to be absorbed. The spaces between each vocal phrase are longer, so the gathering crowds have enough time to review and consider what they are hearing, to become immersed in the new reading and its original, unfamiliar instrumentation, or perhaps to relate the new version back to the original. On the choruses, the mandolinist and fiddler sing harmony, and by differentiating the sound of the verses and choruses, this adds dynamic to the performance. A mandolin solo adds a dimension of continuity that wasn't possible with solo guitar, and when the coda arrives, the sound of all three instruments playing together produces a noise emotive enough to draw the attention of even the most reticent bystander.

The point of the busker illustration is that all songs seek interpretation. Emphasizing both its social function and the individuality of song in its written form, Frith (1987: 97) asserts that songs are always performances heard in someone's accent. As 'speech acts', he claims, songs have semantic meaning but are also structures of sound that convey emotion and character. Even the finest, most brilliantly written words and music can easily evade their compositional potential and conversely, in the right hands, the most unspectacular of compositions can be brought to life.

With apologies to its author Bill Campbell, the music and words of 'One sided love affair', an unexceptional composition given by A&R man Stephen Sholes to Elvis Presley for possible inclusion on his debut album, presented numerous challenges to the performer as he entered RCA studios in New York one winter's morning in 1956. Listening to the eventual recording, we are led to identify with Cloonan's observation that the way lyrics are sung may bear little relation to how they appear on the page (2005: 79). As a composition, the lyrics, particularly those in the verses, project the most straightforward of romantic propositions, altering only to introduce slight variations on the type of romance to be reciprocated. As lyric poetry it is negligible, as conversational language it is basic, an impression amplified by the familiar, generic twelve-bar blues of the music. The lyric in the bridge, which stubbornly favours the tonic chord, ventures into some complex, near-unintelligible colloquial slang, that in terms of continuity bears little resemblance to the mumbling ramble of the character who delivers the preceding verse. For an interval of eight bars, it is as if the narrator has swiftly downed a very strong cup of coffee.

As a composition, 'One sided love affair' is random enough to sound unfinished, so Campbell must have thought it was all his birthdays rolled into one when he heard what Elvis, Scotty and Bill had done with it. In his percussive delivery of the words and in particular his ability to fuse the surly and the comedic by inventing a version of himself capable of bridging the two, Elvis uses his musical and phrasing skills to project the song, as a recording in vivid technicolour. Aware of the interpretative dynamic best suited to an optimum performance, the band stays in the background while Elvis, bouncing consonants around the vocal booth, miraculously forges the text into a convincing patois.

In essence, song text and song performance are two different things, and to speak of one without the other is – as the widely attributed saying goes – to dance about architecture. This duality of forms, argues Sheldon (2004: 367), presents a kind of figurative language that is often indirect, circuitous and ambiguous, containing some terms that appear closer to the meaning of the central idea than others, sometimes resulting in the obscuring of communication. This, claims Sheldon, is both its trouble and its beauty.

This doesn't mean, however, that performers *need* to possess interpretative genius; they do however need to acquire performative sensitivity, or a sense of the parameters of what will work. Speaking to an invited audience in Leeds in 2013, Simon Aldred explained how he is able to identify a good song of his own, *because* it can be interpreted. 'If you write a good song you can twist it any way you want', he explained. 'Pull it apart and it will still form its original shape. Try a number of different tempos and styles; you may come back to the original idea. It should withstand whatever you do to it.' There is a subtle interpretative difference between Simon's modus operandi and the Bill Campbell/Elvis example here; few ever heard Bill Campbell's original version of 'One sided love affair', but most of Simon's recordings feature him as the central performer and producer. As a consequence, the songs he writes can be interpreted within the scope of his own direction, within the parameters of his own tastes as an arranger.

In Manchester's Blueprint rehearsal room one grey spring afternoon in 2014, Simon, fellow Mancunian songsmith Josephine Oniyama and I ran through some acoustic versions of the Cherry Ghost songs '4 AM' and 'Clear skies ever closer', both of which were penned by Simon. Every iteration, from Simon's initial bare acoustic sketch to our full vocal trio harmony treatment, worked, but without negotiating the issue, Josephine and I took care to play and sing as the song suggested. Returning to the earlier observations made by Frith and Cloonan, we understood the song to be in Simon's accent, and consequently we were obliged to interpret the song *in the air*, not *on the page*. Similarly, when Birdy recorded another of Simon's tunes, 'People help the people' in 2011, she was careful not to alter the core aspects of melody, lyric or structure of Simon's original Cherry Ghost version. Adding drums around a quarter or a third of the way through, the tempo on both versions hovers around 75 to 80 beats per minute and both use piano and strings extensively. It is an appropriate setting for the song.

There are other examples of the parameters implied by excellent composition. While Adele's 2008 version of 'Make you feel my love', initially written and recorded by Bob Dylan a decade earlier, calls upon a different range of instrumental sounds, preserving some of magic of the original interpretation it comes in at an identical 3 minutes and 32 seconds. There is still room for the song to be done 'wrong', perhaps by singing it without passion or too passionately, but neither Dylan nor Adele fall into those traps. Conversely, while Nina Simone's spare version of James Shelton's song 'Lilac wine' captures what *feels like* the intended state of intoxicated bliss, Elkie Brooks' heavily orchestrated version, recorded a decade later, has a sober and formal grandeur that showcases Brooks' magnificent voice, but fails to capture any of the reverie or abandon located by Nina Simone.

Is performance more important than text? While Godlovitch (1998: 14) makes a compelling argument that recordings are not performances, the iTunes and Spotify generation tends to view songs not as texts but as recorded performances, fully dimensional in production and arrangement. Words and music are of course important, not least because few performers possess the interpretative genius of Elvis. As if one of the elements barely existed, song listeners often categorize themselves as predominantly interested in words or music. In all song, however, the two are finely and deliberately balanced, each seeking to guide the listener through finely nuanced and sometimes contradictory fields of expression. From the perspective of the songwriter, to assume the listener possesses the capability to hear and translate every tiny nuance or detail of what is being expressed in a song would be a mistake. Too much information leaves too little to the imagination; all cannot possibly be revealed.

As CEO of Chrysalis, Jeremy Lascelles signed deals with Fleet Foxes, Bon Iver and Laura Marling; to say he has an ear for a good songwriter would be an understatement. In a West London café, Jeremy explained that great songs combine melody, lyric, concept and what he characterized as soulfulness of delivery. Adding that any judgement on which of these qualities is more important is entirely subjective, he continued: 'I would place melody as more important than lyric; there are dozens of great songs with average lyrics and great melodies, but there are very few great songs with great lyrics and poor melodies.' Jeremy acknowledges that the songwriter faces a significant challenge in seeking to create work that can withstand more than one listen, observing: 'The best songs, the profound ones, tend to take a few listens before they burrow their way into your soul. "Like a rolling stone" is my favourite song ever, but it took me ten years to listen to the lyric!' The role of the songwriter, like the protagonist of any other art form, is not to prescribe, but to *suggest*.

Where the expressive scope of the lyric needs to be complex, as it does in Bob Dylan's 'It's alright ma, I'm only bleeding', to meet the ambition of allowing all of the words to be heard, to allow the listener to make some sense of, interpret and absorb the hailstorm of words and images, Dylan creates musical space between the verses. On the original recording, Dylan and his producer Tom Wilson set the tempo of the performance precisely, so we can hear each line at a dizzying, almost disorienting speed, the restlessness of the text amplified by melodies that alternate between the comforting and the demanding, the harsh and the inviting. Although he could have recorded it with a band and put it on the 'electric' side one of 'Bringing It All Back Home', Dylan wants us to hear the words and not to be distracted by any sound other than the guitar. In refusing to vary the musical shape of each section, Dylan effectively invites us to stop listening to the revolving and repetitive music and to focus on the lyric, which from his perspective carries the message. An effective way of drawing attention away from the music, it is a method of songwriting Dylan has revisited often, perhaps most definitively on 'All along the watchtower', which never deviates from its revolving three-chord sequence. Listening to 'All along the watchtower' while the mystery of the verses holds court, it is actually a challenge for the ear to remain with the music, which repeats hypnotically into the mist.

Another hypnotic chord sequence recorded a couple of years later, The Beatles' 'I want you (she's so heavy)' does something very different. Here, an unequivocal verbal cue anchors an ensemble performance that in terms of sound production seeks to envelop us in its affective realm, to draw us into its dream world. The images we see as the song stretches out across 7 minutes and 47 seconds will vary according to who we are and what we have experienced. Unlike Dylan's 'It's alright ma, I'm only bleeding', we are told very little, but we tell ourselves a lot; the effect is less intellectual, more visceral.

Occupying a compositional middle ground, The Shirelles' 1960 reading of Goffin and King's 'Will you love me tomorrow' has an almost constant movement of music and lyric that compels the listener to flit between the two. While we are busy trying to interpret meaning from the music and lyric, we are also tempted to examine and evaluate the vocal accents and instrumental sounds. Is there any way we can slow it down? It is not a poem or a painting that we can mull over at leisure, rather a hurricane of sonic information coming at us in real time. To interpret words and music simultaneously is impossible, so for every signal we receive, others fade or are obscured. Most of what we hear tells us *something*, though. Perhaps we should listen again?

In the modern era, when so much music can be consumed free of cost, the pressure increases on song to stand out, to speak on its own terms and to demand its new value: the listener's time. As the global culture continues to embrace single song listening, we are increasingly inclined to expect each song to have its own fingerprint; to have a beginning, middle and end capable of alerting and absorbing us under all circumstances, in all conditions. For a song to be indispensable, the importance of a signature sound – a texture, vocal intonation and rhythmic identity that make it immediately identifiable to the listener – is paramount. Conversely, the ubiquitous portable iPod device significantly decreases the need for songs to be compelling, or demanding of the listeners' exclusive interest. With iPod in place, we are free to simultaneously tend to other commitments that require our primary attention. While the earphones are in, it may even be preferable to listen to music that does not entirely consume us, to create an unintrusive soundtrack to everyday life. How would anyone write that song?

Returning to our 'Hey Jude' trio, if they are to walk into a studio with an empathetic engineer they will be able to make a recording that some of us will want to hear, and maybe even possess. If, on the other hand, they decide to record it on a mobile phone placed right next to the fiddle, it will challenge not only our sense of instrumental balance, but also our notion of commercial sound quality – the sonic watermark that withstands repeated listening. Once the studio version is mixed and mastered it will meet the level of quality we have come, as listeners, to demand from fixed media song; it will sound *right*.

Songs are also defined not only by recordings but also by performances. Over time technology has moved song out of the dance hall and into virtually any environment imaginable. In this sense, the location and environment in which song is heard can also be definitive. Established by Edward T. Hall in 1959, proxemics is the study of communicative distances between the transmitter of a message (i.e. the songwriter) and the receiver (i.e. the listener). The study of proxemics questions how our relationship with song changes the closer, or further away, we get to it. Is listening on headphones, for example, the same as absorbing amplified sound in an amphitheatre? The song remains the same, yet our perception of it changes.

These questions have implications for the way songs and song sequences are framed for the purpose of being heard. While touring to promote their second LP 'This Year's Model' in 1978, Elvis Costello and the Attractions rearranged and restructured many of their recently recorded songs to sound more immediately effective in a live setting. Of thirteen songs filmed in Cologne on 15 June 1978 for broadcast on German Television, only four – 'Lip service', 'No action', 'Pump it up' and 'You belong to me' – are structured as recorded on the LP. Every other song is altered, from the opening 'Mystery dance', which adds a newly invented introductory drum solo, to the almost double length, improvisatory reading of 'Watching the detectives'. The possible reasons for this are numerous; obliged to play a similar set night after night, the band – who at this point still have less than thirty songs to their name – are perhaps inclined to indulge their own sense of the original structures, to explore the recorded versions and see what creative amusement can be extracted from them. In addition, the adrenalized tempo at which the band evidently feel the songs should be delivered on stage means regular and extended instrumental breaks are needed to make it physically possible for Costello to sing the set with a semblance of the musicality captured by Nick Lowe on the equivalent studio recordings. The vocal production qualities on both 'This Year's Model' and its predecessor 'My Aim Is True' allow the voice to be dominant and durably melodic, so, strangely for such a tuneful singer, whenever Elvis stops singing on stage in Cologne the effect is to increase the musicality. While the voice generates a great deal of the drama on record, it is less able to do so over a sustained period in live performance, and the exploratory solos on 'Lipstick vogue' and 'I don't want to go to Chelsea' combine with numerous 'Who'-style extended endings to create a greater metaphorical sense of drama. Tilting the audience's perception, these shifts in the way the songs are defined and projected alter their meaning.

On a related note, the re-sequencing of songs from original album to stage can allow the same songs to acquire a different prominence or energy. When I saw Elvis Costello and the Attractions in 1984, they chose to open the show with 'Sour milk cow blues', a relatively minor and unsophisticated tune so unprepossessing in its spot midway through side two of the

'Goodbye Cruel World' LP that, on vinyl, it barely registered. In a live setting, shorn of its long player context, the track served as a vehicle for the band to arrive with a loud, intellectually undemanding and confrontational wall of sound. Earlier that year, Costello had chosen to open 'Goodbye Cruel World' with 'The only flame in town', a song originally written and performed as a solo acoustic ballad for voice and guitar. On record, with horn section and full band, the mood changed from mournful to bright and optimistic. The twelve-inch remix of the song released later that year changed it again, this time opening up previously uncharted incidental spaces where more overtly expressive gestures once dominated. In this way, the life of the song evolved to match its surroundings.

To summarize, it could perhaps be argued that songs are mobile and portable works of individual accent that possess, with varying levels of affective, dynamic, intellectual, visceral, repetitive, contrasting, expressive, literal and metaphorical qualities: words, performance, production, arrangement and importantly, music.

1.2 Music

Speaking on behalf of musicians in his book on music philosophy, Allsup (2009: 43) admits: 'We understand deeply and intuitively the value of what we do, but there is no universal agreement as to how we define or explain our craft.' Suggesting that no two people are ever likely to explain or interpret the same piece of music in the same way, and that any enquiry into its meaning would be likely to elicit a variety of different responses, music educationalist Keith Swanwick (1979: 13, 16) asks whether music means anything at all.

Interpretation wasn't always a pressing issue, however, since for the Ancient Greeks music was primarily a means of storytelling, of handing down tradition (Abeles 2010: 42). Typically, the music students of antiquity did not discuss the meaning of the music, but were required to memorize musical works as a means of preserving a record of their historical ancestry. Skilled in the art of memorization, they were the folk traditionalists, the tribute bands of their time. Moving forward through time and sounding the first faint echoes of what was to become pop star mythology, Kivy (1997) recalls how philosophers during the 'Age of Enlightenment' considered music to represent otherworldly knowledge beyond pure reason, worthy of being accorded a type of secular divinity.

Making the case for a tangible link between music and the individuals who create and interpret it, Reimer suggests that music be considered a means by which humans come to know themselves and their world (1989: 89). From Reimer's perspective, the study of form, or critical analysis of works, reveals not only information about the work itself but also portrays something of the quality of our lives. But as Swanwick (1979: 13, 26) enquires: 'How do we know what the composer felt during the period of time spent working on his movement?' Adding further weight to the argument that we should be cautious in attributing meaning to music, Philpott (2001: 34, 35) suggests that, given the relatively lengthy amount of time it would usually take to write a musical composition, it seems unlikely that a composer would be able to formulate and distil a quantifiable communicative expression.

While some are inclined to accept the view of music as a reflection of the life and feelings of the composer, as Allsop (2009: 45, 47) notes, others consider it an activity that has reference only to itself. Although the inclination to link music and feelings is said to be common to all cultures, the principles of aesthetic autonomy indicate that music is unable to refer to anything specific at all, whether it be feelings or ideas (ibid.). Adopting this functional perspective, Stravinsky (1970) argues that music should be contemplated as pure sound; that its functions should be appreciated free of any extra-musical allusions. In this paradigm, the listener is invited to observe how the composition changes in strength, motion, ratio and intensity, and 'meaning' lies in an educated appreciation of the relationships between these elements. According to this perspective, to be admitted to the club, the listener needs to understand the mechanisms, the inner workings of music.

Conversely, Sarup (1988: 52) argues that music *is* a language in the sense that it transfers metaphorical meaning. Emphasizing its interpretative power, Langer (1956: 218, 222, 244) contends that music is a metaphor for human feeling and experience in the broadest sense, and not any particular expressive impetus. Langer proposes that music has semantic meaning in the sense that it has a symbolic content similar to that of language. However, she adds, 'the real power of music lies in the fact that it can be true to the life of feelings in a way that language cannot; for its significant forms have that ambivalence of content which words cannot have'. Ultimately, Langer views music not as a form of self-expression but rather an offering by the composer of the universe or spectrum of human feelings for exploration by the listener. For her, the composer is not inviting listeners to relate to the music by transporting them into the composer's place, but rather the composer is inviting the listener to access the world of feelings with permission to attach whatever meaning he or she sees fit.

Following this line of argument, the songwriter should be aware that the musical element of his or her songs is likely to evoke a range of interpretative responses, all of which might be equally anticipated in the sense that there could be no right or wrong critical reading of the musical content. With this sentiment Swanwick (1999: 2) concurs:

> The act of understanding a piece of music is remarkably similar to the understanding of any text; understanding requires a cognitive act of interpretation, of engagement with the dynamic processes of meaning construction.

In *The Musical Mind*, Sloboda (1985) seeks to identify similarities between music and language: both are particular to humans; both contain the potential for infinite possible combinations; both can be learned by listening to models; both use vocal and auditory sound processors as their natural medium; both involve the use of notation systems; both require necessary skills to be received and absorbed before they can be used; both share some universality of form across cultures; both can be examined in terms of phonetic, syntactic and semantic structure; and both contain an underlying structure over which various transformations can take place.

As a counterpart to lyric, music evidently plays a significant role. Differentiating between linguistics as the phonological field of words and associated noises, and Trager's (1958) definition of paralinguistics as communication *alongside* language, Wilkinson (1975: 7) asserts that not all communication is mediated through words. To emphasize the point, Hills (1986: 48) states that non-verbal behaviour can support or deny verbal communication, take the place of verbal communication and show conflicting emotions or attitudes. Music might, therefore, possess a communicative meaning that opposes the inference of the words. Further, the paralinguistic meaning might be dominant, since Birdwhistell (1972) estimates that in a two-person conversation the actual words spoken carry less than 35 per cent of the social meaning of the interaction, with 65 per cent transmitted by non-verbal exchanges. In seeking to convey meaning, while the poet has the sword of the written word, the songwriter has other weaponry at her disposal.

Because its meaning cannot be agreed upon or a specific feeling or emotion assigned to any given piece, Reimer (1989) agrees with Langer (1956) that music is not a language. In a text dedicated to the resolution of the question 'Is Music a Language?' Philpott (2001: 34) lists a number of key provocative arguments: Why does 'major' music sometimes feel sad? Why are there no dictionary definitions of musical meaning? Why is there no sense in which musical meaning can be negated or proved wrong? Considering music untranslatable, Philpott (ibid.) cites as an example the difficulty an aboriginal audience might find interpreting the precise meanings intended by Mozart. For the songwriter, such discussions make the writing of music extremely challenging to navigate. If it is indirect, constantly changeable, open to interpretation and untranslatable, why is some music more beloved than others? Perhaps more often than not, the music we treasure has *some* meaning to its creator, and subsequently *some* meaning to us, that an exchange of meaning takes place.

Another possible answer to the conundrum lies in Hallam's observation (2001: 62) that, uniquely, musical learning is considered a natural process and humans are naturally generative, continually creating, recreating and developing new ideas. From the beginnings of life, Hallam claims, children are able to perceive, structure, make sense of and reproduce their sound environment. Those of us who develop a love for listening to music and at a young age, with time to spare, discover an antique piano or a battered old six-string have the means to construct a unique musical persona. Further, according to Durrant and Welch (1995: 20), children imitate musical sounds in the same way they imitate language sounds, and make up rambling phrases that could be considered improvisational, or the beginnings of composing.

As we move towards adolescence, structural and cognitive skills associated with music are collected during a process of 'enculturation', enabling almost everyone to become a musical expert (Sloboda, 2005: 248). As Duke Ellington once said (cited in Tucker, 1993: 6), there are only two types of music: good and bad; and whenever we disagree with an opinionated judge on one of the singing talent contests that have sprung up in every corner of the globe, it is because we feel that we instinctively know and understand our subject – we all possess a lifetime's worth not only of linguistic, but also musical expertise. It follows that, already extremely well acquainted with music, whether tutored or untutored, each songwriter brings a significant level of understanding of music, tacit or learned, to the songwriting process.

In October 2014, without disclosing the title I played a group of postgraduate students an instrumental track,

'Quadropuss Island' by the New Zealand-based psychedelic artist Connan Mockasin. Once the track had ended, I asked the group what meaning, if any, they had been able to discern from the music. While some found it eerie and unsettling and one student found it reminiscent of airport music, about half said it put them in mind of an island setting. Although Connan Mockasin was unable to *control* the transfer of an intended meaning, he was able to *infer* it through suggestion in the chords, notes, arrangement, production, performance and structure. Returning to Sheldon's earlier observation, what might be troublesome for the songwriter as a composer of music might, in terms of thematic variation, be the beauty for the listener.

How powerful can these musical suggestions be? Powell (2010) is not alone in his observation that major chords tend to possess an assertive, positive character while minor chords tend to be more melancholic. Howlin' Wolf only needed one major chord for 'Spoonful'; The Ramones daringly upped it to three for 'I want to be sedated' and Bruce Springsteen scaled it back down to two with 'Born in the USA'. From a listening perspective, there is no perceptible measure of doubt in any of these three songs, each of which roll along with self-assured confidence. Other songs composed entirely of major chords are less stable, however. 'Get up' by REM, for example, feels angular and unresolved, while The Kinks' 'All day and all of the night' is tense and agitated.

Seeking to describe the effects certain musical chords have upon the listener, Rooksby (2003: 32) claims:

> Second inversion chords are harder to describe. I call them dreamers. Not as assertive as the root chord; not as mobile as the first inversion, they have a dreamy indefinite feeling that can lend itself to impressionistic effects that work well in intros and bridges.

Similarly, citing 'Losing my religion' by REM as an example, Bradford (2005: 146) characterizes minor triads as sad, and, with reference to Neil Finn's 'Better be home soon', Bradford links dominant seventh chords with the impression of a 'toughening' effect. Minor triads undoubtedly contribute to the creation of a melancholy effect in some contexts, but their frequent presence in the harmonic structures of modern R&B, a genre rarely associated with melancholy, would suggest other possibilities. Further, the lyric for 'Losing my religion' finds lyricist Michael Stipe referencing laughter and smiling, perhaps indicating that, if a melancholic effect is in intended, the inclusion of a minor triad may be sub-textual, not reinforcing or reflecting the lyric, but instead offering the listener a separate option for engagement. When heard within the context of the words that accompany it, the dominant seventh chord in the chorus of 'Better be home soon' by Crowded House could equally be considered the most unguarded and celebratory moment in the song. From the perspective of the songwriter, the interpretative complexity generated by the contexts in which first and second inversions, minor triads and dominant seventh chords appear needs to be borne in mind when seeking to create or suggest a specific effect.

To add further complexity, as listeners we are encultured, through centuries of attentive listening, to favour a degree of unpredictability within this musical soundscape. When we hear unusual chords we sometimes hear what Cat Cohen refers to as unsettled notes (cited in Braheny, 2006: 114). Two illustrations of this effect can be found in the verse-to-chorus movement of The Beatles' 'Norwegian wood' and 'Things we said today'. Lulled into a sense of security by the bright positivity of the major chord verse of 'Norwegian wood', our perception of the prevailing mood is jolted by the sudden arrival of the same chord in its minor form, a compositional movement rare enough to challenge our initial assumption of the prevailing mood. Conversely, in 'Things we said today', as the revolving, repetitive minor-chord suppression gives way to its major counterpart, our notion of what the music seems to be suggesting is thrown again. Both songs challenge us to become more deeply involved as interpreters, to consider how the unanticipated might be part of the natural flow.

In other settings, music can be made repetitive to create stability – for instance, in Beirut's 'Santa Fe', where the circularity of the chord sequence gives the expression a sense of permanence. 'Transmission' by Joy Division uses a similarly repetitive chord sequence to develop a rising claustrophobic intensity, while Bill Callahan's album closer 'One fine morning' uses chord repetition to evoke a meditative hypnosis. Among other effects, music is also used to chapterize songs by harmonic and melodic contour, as in 'The way you move' by Outkast, or to create startling dramatic peaks, for example in Bjork's version of Lang and Reisfeld's 'Oh, so quiet' and Elbow's 'Starlings'.

In songwriting, music always suggests *something*, but its meaning in relation to the lyric is malleable. Generally, if it doesn't sound wrong it will sound right. Dull or familiar words often benefit from original music and dull music tends to make words more prominent. Bold musical statements sometimes bear little relation to the lyric and sometimes accentuate it; there is no prescriptive or set approach. We don't hear music or song in black and white, but in technicolour, and the challenge of controlling music projection and perception is as demanding for the composer as it is for the listener. Fortunately for the songwriter there is another medium to call upon.

1.3 Words

While Formalists, such as Hanslick (1957: 30), contend that the 'true character' of music allows it to offer a directness of meaning that cannot be generated by the ambiguities of spoken language, Allsup (2009: 45) argues that music might only attain clarity of meaning with clearly communicated lyrics. Even with clearly communicated lyrics, however, it seems inevitable that song words, like music, are likely to have different meanings for different people.

It may seem natural to assume that 'successful' songs consist of skilfully written lyrics and skilfully written melodies and harmonies, written by a skilful lyricist and a skilful composer of music. Bob Dylan's work is regularly discussed solely in terms of its lyric – sometimes even by Dylan himself, while chapters of published analysis of Dylan's work barely mention the musical aspect of his writing (Gray, 2000; Dettmar, 2009: 43–4). This narrowing of analytical focus would seem to suggest that Dylan's most remarkable skill lies in the realm of lyric writing, and that his music is less remarkable.

Conversely, Coldplay have been criticized for combining emotive music with meaningless lyrics. In his 2005 *Guardian* review of 'X and Y' Alexis Petridis writes:

> Dealing only in generalities, the lyrics have been buffed until anyone can see their reflection in them … At their worst they are so devoid of personality that they sound less like song lyrics than something dreamed up by a creative ad agency.

It could perhaps be argued that, by opting to use their respective strategies, Bob Dylan could be seeking to primarily engage the listener at a verbal level, while at the other end of the songwriting spectrum, Coldplay could be trying to engage the listener in the realm of emotion or feelings, purposefully avoiding a situation where the listener might be distracted from the music by the lyric.

As previously mentioned, lyrics do not necessarily reinforce musical meaning; they may be used to create a subtext or meaning other than that inferred by the music. For example, 'Where did our love go?' by Holland, Dozier and Holland has a lyric that on the page appears desperately sad. On the recording made in 1964 by Diana Ross and the Supremes, however, the band plays the text with gregarious swing and, as if the question asked in the title of the song has already been answered, the mechanically revolving chord sequence offers no dramatic contour. For just over two minutes, it relentlessly rolls along in its jolly major key behind a vocal performance bordering on sensual. Pulling in a number of different directions and seeming to convey a number of contradictory messages, somehow it all makes sense. How can this be? Perhaps the recording feels authentic because it speaks to us of how life is – with nothing ever particularly simple, merely the occasional snapshot of clarity glimpsed through a series of masks and layers. Led by the mood and circumstance of whatever moment we find ourselves in, when we hear this spectacularly ambiguous recording we are given a range of affective sonic wavelengths to tune in to.

Words are sometimes used to take us to locations we have never visited. In 'Texas 1947' and 'Car wheels on a gravel road', Guy Clark and Lucinda Williams guide us back to their childhood, not as if recanting a memory but as if they, and by extension we, were *actually* there. Present at the scene we are able to sense innocence and anticipation, to feel the movement of trains and cars, and to smell the frying of eggs and bacon. Our imagination sparked by a filmic quality, we are prompted to relate by summoning some of the poetry and magic of our own experiences, the most fondly remembered of which might evoke a similar sensory clarity. Using music as an escapist subtext for the lyric, the songwriter can also take us to places we might otherwise not want to go. The rural poverty of Clarence Williams' 'My bucket's got a hole in it' (recorded by Hank Williams in 1949) and Morrissey and Marr's similarly bleak 'Girlfriend in a coma' both employ a jaunty musical subtext to sugar-coat the harsh reality of the lyric. In doing so, they manage to reflect our common capacity to make light of hard times; no matter how grim the diagnosis, the spirit endures.

Echoing the splintered pictorial and written narratives of Braque and Joyce, in the dreamlike 'Madame George', Van

Morrison leads us through a fractured series of localized visual scenarios to bring us within touching distance of his own experience. The lyric is fragmented and kaleidoscopic, and in the hypnosis of the musical spaces we are invited to make our own way. We glimpse the artistic visions, and leave with a feeling that maybe that's all he did too. There is no full disclosure, nor should there be. If the story of Madame George had been told in its entirety, would we, half a century later, still be venturing with Ford and Fitzroy down Cyprus Avenue?

For the purpose of analysis, love songs can be divided into four quarters, the first of which involves worship from afar. With the aspirations of the narrator at the core of the expression, Roy Orbison and Bill Dees' 'Oh pretty woman' aspires to strike a universal chord. Authentically rational as a song expression, the emotional jolt felt by the storyteller is immediately recognizable as something worth singing about. Usually in a major key and upbeat, these phase one love songs tend to be lyrically uncomplicated, bright and approachable, perhaps reflecting the way the narrator might initially like to be seen, or noticed.

In the love song 'My girl' by Smokey Robinson and Ronald White, famously recorded by The Temptations in 1964, the mood is similarly upbeat; after all, who would want being in love to sound like hard work? Alternatively, true love travels on a gravel road, and on the 2003 hit 'Crazy in love', co-written with Harrison, Carter and Record, Beyonce Knowles uses a wilfully distracted structure to enable the words to convey an amplified sense of disorientation. John Lennon's penitent 'Jealous guy' and Carson, Christopher and James' similarly rueful 'Always on my mind', recorded by Elvis Presley in 1972, have identical forms, suggesting that the structure offers a compelling framework for a worded apology. Likewise the relentless pacing movement back and forth from verse to chorus of Marvin Gaye's reading of Whitfield and Strong's 'I heard it through the grapevine' echoes, and makes more dramatic, the frame of mind of the narrator trapped like a caged lion, torn between the heaven of what could be, and the hell of what seems inevitable. In this way, love song structures not only shape musical continuity, but also frame lyric expression.

When in phase three it all starts to go wrong, as in the Bee Gees' 2001 recording of the Gibb Brothers' 1982 song 'Heartbreaker', we find the music contracting mid-song, halving the words as if in a despairing effort to make things right. Here, the verse, pre-chorus and chorus are all halved as, in a musical sense, the narrator tries everything he can to find a resolution. Perhaps because they represent the state of mind most of us spend the least time in, post-love songs, with their predilection for jealousy and rage, are in the minority. Almost fifty years apart, only Vimmerstedt and Mercer's 'I wanna be around', written in 1959 and recorded by Tony Bennett four years later, and Lily Allen's 2006 hit 'Smile', co-written with Babalola and Lewis, have made an enduringly significant mark. A surrogate voice for the romantically disaffected multitude, silver linings are more prominent, from the Zen contentment of George and Ira Gershwin's 'They can't take that away from me' to the unmistakable musical, if not lyrical optimism of Bacharach and David's 'Walk on by' and 'I'll never fall in love again', both famously recorded by Dionne Warwick.

Song lyrics are often delivered in conversational prose and in American roots music, where the representation of the common voice is the default medium, authenticity of expression is prized. As plain conversation in itself is not usually a commercial entity, within all the straight talk something a little outside the bounds of normal conversation often needs to be said. Reflecting upon what at first seems a blissful experience in 'Perfect day', Lou Reed initially warms the collective spirit with a series of fondly remembered verse phrases before using the chorus to disembark upon a glorious melodic run. Is it enough, though? Sensing the need for another dimension, some dark sunglasses to counteract the overwhelming lightness, Reed chooses to conclude both the chorus and the song itself, with a menacing verbal under-current. It is, eventually, a remarkable narrative.

Some conversations are short, and lyric minimalism exists in song in a number of ways: Brian Wilson and Mike Love's 'Meant for you', Tom Waits' 'Johnsburg, Illinois' and most of Wire's 1977 album 'Pink Flag' are miniature in length and structure, ending long before they outstay their welcome. Within a popular culture that tends to anticipate proportion, these songs are arrestingly short; brief despatches when we expect more. With its absence of words and inclination towards textural absorption, side two of Bowie's 'Low' LP evokes a sense of minimalism, as do broad swathes of Wilco's more overtly expressive LP 'A Ghost Is Born', where instru-mental sequences are exaggerated to stretch our concept of what pop composition might be. Listening to the extrava-gantly elongated 'Spiders (Kidsmoke)', after a while, we are obliged to bend our notion of lyric and song structure to the will of the band.

While it has been argued that there are inherent difficulties in the task of evaluating lyric outside of its musical and performative context, the *timing* of lyric delivery may have a bearing on the extent to which the listener finds the song communicative. Notwithstanding the inevitable suggestive and metaphorical effect and influence of music, perhaps some communicative traits observed in speech may be transferable to song. In her study of human speech patterns, Goldman-Eisler (1958, 1961) found that there were lengthier pauses before unpredictable words and that pauses in speech tended to relate to emotional activity. D'Souza (1981: 43–7) found that intonation patterns, which are said to communicate to the listener at an unconscious level, help the listener to organize the meaning of sentences. Further, D'Souza (ibid.) found that people often indicate the end of a thought by inserting a slight break. To enable the listener to absorb and interpret meaning, in other words, particularly detailed sections of lyric might usefully be followed by a pause in verbal content.

Differentiating between written, oral and 'inner' or thought pattern speech, Vygotsky (1956) considers written speech likely to be the most precisely developed and expanded, oral speech between two subjects to be the most likely to use abbreviations, and inner speech (within which the subject is always implicitly understood) to usually be the most disjointed. A memorable scene in Wim Wenders' 1987 film *Wings of Desire* translates the random thoughts of Berlin underground travellers into subtitled speech. While thematically disjointed, it feels entirely natural to watch and perhaps provides a clue to why we find The Beatles 1967 song 'I am the walrus' such a rewarding listen; if we contemplate the narrative as Lennon's 'inner speech', we are less obliged to seek a thread of narrative meaning.

First lines of songs are often considered important as a way of attracting interest and earning trust, and consequently songwriters are frequently preoccupied with making a positive first impression. On the organization of verses, Rodgers (2003: 56) advises:

> If the opening lines amount basically to throat clearing, and the song's real statement doesn't arrive until verse two or three or the chorus, consider whether that later section might actually work in the beginning.

While this advice helpfully encourages the songwriter to think laterally about how lyrics might be improved, it overlooks the possibility that, in song, the 'real statement' often arrives at an unconventional point. 'Christmas card from a hooker in Minneapolis' by Tom Waits, for example, holds off until the final verse before introducing a verbal conclusion that gives the narrative of the song its full meaningful dimension (Kessel, 2009: 81). Similarly, the lyric of 'Sign o' the times' by Prince appears to consist of a series of dispassionately delivered social observations (Perone, 2008: 43) until the observations are contextualized and given greater meaning by the questioning nature of the lyric in the bridge. Further, it could be argued that in some instances the 'real statement' of a song is implied not by the lyric but primarily by the music. Led by guitarist Brix E. Smith, 'Cruiser's Creek' by The Fall makes its most immediate and memorable statement through the unrelenting swagger of its motif.

Songs use a number of narrative dynamics to convey lyric meaning and the selection made by the lyricist shapes and directs our involvement as listeners. Each type of dynamic has a different distinctive effect. 'I to You' lyrics, for example, are written in the voice of the singer, who is singing to another. As listeners, we are given a series of options. We might relate to the singer or even imagine ourselves to be them. Alternatively, we can imagine that we are the one being sung to. A third possibility exists, for us to adopt the role of outsider listening in to the lyric conversation. We may, on repeated listens, eventually hear and perceive the song in a number of different ways. An example of an 'I to You' lyric is the Bee Gees' 'How deep is your love'. Here, as with most song lyrics, once the narrative dynamic has been established, it is held for the duration of the song.

Flawed 'I to You' songs often lack a balance between 'I' and 'You' characters. Either too much is said about the 'I' or too much is heard about the 'You' and consequently, one of the main characters remain undeveloped, giving the listener a restricted view. In his 1995 song 'The words we never use', Ron Sexsmith addresses this by using verse one to sketch his own feelings, verse two to convey the feelings of the 'You' character, and verse three to join both together as 'Us'. This narrative balance allows us to gain a fully dimensional perspective on what is happening to those involved. Rather than engage in larger-scale guesswork or invention, we are left to fill in only the finer details.

If Lennon and McCartney had written 'And I love *you*' in 1964 rather than 'And I love *her*', they would have followed a similar dynamic to that used for 'How deep is your love'. Significantly, the last word in the title evokes a very different narrative emphasis, that of the singer singing to *us* about *her*.

We are on the outside listening in. Perceiving the difference at an almost subconscious level we understand we are under no obligation to be involved. With this lightening of the load, we might feel inclined to seek meaning in more than the lyric, and in 'And I love her' the use of minor chords to accompany a simple tale of affection adds a subtext. What is the meaning hidden behind those revolving autumnal guitar sounds hanging shadow-like over each verse? Perhaps the outlook is not as sunny as it seems, and a darker undercurrent lies beneath. The subtext gives us something to think about, and without it the lyric statement risks coming across as bland. Without the sub-textual suspicion of doubt, would the discerning listener engage, or even hold a passing interest? With its minor chord undercurrent, 'And I love her' offers a way in for the listener, who is likely to be intrigued by the tension, or apparent cross purpose of meaning that exists between the lyric and music texts.

Of course, if you are female, there is every chance that Paul McCartney could be singing 'And I love her' about you personally. Narrowing the scope for inclusivity in 'Alison', Elvis Costello sings to a specific character. Unless our name is Alison or we know an Alison we would like to sing to, we are obliged to adopt the position of voyeur. Going a step further, Robert Palmer offers even less interpretative room in his 1980 song of domestic strife 'Johnny and Mary', which describes a taciturn and volatile relationship in the third person. In 'Johnny and Mary' we are invited to hear the tale of two specific characters we will have never met, although, thanks to a dimension of theatrical authenticity that elevates the lyric above mere observation, we probably know of a couple like them. This uninvolved and dispassionate lyric writing style stretches back through the history of folkloric storytelling via Richard Thompson's tune 'Vincent Black Lightning 1952' where there is similarly nothing at stake for the singer, who merely watches and reports the drama as he sees it. Inevitably, interesting lyric images and the empathetic drawing of human characters with dramatically believable traits and frailties are needed for these types of observational songs to flourish. Significantly, suggesting that Johnny, Mary, James and Red Molly are people the two songwriters are warmly inclined towards, both 'Johnny and Mary' and 'Vincent Black Lightning 1952' are musically bright and momentous.

When sketching the lyric for 'Yesterday' in 1965, Lennon and McCartney will probably have noticed a collective resonance in the poignancy of its introspective lyric theme; regret is a condition most of us can relate to. Similarly, Sheryl Crow's meditative 'Home' is a song that might be considered inward-looking in nature. Again, while we are aware that the song is 'sung to self', there is a sense that the narrative seeks to appeal to a universal empathy for the temporary state of isolation, and this, in the grand scheme of the songwriter, is where we become involved. Made even more engaging and relatable through a hazily introspective vocal performance, a finely contrasting set of melodies and some West Coast production textures that imply a definite location, Sheryl is saying something interesting about herself that we might say, with our equivalent lexicon, about ourselves. Like her earlier hit 'Leaving Las Vegas', 'Home' is peppered with idiosyncratic lines clearly intended to convey Sheryl Crow as an individual spirit. This authentic individuality is, ironically, an aspect of universality, for after all we each recognize ourselves to be unique. Further universal dimension is evident in the chorus lyric and melody in both songs, each of which invite us to sing along and share in the expression. In both instances the choruses are examples of what Stephanie Pappas (2013) calls reward: simple, memorable sections that offer the listener relief from the relatively dense and engaging verse imagery.

Conversely, in 'Addicted to love', Robert Palmer mentions himself only once in five minutes, instead focusing obsessively, addictively upon the object of attention. As the lyric progresses, the possibility of the singer intervening in a self-referential way seems to gradually dissolve, leaving us with an intense portrait of the *other*. Returning to the subject of balance between main characters, if the singer says next to nothing about himself, what can we know about him? In this instance we find ourselves looking for clues in the accent of the voice, the insistence of the vocal phrasing and the bravado of the music.

Going even further by removing himself from the narrative action entirely, in his 1980 song 'That's entertainment' Paul Weller lists a seemingly random, imaginatively assembled series of sensory snapshots, in equal parts violent, romantic and mundane. Within the scope of the narrative, the listener is moved not only by the emotional exchanges that occur in sharp relief to incidental events, but also by the author's skill in daring to reveal, on an equal compositional footing, experiences both permanently memorable and instantly forgettable. Within this image-laden kaleidoscope, all human life seems to reside. Like John Lennon's narrator in 'Good morning, good morning', he has nothing, but everything to say. Exceptional though 'That's entertainment' is, a counter-argument could be made that in popular music lyric, sensory imagery is often barely required. Like 'Hello goodbye' by Lennon and McCartney, songs such as 'Can't get you out of my head' written by Cathy Dennis and Rob Davis for Kylie in 2001 make minimal use of sensory images in the lyric, relying instead upon performance, arrangement, melody and structural repetition to gain expressive effect.

As noted earlier, most lyrics do not stray from their initially established narrative dynamic. The most compelling reason for this lies in the risk that the listener, confronted with a sudden and startling change of narrative dynamic emphasis, will spend precious listening time trying to figure out *who is now singing to who*. If a singer sings to *you* one moment and *her* the next, such a development challenges the listener to seek resolution through interpretation by reviewing the nature of the switch as the song continues to move forward. As listeners, we are encultured not to be distracted in this way; rather we are accustomed to anticipate a singularity of communicative expression. This is not to say that songs cannot be about more than one thing – merely that, in terms of narrative dynamic, they rarely change horses in mid-stream.

Some honourable exceptions to the rule exist, notably in the songs of Robert Johnson. In many of his greatest works the dynamic switches unannounced, wilfully disorientating the listener, who is left with a scattergun impression of voices both clear and shadowy, heard from numerous unspecified viewpoints. Importantly, the canvas that holds Johnson's 'Kind hearted woman blues' together, that saves it from overpowering the listener with complex and fractured lyric information, is the relentless insistence and predictability of the chords over which Johnson's troubled and chaotic thoughts wander. Fairly soon we realize we know where the chords are going, and consequently we have enough of a sense of grounding, of attentive listening wherewithal to gain a full sense of the narrative entanglement, to appreciate its poetic quality. Sensing something of his own frame of mind in this duality, Dylan's post-millennial writing regularly creates a similar effect: a weary narrator treading the same old familiar tracks, encircling and glimpsing, yet never quite finding the elusive truth.

1.4 Structure

Although standard song forms have existed since the dawn of recorded sound, song structures, the sequential placement of different musical sections, are almost infinite in variation. Structure can be used to add emphasis to expression, add continuity, provide variation and create diversion. In essence, an effective structure ensures that the listener's imagination is always drawn to *something*.

It is not always clear-cut. Confusingly, a section considered a verse by the songwriter might be a chorus to the listener. Further, within the songwriting community, British middle eights and American bridges are often the same thing, and commentators who observe the convention of the American songbook, including Pollack (2006), refer to the introductory section as a chorus. To avoid confusion and to give the section a name that reflects its purpose, I will refer to the section which offers a musical variation on the verse and chorus as a bridge. It is common for a bridge to exist in a song if necessary, although Lennon and McCartney used two in the highly unorthodox 'I'll be back', and latterly Sting in 'Every breath you take'. Having written two different bridges, they simply decided to include both.

While the analysis of structure is far from an exact science, in broad terms, we can say that songs tend to be assembled by using a combination of elements: Introduction, Verse, Pre-chorus, Chorus, Post-chorus, Bridge, Solo and Coda. As a rule, songwriters use the following code for each section: A – verse, B – chorus. When a pre-chorus is used to link the verse and the chorus, the verse remains A, the pre-chorus is B, and the chorus C. Bridges, Solos and Codas retain their names. Once written as separate pieces of music, these elements are selected for inclusion by the songwriter and are often repeated, sometimes with alterations. Immensely influential, the *right* structure predetermines if a song will work or not. Imagine the verses of The Beatles' 'She loves you' and 'Can't buy me love' preceding their significantly more memorable choruses and you might hear why, to avoid the audience becoming disinterested, Lennon and McCartney took the unconventional step of placing the chorus at the outset of each composition. In each instance, the unsuspecting listener, used to hearing verses first, is initially caught off guard, yet is eventually able to resolve the structural issue upon hearing the comparatively monochromatic verses that follow.

Song introductions can be voice-led, as in The Beatles' 'Help' and Elvis Costello and the Attractions' 'Accidents will happen'. In both instances the introductory lyric phrases infer immediacy and the absence of a musical cue is apt. Using a melodic riff or motif that contrasts with the one used in the vocal melody of the verse, Bruce Springsteen's 'Born to run' transports the chord sequence used in the verse to the front of the song structure. When the verse arrives, its harmonic setting is familiar and the listener is skilfully directed towards the lyric. For the similarly iconic introduction of 'London calling', Strummer and Jones extracted the tense E minor and F chords from the sung verse, saving the resolving G chord to support the eventual arrival of the lyric. In making this chordal alteration, the writers withheld the G chord to build tension and delay resolution.

Simply structured AAAA songs, like Steve Earle's 'Tom Ames' Prayer', use chordal repetition to allow the initial sensory assault of the music to gradually fade into the background, directing us to focus exclusively on the lyric story. Brilliantly, 'Tom Ames' Prayer', also uses instrumental breaks to punctuate the chapters, on each occasion suggesting time having passed. For Steve Earle, this will have been an editorial task; once the verses have been written – and in an AAAA song it is likely that the words we hear will be a fraction of those drafted – the songwriter can assess the narrative to see where breaks might occur that will allow the listener to take stock of what has happened so far. In collaboration with Fred Rose, master storyteller Hank Williams uses a similar strategy in 'Mansion on the hill', where the instrumental breaks that punctuate the verses become increasingly shorter, creating a quickening feel; we feel we are moving closer to the mansion. Conversely, to generate an impression that the narrator is increasingly being cut adrift, on another of Williams' classics 'I'm so lonesome I could cry' the band is instructed to play increasingly lengthy instrumental breaks. The harder it becomes for Hank to sing, the more lonesome we know he is.

AABA songs were extremely popular in 1944 when Duke Ellington and Bob Russell's 'Do nothing till you hear from me' came to popular prominence. Typically, an AABA structure is neatly proportioned to establish a theme, re-establish it from a slightly different angle, set it within a new musical framework, and finally return to it with a further variation. Three musically uniform verses are interrupted by a new piece of music, giving the song continuity and a measure of musical unpredictability. As the words and music are heard for the first time in verse one, the listener is required to listen attentively to try to absorb both compositional elements simultaneously, and consequently the tempo of the song is set to allow the listener to make sense of and evaluate both the verbal and metaphorical strands in real time. In many of the classic compositions we know, perhaps a complex and demanding musical pattern will be counterbalanced by a simpler, more direct, unambiguous lyric, or vice versa.

Verse two repeats the music of verse one, and the listener, now familiar with the music, is drawn more closely to the words, which, with exception of the refrain, will be entirely new to the ear. Obliged to involve the listener in a verbal sense, the songwriter is sometimes inclined to see the second verse as a chance to explore the opening expression of verse one in more depth, or with a greater degree of abstraction. As 'Do nothing till you hear from me' illustrates, the lyric used in the second verse may be less memorable or immediate. Three verses need to be written and the songwriter may be tempted to write more verses than are needed, and to choose three at a later time. Ella Fitzgerald's bawdy full-length 1956 reading of Rodgers and Hart's classic 'Bewitched, bothered and bewildered' shows how a relatively unedited framework of this type might sound.

Bridges are often the last part of the song to be written. Here, more than in any other section, the songwriter is given free rein to improvise, and historically this improvisatory section has fulfilled a number of roles. Sometimes a bridge will move to a predictable fourth chord, a movement so seamless and familiar that our ear barely registers a change. 'I saw her standing there' is a song that needs a progression of this kind to sustain its impetus. The verse-to-bridge transition isn't always musically smooth; 'From me to you', for example, uses a relatively unpredictable and unstable chord change to balance its relatively predictable verses. Alternatively, when the repetitive musical tension of the double verse is at breaking point, bridges provide melodic relief; this happens in another Beatles tune 'I'm looking through you'.

Something that doesn't always occur to songwriters during the creative process is the way a bridge can use a new musical framework to reintroduce a variation on an expression that already exists within the lyric, for example Lennon and McCartney's 'Eight days a week' and Goffin and King's 'Will you love me tomorrow'. In each case, where the temptation may have been to look for something new to say in words, safe in the knowledge that the music is saying something new, the songwriters effectively reprise the lyric theme. Skilfully bringing the listener into the dialogue, in 'Sign o' the times' Prince uses a bridge to stop making statements and start asking questions. Ron Sexsmith does the reverse for 'Secret heart', where the bridge is used to stop asking questions and make a statement. A further potential role for the bridge is its potential capacity to introduce musical release in the form of a melodic legato with longer-held vocal notes that contrast the previous staccato notes, as exemplified on Tony Bennett's recording of Irving Berlin's 'Let's face the music and dance'.

Allowing time for the listener to absorb their resolving phrase before the next section begins, AABA song titles are often found at the end of each verse. The standard 'The devil and the deep blue sea', originally recorded by Cab Calloway and his Orchestra and written by Harold Arlen and Ted Koehler in 1931, illustrates how this works. As it is much easier for the songwriter to write *around* them than it is to ramble along and suddenly *discover* them, these titles are often the first words of the song to be written. As such they play a pivotal role in anchoring the composition, acting as a slogan around which satellite expressions revolve.

Sometimes, the songwriter will opt to use these satellites, or verse phrases, to lead the listener in a perceived direction before concluding with an opposing 'surprise' emphasis.

Irving Berlin's refrain 'I've got my love to keep me warm' is, for example, preceded by a series of lines that emphasize cold; similarly, the narrator of 'I'm beginning to see the light', written by Ellington, George, Hodges and James in 1944 and reprized by Ella Fitzgerald and Count Basie in 1963, lists a number of things they *don't* do any more before arriving at what they now *do*. Turning our expectations upside down by establishing an expression as a refrain and then writing preceding verses that stress the opposite, the refrain effectively becomes a punch line.

It is a lot to ask of the listener to be compelled by four musical sections, and the writer of the great AABA song needs to be resourceful in ordering the raw music and lyric materials. Whatever the original verse order of Felice and Boudleaux Bryant's 1958 classic 'Raining in my heart', it will soon have been obvious to its writers that the most memorable verse, the one usually sung by the listener when the song comes to mind, is the first one. By placing it first in the order of the composition, the songwriters and the artist effectively earn the trust of the listener. Once captivated by the quality of the opening lines, each verse gradually becomes less memorable until verse three of 'Raining in my heart', which in a comparative sense lacks revelation and effectively gives us a chance to appreciate the melody.

In terms of structural placement, the trust of the listener can also be achieved by overturning this principle. In piecing together 'Don't know why', evidently aware of the power of the melody and its potential to compel the attention of the listener, Jesse Harris withholds the most singable and direct verse until the second round. As an introduction to the voice of Norah Jones, who covered the song soon after its original release, the strategy used to structure 'Don't know why' has a number of appealing qualities. On Norah Jones' classic reading, by the end of verse two the listener has heard, in sequence, some intriguing music, *that* sublime vocal texture, and *then* some relatively accessible lyrics. As a construction, in this setting it works best that way round.

Mirroring literature and film, both of which have conditioned us to anticipate a dramatic development a short while in advance of the conclusion, another frequent trait of AABA songs can be found in the dramatic peak that often emerges around the three-quarter mark, typically during the bridge section. Kris Kristofferson's 1970 ballad 'Help me make it through the night' and Bob Dylan's 'Make you feel my love', recorded in 1997, both use the bridge to move from descriptive to emotive, from warm to demonstrative. Here the compositional change symbolizes and reflects the singers' need to convey how much what they are singing about means to them and, by inference, how much it should mean to the listener. Without a dramatic peak, how could we be sure they *really* mean it?

AB songs, or songs with lyrics that begin with a verse followed by a chorus, typically use verses to expand upon or add detail to repetitive, often memorable chorus sections. Two examples of this structure are 'Material girl', written in 1984 by Brown and Rans and recorded by Madonna, and 'You know I'm no good', written in 2006 by Amy Winehouse. Both narratives set out to create a distinctive character impression and in both instances the verses are exploratory and the choruses resolute. While Madonna's track uses a familiar contemporary chord sequence borrowed from Bruce Springsteen and Patti Smith's 'Because the night' and Prince's 'Little red Corvette' to channel a uniquely American atmospheric, Amy Winehouse looks to the traditional music of Eastern Europe to add a sense of exotic remove from her narrative. Both intentionally autobiographical, the songs are also similar in the way they use instrumental motifs as compositional punctuation, providing musical space to balance the composition away from verbal detail and towards metaphorical repetition.

As illustrations of how AB songs might develop, Elvis Costello's 1979 single 'Oliver's army' and Bob Dylan's 1966 single 'Just like a woman' have ABABCAB structures that are at once restless and insistent, regularly spiralling away from and returning home to the chorus anchor. Again using verses for detail and choruses to summarize, the effect is simultaneously both definitive and exploratory. Unlike 'Material girl' and 'You know I'm no good' which favour repetitive statement and metaphor, 'Oliver's army' and 'Just like a woman' both use bridges to supply intensity, adding an angular counterpart to a relatively bright, three-chord verse. With only the choruses repeated, as a music and lyric text this structural form demands the attentive involvement of the listener, who is required to adjust to five new sections: verse one, chorus, verse two, middle eight, verse three. Increasingly, in recent decades the trend has been for choruses to rise melodically above verses in AB structures, for example Radiohead's 'High and dry'. Suggesting verse introspection and chorus extraversion, this simple strategy, later favoured by chart brethren Keane and The Script, uses contour to create a sense of emotional containment and release. In terms of structural process, by writing the chorus first, the songwriter of such a song has a number of options for what might potentially happen in the verse, whereas the options for where the chorus might go from an existing verse are relatively minimal.

ABCABC songs like 'Loving you is sweeter than ever', written by Ivy Jo Hunter and Stevie Wonder and released as a single by The Four Tops in 1966, Holland, Dozier and Holland's classic 'How sweet it is (to be loved by you)', recorded in the same year by Marvin Gaye, and, from the following year, Goffin, King and Wexler's '(You make me feel like) a natural woman' have pre-choruses that use repetitive melodic phrases to add tension by disrupting the melodic flow of the surrounding verses and choruses. According the songs valuable gravitas, once removed from the composition these 'stalling' pre-choruses are sorely missed; the songs sound relatively one-dimensional.

In a musical sense, solos, riffs and codas can all add strength to structures that are otherwise too intense to be absorbed in real time, creating room for the listener to take in what has been sung. Van Morrison's 1972 single 'Jackie Wilson said' offers a sublime example of a foundational riff. Unless the songwriter is predisposed to use a motif as a compositional foundation or starting point, as Tom Petty did with 'Honey bee', introductory motifs are commonly chosen towards the end of the songwriting process from a range of options pre-existing in the main body of the composition. Charged with capturing the attention of the listener prior to the vocal, they tend to be critically important.

Soul singers often need space to testify and in Percy Sledge's momentous 1966 reading of Penn and Oldham's 'It tears me up' and the Rolling Stones' 1968 single 'Jumpin' Jack Flash', verses are unexpectedly extended and stretched to allow for this. Similarly, the eminently soulful 'What becomes of the broken hearted', written for Jimmy Ruffin by Weatherspoon, Riser and Dean in 1966, uses a verse, chorus, verse, verse, chorus structure to open up the middle of the song for extemporization. In each song, as the extended section unfurls, there is a sense that the singer can't quit until he has said his piece, yet while it sounds improvised, the section is knowingly constructed – an example of the use of structure to persuade.

In structural terms, there is no law that anything should happen twice. In the early days of popular song, Rodgers and Hart's 'My funny valentine', memorably recorded by Chet Baker in 1956, and Billy Strayhorn's 'Lush life', definitively captured by John Coltrane and Johnny Hartman in 1963, both used meandering, unrepetitive musical settings to frame lyric soliloquy. In each instance there is a sense that the introduction of a repetitive structure would have restricted the power of the narrative by making it more directed, less improvised. Avoiding structural repetition altogether, Paul Weller's 'Trees' and Radiohead's 'Paranoid android', like their predecessors The Beatles' 'Happiness is a warm gun' and 'You never give me your money', use an ABCD structure to move through a series of intriguing, contrasting and sometimes obtuse chapters.

Unlike their American counterparts, the English suites exhibit an uncontrolled sense of adventure that takes the listener on an unsettling and unpredictable structural joy ride before ending mercifully with optimistic resolve. Going even further into the realm of structural adventure, 'In dreams' by Roy Orbison has a structure consisting of musical sections that never repeat (ABCDEF). Possessing a sub-textual structural authenticity, this unfamiliar absence of repetition, which might be said to evoke or reflect a sequence of events typically likened to those of a dream (Lehman, 2003: 80), closely matches the lyric expression.

1.5 Creativity

Songwriting is commonly considered to be a creative act, but what is creativity? What, if anything, defines the creative character and how do creative processes work? Using the answers to these questions, what can we learn about songwriting from the study of creativity?

Getzels and Jackson (1962) and later Weisberg (1986) consider creativity to involve the forming of new combinations or conjoining elements that were previously considered independent and dissimilar but, in their new collaborative state are in some way useful. Perhaps, they suggest, it is the nature of borrowed ideas themselves, the novelty that arises from the uniqueness of their combination, that decides whether an artefact constructed from historical cloth is new or orthodox. According to this line of reasoning, creativity arises from associated 'chains' of ideas that originate from a deep knowledge of the field. Creative songwriting, therefore, is not necessarily bound to ideas entirely new to the community, but might instead comprise existing ideas that have not been compiled before. Implying the need for creativity to possess a quality of uniqueness, Csikszentmihalyi (1996: 8, 50) seeks to redefine creativity as 'a process by which a symbolic domain in the culture is changed'; inferring a similar degree of novelty, in 1999, the National Advisory Committee on Creative and Cultural Education published a definition of creativity as 'imaginative activity fashioned so as to produce outcomes that are both original and of value' (NACCCE 1999: 29).

Adopting an increasingly communicative dimension, the value of creativity itself has evolved alongside its definition. In the sixties Torrance (1967: 7) offered a working definition of creativity as:

> a combination of flexibility, originality and sensitivity to ideas which enables the thinker to break away from usual sequences of thought into different and productive sequences, the result of which gives satisfaction to himself and *possibly* to others.

In outlining his systems model, however, Csikszentmihalyi (1996: 27) argues for a retraction of the term 'possibly', insisting that successful ideas must be couched in terms that others can understand. Immediately, within the parameters of these attempts to define it, we can picture a situation in which the quality of creativity is contested, where what is considered by the songwriter to be creative is not similarly valued by the audience.

Challenging the theoretical models of the late twentieth century, Cropley (2001: 45) notes that expertise acquired through the development of familiarity with a field can pre-organize thinking and produce orthodoxy. At the dawn of the present century, it would seem that merely being capable of identifying, sifting and recreating song ideas may not be enough. Inferring that some songwriters may be more predisposed to creative practice than others, Cropley (ibid.) discusses the possibility that those less informed by the weight of history and who lack such constraints, might in fact benefit by using ignorance of convention to produce novelty. The songs of Austin-based outsider artist Daniel Johnston, for example, often evidence only a fleeting relationship with convention, yet enjoy a hallowed reputation among songwriters as diverse as Kurt Cobain and Chris Difford. Cropley proposes that while a low level of subject knowledge might be helpful in precipitating a flood of novel ideas, the unconventional individual would be likely to have great difficulty in discerning which of those ideas were likely to be effective. For every Daniel Johnston, the argument goes, there are many outsider songwriters yet to catch lightning in a bottle.

Perhaps a balance could be reached by combining those familiar and unfamiliar with convention? A number of the most successful British bands of the past fifty years could be said to possess such equilibrium. In a first category of musicians considered technically knowledgeable, we might place Pete Townshend and John Entwistle of The Who, Charlie Watts, Brian Jones and Bill Wyman of The Rolling Stones, Mick Jones and Topper Headon of The Clash, and Johnny Marr and Andy Rourke of The Smiths. In a second category of relatively intuitive band members we might list Roger Daltrey and Keith Moon of The Who, Keith Richards and Mick Jagger of The Rolling Stones, Joe Strummer and Paul Simonon of The Clash, and Mike Joyce and Morrissey of The Smiths. Within each band it could be argued that a balance of technical and intuitive qualities combined to produce creative and novel song recordings.

Identifying divergent thinking as the cognitive basis for creativity, Cropley (2001: 32–3) discusses the differences between convergent and divergent thinking. Convergent thinking, he explains, recognizes and reapplies set techniques, does not produce novelty, but is instead focused upon obtaining a single correct and accurate answer. This type of thinking can be linked to the notion of songwriting creativity as realized abstraction. When Johnny Marr, formerly of The Smiths has an idea for a sound, for instance, he explores the sonic possibilities until he finds it. Produced by Marr in 1986, 'The Queen Is Dead' LP moves from one distinctive sound to another suggesting complete control over the direction of musical aesthetic; the effect is virtuosic rather than explor-atory. When Marr questions the idea of channelling the sound of The Stooges for the title track, or The Rolling Stones for 'Bigmouth strikes again' (Rogan, 1993: 247, 248) using his skills in identifying the sonic texture required, he knows how to answer. Within the context of song, while divergent thinking is considered to be a significant part of the creative process, it is equally clear that as creative artefacts, songs need to be finished; that convergent thinking needs to inform a final series of decisions.

By contrast, divergent thinking involves shifts of perspective, and the generation of multiple answers from the information available to produce novelty. With reference to songwriting, divergent thinking, Cropley says, creates answers that may not have existed before. Returning to 'The Queen Is Dead', throughout the album Morrissey responds to Marr's historically informed sonic settings with often startlingly idiosyncratic lyric phrases; outside of the stability of their metre and phrasing there is little 'correct' about them and they are consistently novel. Further, while Marr is occupied with the convergent thinking skills needed to obtain a correct textural answer, he uses divergent thinking in the generation of chord sequences. Similarly, Morrissey needs divergent thinking skills to create his highly individual lyric ideas but convergent thinking skills to figure out where to place them.

Creative people are thought by some to possess certain characteristics, some of which are said to involve a strong inherited component while others may be largely acquired through experience (Ericsson and Smith, 1991). Dellas and Gaier (1970) found that creative people are distinguishable from less creative individuals in nine ways: independence, dominance, introversion, openness, breadth of interests, self-acceptance, intuitiveness, flexibility, and social poise, a list to which Dacey (1989) adds tolerance of ambiguity, risk taking, androgyny, and preference for complexity. Adopting a behavioural perspective, Perkins' (1981) model of creative

characteristics includes the ability to change perspectives, the
ability to learn from mistakes and the inclination to evaluate
ideas.

In his study of 'high creativity', Gardner (1993: 364–8)
observes a number of characteristics shared by those capable
of producing highly creative ideas: they showed rapid growth
once they had committed themselves to a domain; they were
self-absorbed; they tended to be both child-like and adult-like
in their activity; they considered themselves, and desired to
be, socially marginalized; and were productive each day. All
were able to identify and explore similarities and differences
between their own works and those of others in the field and
the knowledge gathered from these explorations was key
in enabling them to break away from established wisdom.
High creators, claims Gardner (1997) make time to reflect,
are able to identify and thereby capitalize upon personal
areas of expertise, and see failure as an opportunity to learn
from what went wrong. Agreeing with Craft (2001: 59),
Joubert (2001: 19) argues that creativity is an active process
and that learners must want to consciously apply themselves
to the solution of the problem. Even if the solution occurs
unexpectedly or by chance, it is claimed, the individual must
then work to turn the relevant thoughts into creative action.
Amabile (1983) finds that people will be most creative when
they feel motivated primarily by the interest, enjoyment,
satisfaction and challenge of the work itself, not by external
pressures. The key 'creativity killers' she discovered were:
evaluation or concern with what someone else will think
of your work; focusing entirely on a goal or reward; and
competition.

Projecting a model of creativity as a series of levels, Taylor
(1959) argues that a first level is one of expressive creativity
in which the quality of the product is unimportant. A second
level, during which the individual improves technique but
still may not create artefacts significantly different from
those made by other people, is that of productive creativity.
A third level, inventive creativity, concerns the perception of

new and unusual relationships between previously disparate elements. A fourth level, the innovative, results in a modification of the basic foundation of the field. Translated to songwriting practice, as a developmental trajectory this might read as: songs of self-expression; songs that lean towards pastiche; songs that exhibit thematic juxtaposition; and new, original art.

In research conducted by the author (2006), several professional songwriters recalled having independently followed a similar transitional process. Reflecting upon their first efforts, they remembered being aware of the unedited and over-introspective nature of their compositional ideas. Should the fledgling songwriter perceive this initial work to be of no value to the community, the temptation to either cease writing, create work typical of the zeitgeist, or jettison indulgence in favour of mediocre moderation could be significant. Over time, according to Taylor's proposition, as the songwriter becomes increasingly adept at selecting sounds and ideas that co-opt within an emerging aesthetic template, the individualistic and referential strands integrate to form a voice capable of projecting individual character within familiar soundscapes.

Expanding upon Taylor's notion of the fledgling songwriter as uncritical generator of ideas, it is held that brainstorming, or the outpouring of ideas without evaluation can be effective as a means of avoiding the tendency to slow down the rate of the production of creative ideas (Barron, 1969: 132). Barron's text advocates a process of 'deferred judgement' in which the creative individual seeks to brainstorm ideas in an environment free of criticism before later looking for ways in which to combine and improve the ideas. Referring to the phenomenon of 'Synectics', Gordon (1961) considers the process to involve the fusion of diverse elements produced by the creator during the spontaneous and free flowing generation of ideas. Significantly, Gordon suggests that brainstorming should occur without the intervention of criticism; that the ideas should be allowed to exist without filtration.

Creative songwriters are said to be those who free-associate without evoking critical interference. This free association is, however, in itself insufficient as a means of solving the compositional problem of how to turn the abstractions of the extrovert subconscious into words and music that at once reflect the spirit of the initial impetus, and allow for that spirit to be accessible to the listener.

Overlooking the initial solipsistic phase identified by Taylor, Boden (1990, 1994, 2001) cites three types of creative thinking: combinational, exploratory and transformational. Dependent upon the individual having knowledge of disparate things and being sensitive to subtle similarities, combinational creativity refers to the production of new ideas by making unfamiliar associations that are unexpected yet valuable. Exploratory creativity happens, according to Boden, once the individual has learnt some of the rules of creative activity in question and proceeds to stretch, tweak or significantly alter the rules. Transposed to songwriting, this implies that skills of editorial judgement rather than the mediation of individual character are at the core of progression.

Recognizing the critical listener to be the ideal sounding board, numerous theorists emphasize the notion of creativity as a multidimensional interactive process between the creative individual and his or her environment (Rhodes, 1961; Chambers, 1973; Treffinger, Sorore and Cross, 1993). Jackson (2006: 1–4) identifies a number of obstacles to the successful realization of this paradigm, including the difficulty in translating creative processes outside of the original sphere of expertise. While the creative work might be considered innovative within the immediate circle of songwriting practitioners, it might not be heard the same way by an audience of non-songwriters. Songwriters, it seems, cannot expect to be rewarded by the wider critical community for creating peer-approved work of innovative songwriting character; many listeners desire and value music that is not challenging. To bridge the divide, songwriters are obliged to engage with *degrees* of creativity.

The relatively rare transformational creativity concerns the generation of ideas that could not have been predicted prior to their generation (ibid.). This type of creativity would perhaps apply to ideas that have no identifiable point of reference – those considered works of genius in the sense that they are both unforeseen and unforeseeable (Moore, 2004). While the scope for argument over songs that might be worthy of inclusion in this category is colossal, Kate Bush's 'Babooshka', David Bowie's 'John, I'm only dancing' and The Fall's 'Touch sensitive' might be considered as recordings with roots that are particularly difficult to trace. Ultimately, the songwriter is obliged to make the leap beyond imitation into a world in which elements previously unforeseen in the field of song co-exist to a greater or lesser extent with familiar signifiers. To be creative as a practitioner, songwriters need to know both what it is about their original practice that is new to the domain, and what those signifiers, or markers of song tradition are. To be a songwriter, what is needed is to know what makes communicative songs work.

1.6 Communication

Sean Devine, vice president of international membership at the American Society of Authors, Composers and Publishers, firmly believes that songwriting is about communication. 'The people who write popular songs', he says, 'are masters of communication who communicate in ways that most of us are unable to do.' As previously discussed, while a lyric writer may have a highly developed sense of conversational or written language, he or she is not entitled, within the multidimensional format of song construction, to convey lyrics on extra-musical terms. Rather the presence of music in song requires the songwriter to mediate and adapt a melodically structured verbal language to create a new form

of communicative language. Further to the previously emphasized areas of music, lyric and structure, the dimensions of
arrangement, performance and production are key in allowing
songs to communicate. With the addition of these comple-
mentary elements, each of which compete to occupy our
attention, how songs communicate meaning becomes a more
complex study.

As Sim (1992) observes, like language, music is said never
to refer to something directly, always attaching a complex
web of meaning. Similarly, the meanings of texts, languages
and words are unstable and hard to determine, making it
impossible to lay claim to a 'correct' interpretation (ibid.).
Building upon the notion proposed by Cooke (1959) that it
is possible for musical ideas to be expressed by the artist and
received by the listener intact, Tolstoy (1960: 44) argues that
the purpose of the artwork is to communicate or transmit
feelings from the artist to the receiver, and that the degree to
which the work is a success depends upon the degree to which
the receiver is 'infected'.

Echoing Swanwick's observation (1979: 20, 38), Philpott
(2001: 34, 35), however, claims that the listener can never
be certain that the message he or she is receiving is the one
intended by the composer, and that therefore it is the work
rather than the composer who is communicating something
to us. In songwriting, meaning can never be truly conveyed,
rather meaning can be made accessible or inaccessible. To
stake an interpretative claim on what the songwriter intends
to convey is to indulge in guesswork; no matter how much we
think we understand we may be wrong.

In a meditation on the time and place in which musical
works exist, Gadamer (1975: 130) alludes to the continu-
ously changeable nature of the performance contexts of
musical works and, on a similar theme Philpott (2001: 33,
40) notes that a number of semioticians have suggested that
the relationship between signifier and signified, performer
and listener, is constantly shifting, and that consequently as
listeners we never arrive at a definitive meaning. Understanding

is therefore 'a playful and dynamic process of interpretation'. Slowed down by distribution and critical deliberation the argument suggests, this year's next big thing might be superceded by the time it reaches the listener's ear. No matter how confident the predominant X Factor judge Simon Cowell may appear, the complexities of songwriting mean we can never *control* the relationship between artist and audience. Exceptional songwriters like David Ackles, Laura Nyro and Nick Drake all had to wait decades until a mass audience was ready to hear what they had to say.

While Shakespeare would have us believe that there is nothing new under the sun, as Fromkin, Rodman and Hyams (2009: 34) observe, much remains unknown about human languages and their use. While all languages use a finite set of sounds that combine to form meaningful elements, these meaningful elements can combine to form an infinite number of possible sentences. Further, speakers of all languages have the potential to comprehend an infinite number of sentences. Similarly, Chomsky (1971: 8) views the most striking aspect of linguistic competence to be the ability of the learner to produce new sentences which despite their unfamiliarity to the listener are immediately understood. Thankfully, as communicators, songwriters are not bound by regulation. For the songwriter, faced with the daunting task of directing a communicative gesture between themselves, who few among the audience will have met or encountered, and the listener, who is almost certainly unknown to the songwriter, the findings of Chomsky might offer comfort; on the face of it, this challenge might seem insurmountable, the scope for disconnection almost infinite, yet the scope of the listener's capabilities cannot be underestimated.

In a discussion of Chomsky's writing on language, Lyons (1970: 22–3) refers to Chomsky's vision of a duality of structure in the way grammar is divided: a syntactic level, representing combinations of meaningful units (words); and a phonological level consisting of units that are themselves without meaning but assist in the identification of the primary units (phonemes). With reference to the reception of songwriting, Chomsky's theory implies that the way words are received by a listener involves more than a simple transferral of text; they also rely on performance to convey meaning. Successful communication in this context requires a combination of verbal, musical, textural and culturally referential signifiers to interact, the subtle backgrounding and foregrounding of phrases to inform and absorb. Thanks to the monochrome nature of its lyric and the colour of its music, The Smiths' 'William, it was really nothing' is a dour read, but a joyful listen. Can these signifiers be controlled in any way other than delineating them?

In seeking to classify language functions, Wilkinson (1975: 56) identifies three kinds of activity he observed during 'interchange': the self-expression of the individual; the establishment and maintenance of relationships with others; and the exploration, description, analysis of and reflection upon the world that was, is and might be. Similarly, Moffatt (1978: 10, 47) asserts that the elements of discourse comprise three elements: a speaker, a listener, and a subject, and that these contributors create a 'spectrum of discourse' concerned with recording what is happening, what happened and what may happen.

Analysis of popular music lyric writing evidences how lyricists regularly frame song sections in past, present and future tenses. One example is the song 'The suburbs' by Arcade Fire, which begins in the past tense, moves to the present and later dwells in the future. It may be that, because these lyrics give the listener three dimensions – context for the existing situation; insight on the narrator's current state of mind; and a glimpse of how he sees the future – the editorial adaptation of such a lyric writing strategy might allow the lyricist to communicate a significant degree of meaning to a largely unknown audience.

Rodgers and Hart's 'Bewitched, bothered and bewildered' is a lyric composition that divides the tenses in equal measure: verse one refers to the worldview of the narrator as it is;

verse two deals with the world that used to be; and, with reference to the communication-based theories of Wilkinson and Moffatt, the third verse is dominated by the world that might be. A standard popularized by Ella Fitzgerald and Frank Sinatra among others, the lasting ability of the song to communicate meaning across time and culture is illustrated by its immense popularity in the twenty-first century, when it has been recorded by artists as diverse as Scottish balladeer Rod Stewart, Chicago-based punk band The Smoking Popes, American-Canadian singer-songwriter Rufus Wainwright, and a 20-million-selling French language singer from Belgium, Lara Fabian. While the consummate music and lyric phrasing inherent in the writing of 'Bewitched, bothered and bewildered' surely account for much of the translatable appeal, perhaps some of the song's timeless quality comes from this deliberate setting of the three communicative tenses.

Alternatively, lyrics that are written in one tense may not give the listener the contextual information needed to be able to empathize. From the perspective of the songwriter, to be conscious of such communicative detail during the creative process would evoke the risk of becoming stifled by critical awareness of how the work will be received, a psychological phenomenon labelled 'extrinsic motivation' (Amabile, 1983). According to this psychological theory previously discussed in the previous sub-chapter, if the songwriter is imagining the reaction of the listener, the focus of the intended expression is likely to be compromised. Consequently, any manipulation of tense is likely to take place in the editorial phase that exists post initial draft and prior to recording.

Writing in 1960, Jakobson proposed a theoretical model of six language functions based upon the communicative process: the expressive function of the addresser's feelings; the conative focus on the person addressed; the referential function based on the context of the speech event; the poetic function in relation to the verbal aesthetics of language; the phatic function that emphasizes the predisposition of the addresser towards the addressee; and the metalinguistic function based on a mutual awareness of the linguistic code. This implies that the feelings of the songwriter are essential to communication; that to write songs that withhold the feelings of the songwriter, and make reference only to what might be perceived to be of intellectual interest to the listener is to overlook a significant linguistic aspect of song composition. Effectively, to omit the affective realm, it is argued, would be to write a song that means little or nothing to the songwriter, and by extension, little or nothing to the audience. A certain amount of emotional self-perception, of effective concept assumes an important role.

Theoretically, to meet the criteria for communication proposed by both Jakobson and Wilkinson, the songwriter is obliged to express his or her feelings and, at some point in the creative process, to think about how the expression of feeling will be received. Again problematically, in songwriting the receiver of the creative work is unknown to the creator, a situation that requires the songwriter to make an informed guess as to which affective expressions are likely to be of interest to the listener. As it demands a surgical approach to sensitivity and a willingness to leave oneself open to ridicule, for many songwriters the weighing and balancing of this element is a challenging editorial skill to acquire.

Further, not only must the lyricist know *what* to say and *how* to say it, but also *when* to say it. The poetic function described by Jakobson may be interpreted to refer to the skill of using words that retain, yet do not place an excessive demand upon the attention of the listener. In written form, the speed at which poetry is absorbed is traditionally controlled by the reader. In songwriting, however, the songwriter must work within the confines of the timescale implied by the performance. Part of the skill of becoming a communicative songwriter therefore involves developing the ability to convey messages of poetic interest to the listener at an appropriate tempo; for the poetic function to work efficiently, either something verbally, melodically or texturally compelling needs to be happening. With its constant chain of bustling horns, bubbling bass lines and insistent narrative, The Beatles' 'Got to get you into my life' is an obvious example of this.

Alternatively, to allow the listener to absorb and reflect upon the poetic material, perhaps within the instrumental parts of the song that exist in relief to the narrative poetry, little or nothing competitive should be happening. In the open musical spaces that punctuate Van Morrison's version of 'Raglan Road', the words continue to chime in the memory long after the voice has ceased its poetic work. Meditative rather than insistent, it is a very different listening experience to 'Got to get you into my life'. While the Beatles' recording requires at least three or four listens for the listener to begin to acquire a quantifiable sense of its multiple lines of expression, 'Raglan Road' can be absorbed and experienced in one go.

While some writers in the folk genre work unaccompanied, in most other genres additional instruments are added to recordings. In the process of inviting the listener to interpret the text as a performance, it is critical that the selection of instruments should enhance, or at the very least not interfere with, the voice. Rather than continually seeking to reinvent the wheel, it makes sense from an arrangement perspective to develop an instrumental coterie of sounds capable of projecting the individual voice.

Vocal intonations, or the 'tune' patterns that accompany speech, are thought to carry messages about the speaker's attitude (Halliday in Kress, 1976) and it is claimed that a significant amount of biological information can be deduced from voice quality – among them gender, size and age (Laver, 1968). Adding that the elements often appear related, Wilkinson (1975: 20) lists the characteristics of paralinguistic communication as: accent, speed of delivery, loudness, relative continuity, voice quality and tone. Wilkinson claims that accent allows the recipient to know where the speaker comes from and that speech rates tend to vary from situation to situation depending on the social context. It would appear important to acknowledge that the way a compositional text is likely to be received as a communicative artefact will rely heavily upon its performance qualities; these elements give the listener, who may not be able to see the singer, key contextual information concerning the singer's identity.

Towards the end of the twentieth century, Michael Stipe of REM used the distinctive frequency and tone of his voice against a basic Rickenbacker guitar, bass and drum backdrop. Not only did the combination of textures sound unique, the earthy familiarity of the instrumental line-up was a counterpart to the otherworldliness of Stipe's original lyric imagery and vocal phrasing. Working in tandem to communicate with character and duality, on REM recordings the voice and arrangement are as one; there is a vivid sense that should either be absent, the mechanism for creating an engaging interpretation of the song text evaporates. Disconnected, the great singer, the great band and the great songs would in all likelihood have never been heard.

As Joe Strummer confesses towards the end of the Clash film *Westway to the World*, there are magical sonic and performative combinations of voice and instrumentation that cannot be replicated. The key, as Strummer realized too late, is to recognize when such simpatico exists, and to acknowledge the correlations, for future reference. As a further example, Peter Gabriel's best work uses synthesizers, the electronic textures of which accentuate and bring a textural, mechanical counterpart to the warm and soulful sound of his voice. Frank Sinatra's vocal tone fits an orchestra, while Tony Bennett's voice works better with a jazz quartet, and so on.

For the songwriter and for the singer, the challenge is not only to find the right sounds to project the vocal, but also to have the critical awareness to understand the sonic parameters or range of options available for the potential modification of sounds. Once the sounds have been identified, through a critical process of trial and error, decisions need to be made concerning if, how and when the arrangement should develop dynamic contour. Content dictates form and some songs are relatively unambiguous in terms of how they can be arranged and performed to communicate. Prince's 'Kiss' is a relatively inflexible song that Tom Jones, noting the lack of room for sonic exploration, only narrowly altered for his own version.

Extending the communicative premise of its initial concept by using arrangement techniques, Prince's 'The most beautiful girl in the world' makes a humble amount of compositional ideas go a long way. Having established its initial instrumental and melodic premise, as the track progresses both Prince and the band extemporize with increasing flourish, altering the listener's expectation with a variety of musical excursions that embellish yet never deviate from the implications of the text. Each new approach to the revolving chord sequence drama-tizes the interpretation, keeping us tuned in.

To ascertain a sense of the expressive intentions of the songwriter, session players in Nashville will typically request an acoustic demo sketch of the song in advance. Hearing the sketch will allow the session player to hear the sound of the song in its core, or foundational mode, and consequently enable the session player, who is tasked with making an ensemble contribution that will amplify the core expression, to apply a more responsive interpretation. As such the session player, often assumed to be merely the messenger, becomes a vital conduit in communicating expressive meaning from the songwriter to the listener.

Some singers are irreplaceable as interpreters: Dionne Warwick's empathy for the compositions of Bacharach and David is a particularly striking example. Some songs, it would seem, have difficulty reaching their potential without an appro-priate reading – a forged understanding of how the text relates to the performance. As their transmission of intended meaning is direct rather than indirect, compared to a non-performing songwriter who relies on others to interpret and convey their feelings and experiences, a performing songwriter could be argued to have greater control over the way in which his or her songs are conveyed.

For a song to be communicative, words may not necessarily need to be clearly projected; the communicative effect may come from expressive performance. In a West London squat late in 1976, Clash lead singer Joe Strummer was beginning to suspect that the demo recordings his band had recently made at the behest of the Polydor record label were not adequately reflecting their live representations (cited in Strummer, Jones, Simonon and Headon, 2008: 95). Seeking to create a more radio-friendly style of annunciation, Polydor had apparently requested that Strummer abandon the guttural, at times unintelligible vocal performance style he had been perfecting on stage and pronounce the lyrics with clarity in the studio. Strummer duly obliged, but neither Polydor nor The Clash were enthusiastic about the newly sanitized sound. Months later, at the behest of rival label CBS, Strummer was back in the studio with The Clash, this time laying down the often indecipherable vocal tracks that added much to their iconic first album.

2

Songwriters

2.1 Tom Waits

In Liverpool, someone with a natural flair for causing trouble can, they say, 'start a row in an empty house'. As the tour guide in 'The house where nobody lives', a stand-out track from the much acclaimed 'Mule Variations', Tom Waits sets himself a formidable task: how, with only a deserted shell of a building at his disposal, can he create a situation engaging enough to warrant a song? Taking his cue from two-well known Liverpudlians, John Lennon and Paul McCartney, Waits uses a 'zoom lens' narrative technique borrowed from The Beatles' 'Penny Lane' that make us feel not only that we are present at the location itself, but also that we are a part of its life.

Both songs introduce us to their respective locations within the first few words. Immediately, we know where we are, and this gives us the necessary context to listen on without scrambling around trying to picture, or imagine the scene as the songs progress. It soon becomes apparent that Waits, like Lennon and McCartney, is more interested in the people who inhabit the place than in the place itself; the title masquerades as the characters emerge. While this may appear to offer the songwriter a way of solving the aforementioned problem, in effect this further compounds the challenge facing the songwriter, who now has the task of bringing to life a cast of characters we have never met, in a place we have probably never been. How do they do it?

In verse one, by observing the barber on Penny Lane from within earshot, or at least near enough to hear the word 'hello', Lennon and McCartney begin to solve this problem by initially placing the narrator (McCartney) at a distance typical of human verbal interaction. Guided by the narrator, by the end of verse two we have zoomed in to the fireman's pocket; we know something about him only he could know: he keeps a portrait of the queen. Soon, the zoom lens allows us to experience Penny Lane at closer than close quarters; in verse three we are placed inside the nurse's feelings, the lens having made its way to the most guarded of locations. The impossibility of the suggested experience is novel as we view Penny Lane from hitherto unanticipated proximities. Through the ears and eyes, the spiritual and incidental perceptions of those who breathe life into the place, we see Penny lane not as it *appears*, but as it really *is*.

Finally, in verse four, the narrator retreats to his initial viewpoint; normal service is resumed and life on Penny Lane continues as before. In using this technique, Lennon and McCartney magically evoke a dual set of allegories for our very existence: some things we feel deeply while others barely register, and we are also reminded that some things belong to us and some belong to everyone. By keeping us constantly on the move, zooming in and out of the lives of those who inhabit Penny Lane, The Beatles give us a great deal more than a voyeuristic experience – they take us behind the scenes.

Tom Waits begins his song at the end of the drive that leads to the house where nobody lives, near enough to know the windows are cracked and the house is empty. Like Lennon and McCartney, he has no intention of staying put for long, and by verse two he is standing on the porch of the deserted abode. Significant in terms of lyric continuity is the idea that things look different at close quarters than they do from a distance, and it is this perspective switch that Waits uses to keep his story moving. And as he moves from verse to verse we move with him, sharing a natural curiosity for what might lie within.

By the end of verse two, Waits has had a look through the windows and seen at first hand the desolation inside. What else is left to say? Is it enough for a singer to tell us that he has found a derelict property? Brilliantly, in the final verse Waits abandons the zoom lens which has so far directed and heightened much of the tension, and makes a personal plea to the listener, never to place earthly possession over love, never to undervalue the spiritual wealth of the community of living, breathing people whose laughter and tears make a house a palace. Once again, as in Penny Lane, the location is the backdrop for the people, real and imagined, who take centre stage.

Back in the early seventies, when Waits was based in Los Angeles, it was similarly the human condition that occupied much of his songwriting. A post-midnight litany of tear-stained ballads and comedic shuffles framed by soft un-intrusive jazz tones, Waits' music from this period yielded many gems, among them 'Rosie', 'Martha', 'Ol'55' and 'Jersey girl', a three-chord tune that Bruce Springsteen was destined to drag from the pool hall to the stadium. While the melodies and the arrangements of this era were imaginatively composed and produced, during this early phase of his recording career, for the most part, it is the lyric, moulded in Waits' unmistakable singing growl, that holds the attention. The lyric narrators – any one of a number of strays, yet inevitably an extension of Waits himself – hold court in thrall to a neon-lit nocturnal universe where the wit is sharp and the scenery transient. At other times, however, the mood is one of almost unbearable sadness: the barfly cut adrift from the warmth of a human touch; the lover whose heart breaks at being torn away from the arms of love. Make 'em laugh, as the mantra goes, or make 'em cry.

As viewers from a faraway time, we have no way of evaluating the authenticity of the community of characters who drift in and out of these tunes like figures in a Hopper painting or a Carver tale. Like his kindred artistic spirits, Waits uses finely observed detail to bring these folk to life; although we never meet them, because of the editorial consistency of the poetry and the sense of place provided by the musicianship, we understand them to be real. Like Carver, Waits never overloads us with back-story, always leaving us room for our imagination to fill in the spaces. And after all, whatever we invent is certain to sound real to us.

Some songs, including 'Jersey girl' and 'The heart of Saturday night', use simple chord sequences that give the impression of having been written on guitar. Others, like 'Kentucky Avenue' and 'Burma shave', would test the most dextrous of guitarists and are more likely to have been written on piano. Half backyard and half orchestra pit, this compositional duality further defines the chasm between the simple humanity of those who inhabit his songs and their grand dreams and hopes. Like a character transported from a Henry James novel, a Minneapolis hooker writes a Christmas card to an old flame, telling him how well she is doing, how life is on the up. Alas, it transpires the story is not true, and by the end of the song the façade drops with an admission that her boasts are mere aspirations. Although, like 'Christmas card from a hooker in Minneapolis', many of the songs of this era are laced with narrative distractions, humanity is never far from the surface and true to its national heritage, the outlook is shot through with glimpses of optimism, sparks of laughter and a spirit of restlessness.

On the 1978 LP 'Blue Valentines', Waits breaks the trend of singing in autobiographical first person by adopting the character of a female prostitute. Allowing us to absorb and accept the switch of gender without distraction, as a mechanism for dealing with any potential ambiguity, the lyric narrative, delivered with trademark vocal gravel, immediately announces 'she' is pregnant. Like John Prine, who opened 'Angel from Montgomery' by announcing himself as an old woman, Waits will have realized that to delay such a statement of identity until a later point in the composition would have led to many listeners lifting the needle to listen again, to need to experience the song in its essential context.

Elsewhere on 'Blue Valentines' Waits' voice moves away from our perception of what it should be or what we might expect it to be. On 'Somewhere' the song is well known enough for us to sense it is being acted rather than lived by Waits. On 'Kentucky Avenue' Waits voices the narrative as if spoken or sung by a child. This child is some poet though, and as we are led through a sensory and ethereal portrayal of how magical the world might seem through the eyes of a child, the effect is one of magic realism. On 'Bone Machine' recorded in 1992, Waits revisits childhood again, this time in the guise of a disenfranchised teenager. In contrast with the elaborate musical voicing used for 'Kentucky Avenue', on 'I don't want to grow up', each monosyllabic lyric phrase and rudimentary chord sequence seems realistically accessible, easily linked to the life of a typical teenager; each compositional move calibrated to persuade the listener to believe they are actually in the presence of someone much younger than the artist himself.

Mount (1988: 62, 63) and Savignon (1997) suggest that creative writers should consider adopting fictional characters, a role-playing strategy that enables them to see and understand motives from multiple perspectives. It could be argued that such creations are only partly fictional in the sense that they are extensions of the imagined self; the characters, their vocabularies and actions inevitably relate to the experience and imagination of the creator. Such licence enables Waits to voice a statement that would otherwise have been impermissible as an authentic gesture in the first person. Who wants to know what the *real* Tom Waits thinks about a prostitute from the Midwest down on her luck? Such a relationship between artist and subject is less removed, more intense as role play. Similarly, in the grand scale of things, how the songwriter Waits imagines a teenager might see the world is not particularly interesting, but by adapting the fictitious persona it becomes compelling. Again John Prine was quick to realize this dynamic in the drafting of his song 'Hello in there', in which he conveys the loneliness of growing old by singing from the perspective of an elderly person. Such a strategy might be considered effective as a means of prompting compassion in the listener, of evoking an empathetic under-standing of the feelings of those marginalized by life.

On the album 'Frank's Wild Years' Waits takes a leaf from Randy Newman's book by using character portrayal to satirize the central figure. Waits' narrator of 'I'll take New York' is disillusioned, yet Waits never states this to be the case, rather he implies it through a combination of narrative and musical language. On Newman's classic modification of 'Old Kentucky home', the narrator comes across as a bigot, a method used liberally on his 1974 album 'Good Old Boys' to create monstrous or marginalized characters who, unlike Newman himself, are ripe for satire. Naturally, as it is actually Newman's voice we hear, there is a risk of misinterpretation, that the listener will believe the obnoxious character to actually *be* Randy Newman. It is all part of the irony; the price the songwriter pays for getting under the skin or into the shoes of someone who is not actually them.

Ultimately, when songwriters are not writing and singing as themselves, in some way they still are. Even the characters who come from the darkest recesses of the author's imagi-nation to represent the voices of innocence or the forces of ignorance are the product of the author's invention and are, therefore, representative in some way of the songwriter's self as creator. Tom Waits may not be Frank, the overly ambitious nightclub singer, but he can certainly imagine being him, and without that facility to metamorphose shared with John Prine and Randy Newman we would have been denied some of the most memorable characters in recent popular song.

After his marriage to Kathleen Brennan in the early eighties, Waits' songs became more playful in design and increasingly unconventional as instrumental arrangements. Following the transatlantic creative journey of fellow realist Henry James by encompassing hitherto unexplored Asiatic and European overtones, on the remarkable trilogy of 'Swordfishtrombones', 'Rain Dogs' and 'Frank's Wild Years', a faux naivety given emphasis by the magnificently angular phrasing of guitarist Marc Ribot cloaks the masterful invention of Waits' new style of writing. Free of Hollywood costume and far away from home, these songs give voice to the ultimate émigré, the elusive loner detached by more than geography. The Stones and Beefheart sometimes literally seep from the grooves, helping to construct a wildly exotic noise so seamlessly connected to the performance of the singer that the elements seem to operate as one. Part of the appeal lies in the unpredictability of it all. Whenever convention threatens to return, as if to deny us what we might expect the anticipated narrative is curtailed with a startling reflex. This is a new America as seen through the rear view mirror of its author; disconnected from the accepted wisdom of its ancestors and refracted through glass harmonicas, talking drums, congas, freedom bells and bagpipes.

Expanding his newly found fascination with the possibilities of character projection through sound, in the nineties Waits' songs are more concerned with texture than words, increasingly willing to allow the ambiguous to represent the real. 'Black Rider', partly recorded in Hamburg with a group of musicians recruited outside the local train station, sets the tempo for the fierce percussive howl heard on 'Bone Machine', 'Blood Money' and 'Real Gone'. More Pollock than portrait, on these records the song often serves the sound, pushing and pulling the form without seeking to direct or define. This wilful abstraction, or widening of sound, imbued Waits' songwriting with a mythical sense of adventure, cementing his reputation as an artist of extraordinary depth.

Observing a career in parallel, in his *Guardian* review of Blur frontman Damon Albarn's debut solo album 'Everyday Robots', critic Alexis Petridis writes:

One of the chief allegations levelled at Blur was that they were somehow inauthentic. Damon Albarn, in particular, dealt with artifice, adopting personas and inventing characters rather than reinventing himself ... As it turned out, keeping himself to himself might have been the smartest move Albarn ever made. It ensured he was never trapped by public perceptions ... and enabled him to spend the last fifteen years or so flitting between disparate projects ... without anyone questioning why.

Perhaps uniquely among his peers, in the present century on 'Mule Variations' and 'Bad As Me', Waits has been able to conjure new and lustrous strands from each phase of his songwriting life, mixing songs disparate in form and style yet unified by his own original, inimitable voice. He is, it seems, given free reign by his listening audience. A victory lap of sorts, such a retrospective approach could easily be forgiven since over three decades, Waits had successfully managed to change horses in mid-stream not once but twice, a highly unusual claim for any songwriter.

2.2 Adele

Adele's 2010 cover of Bob Dylan's 'Make you feel my love' is delivered with a clear reverence to the original, which has a demo quality born of its recording method. In his book *Chronicles* (2005: 190–4) Dylan talks of the need to capture a 'certain something', whether it requires five minutes or twenty takes. Capturing a perfectly written ballad with incomplete instrumentation and imperfect timing as if to ground any delusions of grandeur, his original version of 'Make you feel my love' possesses a genuine humility that stems the sentimental tide. While similarly sensing a need to let the words and voice convey the text, Adele's reading is also careful not to adorn. Undistracted by embellishment, both are as close to demo in spirit as can be found on a modern commercial recording. In recent times, demos, once performances that merely sought to illustrate the basic compositional shape of the text, have become more like records, with the onus upon the songwriter to create a fully dimensional and immersive representation. Nothing, it seems, should be left to the imagination. Dylan's recording of 'Make you feel my love' is therefore something of an anomaly: a gesture harking back to old times as much as a statement from an artist so far into his career, so lost in his art that the delineation between demo and record needn't overly concern him.

For every spare, unaffected demo-sounding track released, there are hundreds treated with forensic care – arranged and produced to enable them to survive repeated listens on portable devices, radio and sound systems of all dimension. Contemporary analysis is informative, with both commercial and independent recordings adopting complex arrangement strategies that portray repetitive or near-repetitive sequences of text in new ways. Deceptively introducing itself as a modern folk song, Adele's 'Rolling in the deep' begins with a verse delivered by voice and guitar. After 23 seconds, to hint at more expansive sounds to come, and to dissolve the initial impression of the song as a 'solo' performance, a drum is added. To sustain continuity, at 42 seconds a new section is presented, a pre-chorus with quickening chord changes that overturn the relatively sedate and undemanding stillness of previous verses. Before the chorus has arrived, we have experienced three different sets of sounds, each one drawing us towards the soaring chorus, which finally arrives after one minute.

After the chorus, at 1:18, we hear another verse, but this time, to differentiate it from the first verse, we hear the newly added sound of a piano. From a recording perspective, the strategy so far has been to alter, either with chords or instrumentation, our impression of what we are hearing approximately every 19 seconds. The scope for regularity in changes of arrangement is limited, however, and the producer, charged with creating a recording that audiences will be able to return to on numerous occasions, needs to temper predictability by ensuring that new textures do not arrive at easily anticipated points. So, at 1:28, midway through the second verse, extra percussion is added. The new sound not only breaks with the established tradition of a change every four bars, it also signals a quickening of the pace; the more familiar we become with the verses and choruses of the song text, the more changes our ear will tolerate, and eventually welcome.

At 1:37 we hear a second pre-chorus, this time with backing vocals, and at 1:55 we hear the second chorus, again with additional backing vocals. As the track progresses, the dimensions of sound snowball. More compositional variation is needed, and at 2:12 we hear an entirely new section that is effectively a repetitive reinforcement of the title. At a little over 2 minutes into the track, it is the fourth new piece of music we hear, but in terms of arrangement it is the ninth. So far, everything that has happened has inferred a build: more instruments, more voices, more music. To continue building the sound will eventually become impossible or at the very least predictable, so at 2:31 the arrangement is reduced to just voice and drum. Retaining this minimalist approach to present the third pre-chorus in a new sonic format, at 2:50 we hear the pre-chorus with no drums, and then at 2:58 there is a structurally unpredictable extension of the pre-chorus with handclaps.

The shifts in sound come with increasing regularity as the song nears its close; at 3:08 we hear the chorus with extra cymbals and then finally an ascent to yet another peak in the form of a concluding chorus with added high register piano at 3:27. As a compositional text this is a relatively simple song. As a single, however, it is also an extremely complex arrangement that leads the song to shift shape no less than fourteen times.

Given the complexity of this recording, and the evident ability of her voice to withstand and even benefit from a broad range of instrumentation, why did Adele barely use any dynamic variation in her version of 'Make you feel my love'?

Across an album of songs, to continually shift the spectrum of sound would soon become tiring on the ear; it works well for four-minute singles but not necessarily forty-minute albums. To combine inventive and less inventive arrangements is to extend the dynamic of the sequence and make the album more durable, more shared and ultimately more known. 'Make you feel my love' is therefore a fine album track, but singles are something else entirely, and in the parlance of the global hit, 'Rolling in the deep' tells us that a significant amount of sound movement may be required to make us to want to hear it, either passively or attentively, again and again.

2.3 George and Ira Gershwin

While Tom Waits and Adele are masters of fiction and autobiography, songwriting isn't always tied to persona. With 'The man I love', George and Ira Gershwin succeeded in creating a song universal enough to be sung by all. Ella Fitzgerald performed it as part of her landmark 'Gershwin Songbook' on Verve, and three decades later, singing the tune as part of his ground-breaking MTV set, Tony Bennett, altering the gender without skipping a beat, switched the word 'man' for 'girl'. The malleability of the title speaks volumes for the inclusivity of the words and music, which are convincing enough to withstand either setting.

It is sometimes advised that the opening lines of a song might benefit from telling the listener who, what, when and where (Braheny, 2007: 65). The four 'w's, it is argued, give us the parameters within which the following narrative detail can be contextualized, deciphered and understood. In 'The man I love', however, we are given this information in only the most vague of terms. As it is a song purposefully intended for any singer, we don't know much about who is singing or anything about who is being sung to. Equally ambiguously, the when is someday and the where unspecified. All we know is that the singer believes that *someone* is out there somewhere, and that *someday* they will appear. A master-class in figurative and emotional generalization, these opening words effectively encapsulate the entire song. Four sections later we still know nothing about the other. How could we? They don't exist yet. From the songwriter's perspective this is deliberate, as it creates the potential for a blank canvas, open to the improvisational realm of each individual listener's imagination. In 'The man I love' George and Ira Gershwin invite us to imagine our own, idealized version of the man or girl in question, knowing that we will choose our ideal image. Unwittingly we write part of the song ourselves.

Using another strategy designed to create a sense of universality, the Gershwins' 'Someone to watch over me' recreates the theme of longing mined by 'The man I love', this time adopting a different yet similarly inclusive approach. Within a classic AABA structural setting, the lyric narrative of verse one focuses entirely on the person being sung to. As the person being sung to doesn't even exist yet, he can be substituted for she. Again the absence of detail involves us in the song: what does somebody we are longing to see look like? By contrast, verse two trains the narrative focus upon the singer, who tells us something of their own personality. In equal compositional measure, we have now 'met' two figures, one real and one imagined.

Now we have been introduced, what next? A bridge that tells us more about the singer herself will tip the scales of self-absorption, while a bridge that reiterates the anonymity of the 'someone' character promises little; after all, there is a limit to how much we can be told about a figure who hides behind the mist. Alternatively, to write lyrics that tell us about the setting, incidental features that locate the narrative, will risk negating the mood of open intimacy created by the opening stanzas. If the 'someone' suddenly appears, the refrain due to be repeated at the end of the third verse becomes redundant. Ruling out these options, the Gershwins need to rule one in.

Inventively, the middle eight that comprises the third chapter of the song switches the narrative focus to onlookers, those who can actually and realistically tell us something of the 'someone'. Equally effectively, verse four involves us directly, as the singer pleads for our help in persuading that longed-for someone, now identified, to step forward. Gradually we find ourselves encircled by characters: the real, the imagined, the distant and near, all part of a community brought together by the song. Why should we fall for such a finely crafted, calculated strategy? Enchanted by such a melody, how could we resist?

2.4 Lucinda Williams

Grinning widely and clearly in thrall of her duet partner for the evening, Lucinda Williams introduces Elvis Costello to the CMT audience with a barely disguised tone of reverence: 'He has written about 300 songs, I've written about, I don't know, fifty maybe'. Following a round of applause, Elvis, whose critical ear rarely lets him down, replies: 'Yeah, but they are fifty really good ones, you know what I'm saying?'

While Tom Waits always seems comfortable standing in another man or woman's shoes, some songwriters, like Lucinda Williams, are predisposed only to tell it like they see it. For Williams, songwriting is less an adventure of the imagi-nation, more of a form of catharsis. In a 2013 interview with Jane Shilling of the *Telegraph*, she says:

> This is my way of dealing with life. It's therapeutic ... I remember talking to my dad once, because I was worried that I wasn't keeping a journal ... My dad said, 'Honey, you don't need to do that, because you write songs instead'.

Like Waits, Lucinda's songwriting took a while to evolve. 'They kept telling me I fell down the cracks between country and rock', she recalled. 'Back then, there was no Americana, no alternative country, no alternative anything.' Singular in sound and in possession of one of the most recognizable voices in American music, Lucinda called upon her love of blues tradition to frame her early recordings. Later, having moved to Tennessee, she forged a more Nashvillian identity, recording with players who had developed a sound that typifies what *No Depression* magazine calls Americana. Perhaps unsurprisingly for a student of blues tradition, repetition is key to many of Williams' songs: chord sequences revolve to draw the ear to the lyric, while choruses often repeat phrases as if to ascend them from the conversational. Middle eights, often used by others to frame dramatic peaks, are rarely needed – there is more than enough autobiographical drama elsewhere to suffice. The surprises are rarely in the music, which is inevitably structured with an assured predictability, but often in the words, which frequently spark.

Revealing her impetus for writing songs, in a 2012 interview with Madeleine Schwartz published in the San Francisco-based *The Believer* magazine, Williams reflects:

> I feel like I usually know [when a song is finished], sometimes I know if I cry. If it's so emotional for me, that I get so far into it … I know right then; OK, there might be some editing that needs to be done, but I've got the crux of the song. I've got it. Because I've reached that place – I've gone inside and reached that place. Then I just need to clean it up a little bit.

This reflection implies that the songs don't arrive perfectly formed. They are not pre-planned or conceptualized in advance; rather, they initially emerge free of critical judgement from within her being. In a secondary creative phase, the songs are shaped, perhaps with some words and chords added and some taken away. This process continues for as long as needs be, until in Williams' judgement the song is both authentic to her own experience and ready to be shared. 'Sometimes it takes longer to finish', she tells *The Believer* (ibid.). 'Certain songs, I get the initial idea, but I just won't be able to finish them right then. For "Soldiers' Song", I had some lines written down several years ago, whenever it was. I keep everything.'

Elvis Costello, whose admiration for the unflinching lyricism of Lucinda's namesake Hank is evident in his own recordings of songs made famous by the Hillbilly Shakespeare, maybe senses something similar here. While 'Essence' and 'Right in time' are arrestingly intimate, 'Joy' and 'Can't let go' have a tensile toughness. Highly unusually in popular song, 'Lake Charles' and 'Sweet old world' deal with the difficult subject of suicide. On this theme Lucinda admits to the *Telegraph* (2013):

> I'm fascinated with the subject of suicide ... I've suffered from horrible sadness, melancholia, and a lot of us do ... My dad used to describe it as like a deep, dark well, and we're all standing around the edge, and some of us fall in. I think what informs my songwriting is my empathy with that. Maybe that's what bothers people. It scares them to go to the edge of the well and look in. But it's what they like also.

In 'Drunken angel', one of many forceful and evocative tracks on the 1999 album 'Car Wheels on a Gravel Road', Lucinda sings directly to Blaze Foley, a Texan songwriter friend who took his own life. As listeners, we overhear a private conversation between this world and the next – the words illuminated by questions, music that kicks with life and an authentic sense of time and place delivered with language of vivid local colour. In the similarly questioning 'Sweet old world', the melodies are more plaintive and the vocal delivery soft, almost as if the departed is being cradled. Having set up a premise for the verses of 'Sweet old world' with the chorus, which will almost certainly have been written first, Williams elects to keep the chord sequence rolling underneath a list of some of the things the subject, now no longer of this world, has lost. As if to bring Blaze back to life to see what he is missing, some evocations are tactile and some sensory. Each breath, each voice and each touch are rendered precious and as listeners, far from feeling downhearted we are reminded of how fortunate we are to be above ground.

When I visited him at his home in West Nashville, I noticed that Guy Clark, a songwriter as revered in roots culture as anyone in modern times, kept a shelf stacked full of cassettes in his basement. Each one was labelled with a title and contained, in work tape form, the seed of an idea, perhaps a chorus, or a verse and chorus. Before starting work in the morning, he told me, he would cast an eye over the sea of titles and select the one he felt like working on that day. Having made his selection he would then listen back to the existing sketch and try to add a verse or two, eventually recording his new updated version over the old one. Working constructively on his songs in much the same way as he used to making seafaring boats in South Texas or whenever he builds one of the Spanish guitars he lovingly crafts and signs for authenticity with his own bloody thumbprint, Guy Clark is not afraid that a song will elude him. As Claire Burge notes in the digital outline of her book *Spin: Taking Creativity to the Nth Degree* (2013), what we expose ourselves to – art, language, people – leaves a mark on our subconscious which we might not even be aware of, but neural patterns are being laid down and in time these impressions will emerge either knowingly or unknowingly.

Like Lucinda Williams, this approach, which allows the subconscious to generate options during fallow periods of creativity, works for those people who imagine or feel ideas very quickly in momentary bursts and, in order to capture them in full dimension, for the song to be as good as it possibly can be, need to step back and take a good look at what is there.

2.5 Ray Charles

The Genius didn't write many songs, but he certainly knew how to write them. Constantly revisited by soul and blues artists around the planet, of the dozen or so songs listed as Ray Charles' compositions, 'What'd I say', and 'Hallelujah I love her so' are among the best known and loved in the genre. Unpretentious and upbeat, viewed within the context of his mighty achievement as an artist, these original songs act as a counterpart to the forthcoming swooning country pathos of 'Georgia on my mind' and 'You don't know me', and the more witty and urbane 'Greenbacks' and 'Smack dab in the middle', all songs famously recorded by Charles but written by others. With his own compositional hand, Charles essentially created a third type of song he could perform.

Extraordinarily for a songwriter with a catalogue so thin in volume, one of his songs, 'I got a woman', has been covered by two of the biggest acts in the history of popular music, Elvis Presley and The Beatles. What is it that makes the song so coveted? As Small notes in *Music of the Common Tongue* (1999: 91, 214), the vocal style used in 'I got a woman', which has its ancestry in the congregational singing of early eighteenth-century New England worship and remains prevalent to this day in the Scottish Highlands and Islands, 'has been remarkably tenacious on both sides of the colour line, no doubt, partly at least, because it is extremely enjoyable to do'. Further, claims Small, secular blues has a sacred function that ideologically ties it to the community:

> Its sound, its melodic mode, its tone colours, its attitude to pitch and rhythms, provide an emotional feeling and a nuance which suffuses the whole musical culture, and unites such varied musicians as Louis Armstrong, Billie Holiday, the Count Basie Orchestra, not to mention Elvis Presley, The Rolling Stones and Bruce Springsteen. It *feels* like the music of the people, a tie that can bind us.

A light-hearted gospel tune that converted spiritual joy into sexual delight, 'I got a woman' struck a chord with the awakening audiences of '50s America and '60s Britain. As Gillette (1996: 226–7) writes: 'Ignoring the prejudices of both gospel traditionalists and teen market sensors, his songs regularly referred to an adult world in which couples not only went to bed together, but brought each other coffee in the morning.' In this setting, it is difficult to imagine the Elvis of the mid-fifties or The Beatles of the early sixties being so impervious to such an overture as to not want to be a part of the community implied by 'I got a woman'. Further, Elvis and The Beatles, both with a mischievous eye for controversy, would have been aware of the sacrilegious nature of Charles' conversion of the spiritual into blues. As Charles' biographer Michael Lydon records, as soon as he heard it, Elvis immediately added it to his act (2000: 118).

Ray Charles' original recording of 'I got a woman' was made at WGST Atlanta on 18 November 1954. Altering the emphasis of the expression to suit his own personal experience, Ray had based the composition on a spiritual song written in 1904 by Will L. Thompson called 'Jesus is all the world to me'. As Lydon (2000: 133) recalls, during 1954 Ray had honed this song, along with others in his live set, to perfection, directing each note played by his ten-piece band and sung by the accompanying female vocal trio. By the time Ray and the band reached Atlanta, both they and their leader knew they had it as good as they could get it.

By 10 January 1956 when Elvis entered the studio to record his version, he had been playing 'I got a woman' for nearly a year – almost as long as Ray had been playing it before the original recording had been made in Atlanta. Given the revelatory fire of the Sun recordings that came out of Memphis in the previous year, and the sense of euphoria surrounding his recent signing to RCA Victor, the stage was set for Elvis to transpose Ray's gospel blues into his own electrifying country blues. Great singer, popular song – what could go wrong?

As Godlovitch explains (1998: 14):

> Recordings of performances ... are not performances.
> Recordings are just traces of records of performances.
> Performances are essentially events. Performance sound
> ceases with the cessation of its generative source, the
> activity of music making, even if some sound outlasts the
> activity through echo say, the entire performance cannot
> outlive all the activity.

While Elvis will have entered the studio with the capacity to recreate his live version of 'I got a woman' equally as well as Charles recreated his, as Godlovitch (ibid.) says, 'Although the performer can seek to eliminate some uncertainties there will always be others'. Listening back, Elvis' recording sounds unusually tentative, lacking in the spirit characteristic of his other recordings of the era. Ultimately, the context for the recording may offer some clues. First it was Elvis, Scotty and Bill's first time recording in Nashville, which at the time would have lacked the homeliness of Memphis and the metropolitan crackle of New York, their only two previous recording locations. Secondly they were working with a producer they were unfamiliar with, Chet Atkins, in a room notorious for the elusive nature of its capacity to capture bass frequencies. Finally it was scheduled to be the first track, on their first session for RCA Victor. The pressure was on and the environment unfamiliar.

'First and foremost adrenalin makes us unusually sensitive to outside stimuli', Gordon (2011: 117, 119) writes.

> Thus environmental factors we might ordinarily take in
> stride, such as temperature, lighting, acoustical properties,
> or getting used to strange venues or instruments, often
> become distractions. Second this high degree of sensitivity
> will probably affect physical processes. So as we start the
> physical activity of the performance, we feel a sense of
> strangeness or newness as if we were doing it for the first

time, and were unsure if we would be able to get started or keep going.

While Elvis settled for take eight of 'I got a woman', the session was only to reach its apex later that day with the dark and unsettling 'Heartbreak Hotel'. Perhaps that studio, on that day, in those surroundings, was more suited to the capture of tension than the realization of musical and spiritual community. Using tape echo to recreate the magical Sun vocal sound, the band shifts up and down without dynamic reason; the effect is of musicians in search of sonic and emotional level. Reacting to the uncertainty, Elvis' vocal is uncharacteristically controlled, as if he can't quite fathom what is happening musically around him, or how he should respond. Consequently by his own standards he plays it safe, going for the take that will anchor the sound and make the recording credible, rather than exceptional.

Gordon (ibid.) continues:

> Experience in performing often builds a sense of knowing just how far to go, in enlisting self-awareness to give the performance an extra kick. Some performers handle this volatile ingredient with expertness, opening the throttle wide during a performance and overreaching themselves. Other equally fine performers prefer more caution, never giving full rein to impulse and opting for a greater measure of control. Moreover a given individual's predilection for one mode or the other may vary from situation to situation, feeling at times comfortable in being freely creative and less cautious during a performance, and at other times less so.

In the cauldron of the moment, in trying to eliminate the variables sent to scramble the spirit, the arrangement of the track seems to have been all but overlooked. Essentially, a key difference between the two recordings is the quality of the arrangement. From the perspective of the songwriter, what can be done to try and eliminate the risk of being restricted by arrangement?

When he is not busy managing his label Efpi Records, Manchester-based saxophonist and musical director Ben Cottrell arranges on a freelance basis. When it comes to arrangement, Ben says:

> There are two principles: keeping the arrangement inter-esting, so there is always something going on. And if there isn't, there is always a reason *why* there isn't. And then also not just putting stuff in for the sake of it, which I guess is kind of the same thing. You should always try to make every instrument do something to justify its existence. For all artists, even orchestras, you've got to make the case for that person, that instrument or that sound being there.

Ben's arrangement process is tied to his philosophy. 'Normally I listen to the song a lot to get it in to my head, and I'll hear it in my head while I'm trying to figure out what to do with it. And then you imagine your version', he explains. According to Ben, with song arrangement the text is the starting point, but the arranger should be given free rein to interpret, to find points in the song to accentuate. In a collaborative setting, this can be a difficult process:

> When you're putting an arrangement behind someone else's song it can go wrong when you get too far away from what they had in mind. Some arrangements I've done are often based on an alternative reading of the atmospheric of the lyric. Sometimes the arrangement suggests a different reading, or a different scenario from what you'd expect reading the lyric.

What should the song arranger avoid? Ben advises: 'Arrangements go wrong when you get too far away from the original song. It's still got to have something of the original in it, whether that's the harmony, the melody, something.'

Sometimes Ben is given direction prior to embarking on an arrangement project. He recalls:

> On the Laura Mvula orchestral record the brief was 'the same but different', so I wasn't allowed to stray too far from the original. I think that's quite a clear brief. We had four or five days to do the arrangements. I had the full orchestra there, but I only used a handful of string and wind instruments because I felt it didn't need to be overcomplicated. It's quite a simple song, with quite a simple sentiment, so I stripped the orchestration right back.

While Ben adheres to the notion that the voice is paramount, he is not averse to playing with the popular conception. 'You've got to leave space for the vocal,' he says, 'but on one of them I thought it would be quite interesting for the orchestra to be overpowering the voice almost. You've go to be careful about doing that I guess!' Ultimately, as Ben says, the purpose of the arrangement is to bring something else out of the song and out of the singer and inspire some extra dimension of performance.

Mimicking Scotty Moore's guitar figures and Elvis' comedic alteration of Ray Charles' original coda, The Beatles' arrangement of 'I got a woman' similarly pales in comparison to the original recording. Again, the context of its capture excuses the performers. Not only was the track recorded for broadcast rather than release, and thus would have been earmarked by the band for a fleeting, rather than permanent, existence, but on the date of the recording, 16 July 1963, The Beatles recorded no less than twenty songs at the BBC's Paris Theatre in London, of which 'I got a woman' was the twelfth. In performative overdrive by this stage in the session and without the critical ear of George Martin for guidance, they could easily be forgiven for overlooking dynamic detail.

When the green light came on, like Elvis, The Beatles seem to have actually been content to not record a *bad* version.

While at this early stage in their recording career both Elvis and The Beatles already had epochal songs like 'That's all right' and 'I saw her standing there' to spare, for Ray Charles 'I got a woman', with all its primal charge, occupied a different space within his existing oeuvre, and as the records show, it simply meant more to him.

2.6 Jeff Tweedy

Radical reinventors of what think we know as rock'n'roll music, Jeff Tweedy's band Wilco are in many ways unique in the recent history of popular music. Equal parts texture, words, music and atmospheric, Tweedy's songs, while he is adept at editing them for solo performance, are written with more than busking in mind. Once the words and music are written, they are given dimension by Wilco, who use guitars, keyboards, drums and voices to pull at and bend the words, chords and melodies, creating intermittent moments of tension and release that defy classification. The collective plays as one, and there is a sense that, through a series of seemly arbitrary lulls and shocks, we are listening in on the deep inter-mechanisms of the unrehearsed personality.

Originally from Bangor and now resident in London, for the past fifteen years Northern Irishman Iain Archer has juggled a career as a solo artist with other lives as a producer, auxiliary member of Snow Patrol and collaborator par excellence, writing global hits with and for Snow Patrol, Example, Leona Lewis and Jake Bugg. A long-time fan of Jeff Tweedy and Wilco, Iain is musing on the subject one winter's morning in a dimly lit hotel in the north of England:

> It feels very intuitive with [Tweedy] – you get the sense in his writing that because of his ability to be so wayward in what he does, he combines words in unlikely ways, but it doesn't feel trite or forced or considered; it doesn't feel

like he's over-thought in any way. And, yet it's littered with emotion. And, I think I've learnt a lot from that to be honest, the avoidance of the true subject for periods of time in songs when you're steering around it. Pointing at the other things; almost highlights more what's really at the epicentre of the song, like in 'I am trying to break your heart'.

The song Iain refers to is on 'Yankee Foxtrot Hotel', the 2001 album considered by many to be Wilco's finest. Seven minutes long, 'I am trying to break your heart' features many of the traits that make its author such a singular songwriter. With minimal sonic interruption, as we are confronted by the scattered, often wilfully abstract thought processes of the narrator, a revolving three-chord sequence is stretched over a whirring, mechanical musical canvas. Most of the lyric is so random in form that without the insistent permanence of the chord sequence, there is a sense the words could at any minute leap skywards. Subsuming the musical aspect much like Bob Dylan in the sketching of 'All along the watchtower', Tweedy wants us to hear the words only, and spares any chordal movement that might draw the ear. Amid the narrative chaos and free-association, he also wants us to know that among the spaghetti junction of thoughts running through his mind, there is a thread of absolute clarity; once every four lines, an unequivocally direct statement is made.

Writing in the *Telegraph* in 2013, art critic Richard Dorment has this to say of George Braque's early cubist landscapes:

We watch as, step-by-step, Braque frees himself of all the attributes associated with traditional painting … in their place, he creates a whole new pictorial space. By breaking up the picture plane into innumerable shallow facets, he can show different aspects of a geometric form simultaneously while drawing the viewer's eye constantly back to the flat picture surface.

In songwriting, as a secondary 'grounding' mechanism, it is a high-risk strategy. As Iain observes:

> That free-associative writing can so easily loose itself in a void. And Jeff Tweedy has this very deft pop sensibility that keeps the whole thing anchored, so he always returns you to something that doesn't necessarily open up the full picture, but gives you a pretty clear understanding of where he's trying to take it.

On 'At least that's what you said', the compositionally adventurous opening track on the follow-up 'A Ghost is Born', Wilco play with song form, moving unpredictably from spare, melodic piano and vocal drawl towards ensemble stabs of jolting dissonance, onto contented progressive guitar rock and finally to a noise of discontented metallic angst. In this final movement, as if to unravel Tweedy's *real* feelings, the forces that lay behind the words initially whispered in the plaintive nature of the opening verse are refracted as a dark, seething undercurrent. Of 'A Ghost is Born', Iain says:

> The private beach in Michigan ... the tax returns ... it's all the kind of stuff you just don't sing in songs. There is something so creepy in that song. It's weird. I don't know exactly what is going on. There's a volatility to what he does, even within the song, you can feel something not violent, but dangerous.

Elsewhere on the album, structures are exaggerated, elongated and shaken free of pop convention. More so than on any of their other studio records, on 'A Ghost Is Born' Tweedy's songs are stretched to breaking point as Wilco tilt, test and bend them until they barely resemble their original shape. Directness, ambiguity, text, sub-text, deliberation, wilfulness, light and shade, having conveyed such fullness of expression, having shown us the *core* from so many angles, it is hard to know what more Wilco and Jeff Tweedy could do to give us what we need. Yet, while we know more than we might, at no time do we feel as if we are seeing the full picture. Summarizing Tweedy's unique fingerprint, Iain concludes:

> He's constantly doing that to you; he sets up a pattern and just at the point when you think you know what he's gong to say, he doesn't do it, he sort of leaves you in these *positions*. That's part of the danger of it, he kind of gets you into a little sense of security and then drags you off the edge of the cliff.

2.7 Holland, Dozier and Holland

While song structure is integral to the Wilco aesthetic, fifty years ago another team from the nearby state of Michigan were doing equally odd things to form in the name of commerce. Historically, certain song structures have appeared more than others in popular song, as Ball (2020: 124) observes: 'Learning is made easy by constant repetition: verse, chorus, verse, chorus.' A chorus written to follow a verse is more likely to provide a sense of solidity than to raise an eyebrow, and for this reason, the canon of popular song is replete with predictably positioned refrains that lack musical adventure yet still delight with the memorability of their musicality and the lyricism of their phrasing. Any songwriter content to operate solely within the constraints of these tried-and-tested compositional shapes should beware, however; as Stephen Sondheim infers in his book *Finishing The Hat* (2010), content dictates form. Having sketched out some musical sections, Sondheim implies, the work of the conscientious songwriter is not merely to piece them together in robust form, but to consider each possible structural variation; to examine all the ways in which the music *could* be reshaped to sound as good as it possibly can.

As history records, Holland, Dozier and Holland often thought laterally about how their compositions might be structured. Writing for The Supremes, the trio had already had a number one Billboard hit with 'Where did our love go?' – a song structured, unusually for Motown, like a folk ballad in strophic verse form. Most commercial songs tend to need discrete musical chapters to provide contrast and contour, yet this recording, deftly arranged to ensure continuity of sound, was so inventively played that any sense of repetition was entirely absent. 'Stop! In the name of love', another Holland, Dozier and Holland number one Billboard hit that opened highly unconventionally with a half-chorus, was already eighteen months old when The Supremes arrived at the legendary 2648 West Grand Boulevard, Detroit studio to record the latest Holland, Dozier and Holland tune 'You can't hurry love'.

From a listening perspective, this 1967 recording flows uninterrupted, moves meaningfully and musically without question. Compositionally, what *actually* happens is that a short verse of roughly eight seconds in length leads us straight to a chorus. This miniature opening verse serves two purposes. First, it allows Diana Ross to open the vocal with the word 'I'. This may not seem hugely significant, but in both Lily Allen's 'The fear' and Rihanna's 'Only girl in the world' it makes an immediate and unequivocal statement that the expression is of personal relevance to the singer. Secondly, the short four-bar verse allows the central premise for the lyric expression, the need for love, to be stated *before* the advice of the chorus is offered. If the chorus had come first, as in 'Stop! In the name of love', these pivotal words would have been delivered without context, and would have sounded more like preaching than maternal advice.

In fact, the song was still being refined on the day of its recording; as the original Take 1 shows, the final structure was only decided once the players and singers had established an instrumental arrangement of the song. Without The Supremes and The Funk Brothers to add the performative gloss, it seems the songwriters weren't quite able to imagine the right structural dynamic for the song. Midway through the first take a section apparently intended to create breathing space causes the mood to drift, perhaps potentially prompting the listener to ask a question of the ponderous section: 'How long does it take to offer advice?' Along with James Jamerson's initial bass line, which hasn't yet melodically locked in, by the time the final master take is recorded it is altered for musical and dynamic effect. In this first run, while the song immediately sounds great and it is clear that all present have an intuitive grasp of how to convey the tune, something is missing; as Diana Ross says towards the end, 'You better fade'.

Going back to the master take of 'You can't hurry love', after the chorus, another strange thing happens: a third piece of music is introduced. Sounding like a bridge, it is strange not just because it is new, but also because from a traditional songwriting perspective the progression comes too soon for most songwriters to even consider adding a bridge. But it is there for good reason. Identifying the risk, in terms of gravitas at least, of the song seeming to comprise little more than a girl dreaming of love and her mother telling her to be patient, Holland, Dozier and Holland essentially bring the dramatic peak, the part of the song that in its first draft might have originally been intended to appear later, a long way forward.

Now absent for two whole sections, surely the verse will return after the next chorus? But no, another bridge follows, making the structure thus far: intro, verse, chorus, bridge, chorus, bridge. At this point we might be persuaded to accept that the bridge is *actually* the verse – but no, after a third chorus the verse finally reappears, three times its original length. Not only balancing the existing compositional elements but extending the final verse, Holland, Dozier and Holland create a space in which the singer can testify. In spite of all this structural unorthodoxy, the song moves naturally, without exaggeration or pretence. As Sondheim insists, there is no such thing as a correct structure, merely a correct structure for the raw, musical ideas at the songwriter's disposal.

2.8 Elvis Costello

Motown music wrapped desperate narrative in irresistible
noise so often and with such soul that it attained an
immovable stature as the voice of the dispossessed – the
sound of a young America in transition. For the listener, it
seems, social and political issues often need to be stripped
of the harshness of their reality and sugar-coated in sound.
There may be an element of longevity in this, since the
songwriter will, on some level, be aware that long after the
issue has ceased to be current, the recording will continue to
exist. Marvin Gaye's LP 'What's Going On' asks the relevant
questions being asked by the African American community
at the time, few of which were new then and, sadly, few
of which have been resolved since. To avoid coming across
as a millionaire preaching from the top of the hill, Marvin
always sings as part of the collective, using the pronoun
'we' as opposed to 'you'. Endlessly inviting to listen to and
acting as a metaphor for the dream, the culmination of the
struggle, throughout the record, the music couldn't be more
luminous.

In 'Shipbuilding', Elvis Costello similarly adopts the persona
of someone directly implicated and again, the transition of
artist to first person brings an essential sense of involvement.
In another similarity, the music, written by Clive Langer, has a
timeless elegance that offers a stark contrast to the lyric theme.
If no longer moved by the passing of time to empathize at an
immediate level with the political core of the composition,
the listener's ear can easily reside in the tune. As Pilgrim and
Ormrod (2012: 84–6) write: 'Langer felt it was the best music
he'd ever written, but was not content with his own lyric. So
[he] asked Costello if he would write some to fit the music.'

In their book *Elvis Costello and Thatcherism*, Pilgrim and
Ormrod explain how the words take us through the contra-
diction for unemployed working-class families at the time of
the Falklands conflict:

The shipyards were being offered work to provide vessels for the military at a time when orders had dried up and they were facing the threat of closure. However, the new ships were in demand to transport the shipyard workers' sons to their death in the South Atlantic.

Untypically separated from the task of writing music to accompany his own words, Costello's lyric is articulated, like Gaye's 'What's Going On', in the voice of those experiencing the hardship. The musician is not outside, but of the people. While Pilgrim and Ormrod (ibid.) speculate that Costello's version of 'Shipbuilding' was included on 'Punch The Clock' to add compositional quality to an otherwise unexceptional collection of songs, this critical revision overlooks the fact that the album was warmly received at the time. Not only was it voted *NME* album of the year in 1983, its musicality was persuasive enough for Costello to invite its producers to work on his following record 'Goodbye Cruel World'. Further, the brass arrangements and backing vocals provided by the TKO Horns and Afrodiziak on 'Punch The Clock' enabled Costello and the Attractions to reinterpret earlier material on stage later that year, breathing new life into road-worn compositions.

Making good use of Steve Nieve's remarkable pianistic ability to glue ensemble sound and replete with Chet Baker's ever-melancholy trumpet, recorded the year after Robert Wyatt's 1982 original, Costello's recording of 'Shipbuilding' is arranged to reflect the bleakness of the subject. Perceptively, Pilgrim and Ormrod note a relationship between the descending harmonies of the opening phrases in 'Shipbuilding' and Bowie's 'Life on Mars', both homages to existential despair with questions at the focal point of expression. As they note, amid the beauty of the music, Costello is effectively posing the central question, 'Will we be re-employed to build tombs for our children?'

Co-written with Harris, Barry and Black, Kanye West's 'Diamonds from Sierra Leone (remix)' is a similarly remarkable

piece of work in which Kanye uses the lyric, shared in delivery
with Jay Z, to deliver a modern-day morality tale. Refocusing
the theme of slavery by placing it in previously unexplored
sociological and geographical contexts, 'Diamonds from
Sierra Leone' asks the listener whether African Americans,
in full knowledge that conflict diamonds are mined by West
African children in brutal conditions of slavery and civil war,
should wear them. Political songwriting at its divisive and
thought-provoking best, the questions asked in the narrative
are polarizing, particularly within the context of the video,
which furthermore ends relatively unequivocally with the text:
'Please purchase conflict free diamonds'.

In a musical sense, it's difficult to know how Marvin or
Kanye settled on their respective textures – where the roots
of this timeless and driven music lay. Similarly, with Costello
the influences tend to surface in strange, almost untraceable,
ways. 'Watching the detectives', for example, was apparently written by Costello after having listened repeatedly
to the first Clash album for 36 hours non-stop (cited by
Crandall 2003). Give or take the rhythmic pulse of 'Police
and thieves', however, little of the guttural phrasing and
humour Costello claimed to be channelling is evident in the
recording that became his first significant chart hit. Rather,
the brittle aesthetic of The Clash seems to have been forged
with other impulses both musical and thematic. Listening
closely, the ghost of Robbie Robertson's 'The night they
drove old Dixie down', recorded by The Band in 1969, can
be faintly heard in the movement from minor chord-led verse
to major chord-led chorus. Perhaps what is at work here on
the compositional fretboard is Costello's muscle memory, a
reflex typical of those with exceptionally good ears and little
theoretical patience, to move the hands in a certain instinctive
way around the guitar. Later, to underpin 'Oliver's army' and
'Two little Hitlers' on 'Armed Forces', Costello drew upon
ABBA and Bowie, two points of reference that in 1979 would
have undoubtedly prompted a credibility crisis. Resemblances
to 'Dancing queen' and 'Rebel rebel' are perceptible yet never

obvious, the strength of musical identity easily erasing any lasting semblance of familiarity.

As with many of Costello's lyrics, at first sight, the words to 'Shipbuilding' are coded and dialectical, but as the meaning sinks in, the force of the narrative lies in the way the composition juxtaposes humble humanity against the enormity of political and mechanical forces we are required to serve. Importantly, given the complex character of the lyric text, the recorded tempo is slowed to allow the listener to absorb and interpret each line. Consequently the words are absorbed and interpreted much more effectively on record than on the page, where only a fraction of the poetry emerges. At the tempo prescribed by Costello and Wyatt, apocalyptic dread and sweet bliss reside together.

Philip Ball (2010: 137) discusses a similar effect in the music of Charles Ives, which he describes as the sound of 'several simultaneous voices that have little or nothing in common almost defying us to weave them into some sort of coherent entity'. As Bell acknowledges, Ives' compositional intention is to recreate the kinds of conflicting sounds we hear in the world to authentically reflect or project how we experience life. Listening to Ives, Bell is able to 'listen with so little effort I was barely aware of it'.

2.9 Kate Bush

Following a live performance hiatus that spanned over three decades, in August 2014 much was made of Kate Bush's return to the stage. As disbelieving fans filed into London's Eventim Apollo like Charlie arriving at the Chocolate Factory, critics raved over the show, a suitably theatrical and visual retrospective of her dazzlingly adventurous career. 'At the end of three hours of untrammelled theatricality,' wrote Kitty Empire in the *Guardian* (2014), 'what is truly thrilling about Kate Bush's comeback is how little her voice, or her essence have changed.' Other publications chose the occasion to review Kate's career, with most, like *Mojo* magazine, presenting an unblemished artistic record, with songs from 1978's 'The Kick Inside' to '50 Words For Snow', released in 2011, receiving equal critical praise. Kate had arrived in the mid-seventies a fully formed talent of extraordinary depth and invention and had remained at a high creative altitude ever since, or so the *Mojo* narrative ran. For the artist herself, however, such fulsome retrospective praise may have prompted a wry smile, for the reception her sophomore recordings received at the time of release was considerably less complimentary.

The UK music press the young Kate Bush had to navigate is characterized by a masochistic critical culture, where in between news items and record reviews, women dress as schoolgirls in cartoon strips, posing suggestively to sell guitars. Published in *Sounds* on 25 February 1978, the advertising copy runs: 'She has never seen a weapon like it before, and the thought of all the uses it could be put to brings tears to the eyes.' It's not only retailers peddling this eye-wateringly sexist narrative; the labels fuel it too. In the rival edition of *Melody Maker* published in the same week, a full-page ad informs the reader: 'Budgie are back, hide your pussy.'

It is indeed a strangely misogynistic critical world that the nineteen-year-old Kate is obliged to enter. How were the very songs that garnered such acclaim in 2014 reviewed back in 1978? Writing in the *NME*, a bewildered Bob Woffinden considered many of the songs on her first LP 'The Kick Inside' to be 'ordinary, constructed in an identical fashion' and 'delivered in a distinctive wailing voice that never settles into any comfortable vocal style'. Warming to his theme, the reviewer considers the record to be 'pathetically contrived, more of a product of 1968 than 1978, with its smatterings of orientalism and mysticism' (1978: 39). Concurring with a one-star review, rival publication *Sounds*' reviewer Sandy Robertson (1978: 29) exclaims: 'This album should have come out on Harvest in 1969 and been deleted two weeks later.' Clearly, Kate had arrived out of time. 'What's this supposed to be?' Robertson continues, 'Doom-laden, meaningful songs with some of the worst lyrics ever, sung in the most irritatingly yelping voice since Robert Plant. Where in the name of all that's rock and roll, and/or art, do they find these people?'

When Verdi's *La Traviata* and Stravinsky's *Rite of Spring* were greeted with civic and public derision in Venice and Paris respectively, the critical hammer blows were dealt to men already acclaimed for *Rigoletto* and *The Firebird*, composers with reputations built to absorb the ire. Looking back through the lens of popular music history, the sight of journalists struggling manfully to figure out whether Wreckless Eric is the truly the saviour of pop rounding with such vitriol on a newly signed teenage girl is particularly unseemly; the onlooker is prompted to marvel at the will of the artist to continue undeterred.

Of course, 'Wuthering Heights', despite having what Woffinden called a 'flaccid lyric', soon superseded its critical reception by proving a vast commercial success, and over time the songs from 'The Kick Inside' have received a very different appraisal. On page 75 of *Mojo*'s 2014 retrospective, Martin Aston calls 'The man with the child in his eyes' 'visionary, assured, orchestral pop', while on page 61 Phil Sutcliffe labels 'Feel it' 'The best sex ever made into one song.' Reaching a retrospective apex, *Mojo* considers 'Wuthering Heights':

> the biggest novelty of them all. Not just peculiar but freakish, untamed, daring, a hallucination verging on hysteria, and yet perfectly controlled, like a sliver of Gilbert and Sullivan operetta complete with pitch perfect soprano, the apex of otherworldliness.

Not only is the issue of originality redressed, what was initially perceived to be ordinary is, with the benefit of hindsight, found to be quite the opposite. Fast forwarding 36 years, even the originally maligned voice is recast from wail to idyll.

Later in 1978, by the time 'The Kick Inside's follow-up, 'Lion Heart', arrived for review, *Sounds*' Dave McCulloch was begrudgingly supportive: 'Now, while the songs aren't individually strong at all, it's more the aura she creates', he explains (1978: 37). Elsewhere his *NME* counterpart, yet another male journalist Ian Penman (1978: 53), is also beginning to grapple with a less dismissive perception:

> Kate's trick is the way she clings to thoughts of innocence, at the same time hinting that she knows more than she's letting on. It may well be an attack on traditional mythical ideas and ideals about the mysterious, silent, seductive woman who wants you and you only.

Hardly the dawn of a new critical enlightenment, but small steps at least toward serious engagement with the work.

Traditionally, the revisionist history of punk hails The Sex Pistols and The Clash as the architects of rebellion against the establishment. However, with their leather jackets, electric guitars and impatience for any female aesthetic not connected to the liberated, barely concealed couture of Vivienne Westwood, it seems the aesthetic of this revolution may have had its most recognizable alibis *within* the critical establishment of the time. Punk wasn't subverting the music media culture; in a definitive way it was reflecting it. Ironically, the teenage girl doing commercial battle with the old guard of ABBA and The Bee Gees was all punk, presenting ideas so confrontational, so revolutionary that the gatekeepers of the traditional press were powerless to absorb them.

In the *Mojo* article, Kate cites David Bowie's 'Star man' as an inspiration – fittingly perhaps, as Bowie as much as any other performing songwriter could be argued to share with her that rare quality, said by Landgraf (2011: 9) to constitute 'Unforeseen artistic performances that go beyond what the participants in the process could have planned or otherwise envisioned in advance'. It is frequently impossible to speculate on where Bush's music comes from, as each new record has only her previous work as a salient point of reference. As Tricky notes in his introduction to *Mojo*'s piece (ibid.), her sound remains untraceable. Almost as great an achievement as the writing of the songs that brought her so determinedly to the public forum is her complete unwillingness to bend or bow in favour of trend. Aston (2014: 75) concludes: 'Kate Bush navigated 1978 by using the record's unique energy to fire her self-belief to trust her music, and she never betrayed it, not even once.'

2.10 Arcade Fire

As discussed earlier in the section on communication, Littlewood argues that a successful communicative inter-action typically involves references to the past, present and future: something of what has happened, what is happening, and what might happen next. When we meet someone we know, for instance, the nature of our response is immedi-ately informed by a sense of context. Our prior experience of them gives us clues as to how they are likely to behave. With someone we haven't met, how could we know what they will be like, or what they will want to talk about? Uninformed, we search for clues on how to begin. Unless we grew up in the same town or street as him, Win Butler has probably never met us before. Unlike us, however, his job as the lyricist in Arcade Fire is to communicate with us, to involve us Arcade Fire fans scattered around the world in his universe. It seems a daunting prospect from the outset. How can he make us feel like we know him, that of all the listeners out there he is talking to us, and us alone?

A recurring motif in the Arcade Fire songbook is the tension between an idyllically remembered past, an emotionally unstable and spiritually bereft present, and the unresolved dream of a future capable of recapturing the idyll. First emerging on the debut album 'Funeral', in 'Neighborhood 1' and 'Crown of love', the notion of childhood surroundings is also a thread in the follow-up album 'Neon Bible', where the theme resurfaces in 'Keep the car running' and 'Windowsill'. Returning to evoke youth on the third Arcade Fire LP, the lyric of the opening track 'The suburbs' begins in the past tense, where it remains for 1 minute and 15 seconds. During this initial chapter of the song, while the option exists for the narrative to be written in the present tense – i.e. 'learn' could be substituted for 'learned', 'tell' could replace 'told' – nevertheless it resides in the past. Either knowingly or unwittingly, Win Butler is giving us the context we need for us to understand his current perspective and motivation.

With its falling movement from major to relative minor, the first two chords of the revolving four-chord riff that underpins 'The suburbs' recalls the emotive effect created by The Smiths in 'I know it's over' and in The Undertones' 'Teenage kicks'. In a metaphorical sense, as the descending chord sequences roll out we hear echoes of other songs about dreams: The Chords' 1954 doo-wop hit 'Sh-Boom' and The Everly Brothers' 'All I have to do is dream', each one whirring away on the jukebox at the back of our minds. In the same way that both Van Morrison's 'Moondance' and Michael Kiwanuka's 'Tell me a tale' use an insistent A minor to B minor chord change to summon a promise of love, the music we hear alongside the words offers a subtle authentication.

The chord sequence used on the track 'The suburbs' is indelibly sentimental, and to imprint the music of Arcade Fire with a similar effect it surfaces on no less than four songs on 'Funeral': 'Neighborhood 2', 'Wake up', 'Haiti' and 'In the backseat'. As a consequence, the album feels emotional, significantly warmer and more personal than its counterpart, 'Neon Bible', which studiously avoids the effect for the first five songs, eventually introducing it on 'Ocean of noise', and after that only sparingly. Taking both music and lyric inferences into account, as we arrive at the chorus of 'The suburbs', we have a sense of the singer's past and of a refracted, emotional warmth, a welcoming and engaging start to our relationship with the record. The third chord in the predominant sequence, a relatively angular F sharp 7 reminiscent of the unsettling chord inserted nine bars into Goffin and King's 'Will you love me tomorrow', asserts its character not only as a measure of musical realism, earthing the dream to the reality, but also as a component of a chordal loop of some durability. While The Cure's 'A forest' and U2's 'With or without you' possess a similar quality, not all four-chord loops can support alternating melody and musical ornamentation without becoming over-familiar.

Then, a communicative shift occurs. Deliberately using 'fall' instead of 'fell' to tell us what is on the singer's mind in the here and now, at 1:15 the lyric moves from the past into the present tense, not just for a moment but for a full minute and a half. The narrative switch almost certainly fails to register in our consciousness, but as our ear meanders between melody texture and narrative, as a consequence of the lyric switch we gain a sense that we are hearing something that *involves* us.

At 2 minutes 45 the lyric moves again to glimpse the singer's future perspective: a typically existential sense of inevitable loss or foreboding, extending a theme interwoven throughout earlier tracks 'Neighborhood 4', 'Black mirror', 'Neon bible' and 'Windowsill'. Here, in a 30-second rumination on times to come, the future tense chapter completes the communicative triad. When the lyric returns to the present tense for the final lyric section, it does so to deliver us safely back to the present, as the coda winds its mesmeric way to a temporary resolve.

In another charismatic signature move, Arcade Fire recordings are prone to switching musical identities mid-song. 'Une année sans lumière', 'Crown of love', 'Wake up', 'Black wave', 'The well and the lighthouse' and 'No cars go' all possess an expressive schizophrenia, a compositional restlessness that, like all of us, seeks yet never finds resolution. Hurling yet another great tune against an invisible spiritual force, as if the better the tune, the deeper the corporate dent, 'Ready to start', the second track on the album 'The Suburbs', revisits the insistent pulse of 'No cars go' and the theme of cultural corruption alluded to in 'My body is a cage'. Here, as well as in track three of 'The Suburbs' LP, 'Modern man', past and present tenses are at play, drawing us into a languid love letter to the wasted hours of youth.

Still waiting and still dreaming, on 'Reflektor' (2013), the band go in search of the self in place, in history and in love, but here, in the opening chapters of 'The Suburbs' and in the recordings that precede and immediately follow them, we are told everything we need to know about a world we can never know. What choices could we have made? Where does the path we never took lead to? A circular trip through the scenery of the soul, listening to Arcade Fire is a journey we can make on endless repeat.

2.11 Pharrell Williams

Writing in the *New York Times Sunday Review* in June 2013, Robert J. Zatorre, professor of neuroscience at the Montreal Neurological Institute, and his colleague Valerie N. Salimpoor, a postdoctoral neuroscientist based in Toronto, argue that science is beginning to find answers to the perplexing question of why, when so many of our pastimes have acceded to evolution, we persist with listening to music. Using brain imaging, their research team has shown how the feeling of pleasure at listening to a musical passage causes the neurotransmitter dopamine to be released in the stratium, a part of the brain also responsive to naturally rewarding stimuli including food and sex. They explain:

Each act of listening to music may be thought of as both recapitulating the past and predicting the future. When we listen to music these brain networks actively create expectations based on our stored knowledge. Composers and performers intuitively understand this; they manipulate these mechanisms to give us what we want, or to surprise us, perhaps even with something better.

In developing his hit song 'Happy', songwriter, musician and producer Pharrell Williams seems to have set himself the task of creating a recording that is unequivocally joyous in all dimensions. Calling upon our shared perception of happy music as exemplified by Stevie Wonder's 'Overjoyed', Katrina and the Waves' 'Walking on sunshine' and George Harrison's 'Here comes the sun', Williams seeks to manipulate our listening mechanisms by delivering a piece of music that both meets our expectations and takes us by surprise. As, in song, the untainted expression of happiness excludes the vast sea of compositional methods related to the creation of negative or dramatic coloration, it tends to be easier for songwriters to write songs that possess ambiguity, and as a consequence few songwriters have succeeded in distilling works of unfettered joy in the modern era.

For a song such as 'Happy' to work, not only do the words and music need to possess a sustained and insistent brightness, each of the instrumental textures and performances chosen must also abide by the code implied by the mood. Perhaps most critically, the vocal performance cannot afford to waver from its heightened emotional altitude; there is no room for performative ambiguity. Further, as a commercial artefact intended to compete in the global market, to gain traction and attain durability among listening audiences, a balance will need to be struck between the memorable, the instantly absorbable and the mildly surprising. Just as the expression of abject misery requires intense focus on behalf the songwriter to avoid any hint of duality, 'Happy' uses every ounce of leverage to accentuate the positive.

Considering it a stellar example of its type, Grammy-nominated producer Will Hicks is a fan of Pharrell Williams' recording. In Will's opinion, 'Happy' is an archetypal example of a song that uses a variety of sounds and approaches to amplify and convey the expressive intentions of the songwriter. To accomplish its mission, it uses, as Will points out, a number of bright sounds including Fender Rhodes, guitars, electric bass, acoustic guitar, drums, male *and* female vocals and happy claps, to reinforce the sentiment. The whole recording concept, says Will, embodies the theme of the song:

> There are no strings or real pianos, because Rhodes is happier, no Hammond, which tends to reduce space and add darkness. The mix is unbelievably trebly, with lots of information at the high end which makes it sound clean and open; short delay on the vocal. All the choices made on that record reinforce the notion of the song and those choices didn't happen by accident.

By contrast, at the other end of the emotional spectrum, Will cites 'Back to black' by Amy Winehouse (2006), a Mark Ronson production that relentlessly applies layers of melancholy to communicate its compositional intent, as the very antithesis of 'Happy':

> It's piano, which is sadder. It's in D minor, which is the saddest key! The bass is playing a single note thumbed on two and the four, so it doesn't move. It builds up tension. The backing vocals are lower in pitch; the top end of the vocal has been completely removed. There are no handclaps, it's tambourine, it's got loads of reverb so it's all distorted.

As Will says, the production does everything within its grasp to coherently and unambiguously project the intended mood of the song.

Yet before these production skills are brought to bear, how does the songwriter create words and music that might potentially alter the mood of the listener to such extremes? According to Pavilcevic (1997: 60–3), as humans we identify music as a whole, using perceptual grouping mechanisms to help us understand how specific musical elements are perceived in their local contexts. This, the author argues, is not necessarily a sequential process, but rather a kaleidoscopic one where each new piece of information changes

our perception of the whole. When we hear the bright introductory motif of 'Happy', we have little difficulty linking it
to the similarly light sounding verse. When we hear the more
unusual and intriguing blue notes used by Williams in the
chorus, they do not, however, strike us as melancholy, rather
they are drawn into our perception of the whole; beautiful
flaws that humanize the expression without possessing the
metaphorical weight to contradict it. Critically, it inclines us
to want to listen again.

Noting how high cluster sounds often stimulate the listener,
and how high-sounding or high-pitched instruments are often
preferred in therapeutic settings, Bunt (1994: 54) observes
how listeners tend to have strong physical responses to pitch.
Further, Pavilcevic explains, to make sense of what we hear,
we group similar sounds together and possess a natural
preference for smaller intervals (1997: 60–3). By grouping
sounds and using relatively small intervals in both the vocal
melody and the motif, Williams succeeds in creating a piece of
music we can all make sense of, remember parts of, and sing
along to.

Offering some insight useful to the songwriter, Andsell
(1995: 7–8) notes:

> Music has, at a fundamental level, similarities of form and
> process with our psycho-physical functioning. In this way
> of understanding we do not merely hear or play, but have
> the prototypes of rhythm, melody, harmony and form in
> our physiological and psychological processes.

Consequently, there will be places within the culturally
acknowledged sphere of sonic and compositional options
the songwriter might go to find the right music for the
right mood. But it isn't that simple. If it were, there would
be more unambiguous mood music in the world. While
ultimately, in the case of 'Happy', the simplicity of the song,
an unquestioning adherence of the words, music and sounds
to the title, is what makes it so singular, so emphatically

undeniable, the artist must also qualify the material with a believably authentic series of performances. To craft emotionally effective and transmutational work, once the scientific processes of composition, arrangement and sound texture have been negotiated, like a method actor or a theatre director, the songwriter must then direct or perform the work convincingly. For the most part, audiences will have little or no comprehension of, or interest in the technical background to the song recording. Presented with sounds that seek to comply with and update our sense of how a happy song should or should not sound, they will either believe or not believe. As the renowned composer Stravinsky (1970, cited in Ansdell, 1995: 178) was moved to reflect: 'I haven't understood a bar of music in my life, but I have felt it!'

2.12 Cole Porter

What better way to create durability for your songs than by writing them so well that multiple versions of them can be recorded and performed? While Ella Fitzgerald recorded a number of definitive versions on her 1956 songbook, the songs of Cole Porter have also been recorded by Doris Day, John Coltrane, James Brown, Dolly Parton, U2, Screamin' Jay Hawkins, Chick Corea, Iggy Pop and George Harrison. It is harder to imagine an artist who couldn't cover a Cole Porter tune than one who could. His songs are similarly broad in scope, celebrating love (I've got you under my skin'), confronting social issues ('Love for sale'), winning bets ('Miss Otis regrets') and in the case of 'Ev'ry time we say goodbye', using the most unequivocal and high-wire of all songwriting methods, prosody. Of the many recordings of this famous tune, the one featured on 'Ella Fitzgerald Sings Cole Porter', the jazz singer's seminal retrospective, is equal to any.

In song, prosody refers to the matching alignment of words and music, where one suggests or closely reflects the other.

It may seem a natural aspiration to match the two, yet over the years, from Bacharach and David to Morrissey and Marr, many have sought to create a subtext by creating a clear division of inferred meaning between music and lyric moods. Some songs, however, twin music and words in a particularly concise way, leading us to be drawn towards an expressive gesture as close to definitive as song can be. When Irving Berlin warns of trouble ahead in 'Let's face the music and dance', he does so over a minor chord, with melodic phrasing suggestive of trepidation; something bleak really is on its way. By the time love and romance join the lyric narrative, we are delivered safe in to the warm tones of the relative major; guided by the prosodic hand of the composer, we can rest easy. Where Irving Berlin is measured in his use of prosody, evoking it once to avoid further suspicion, in 'Ev'ry time we say goodbye' Cole Porter is daring, for if prosody goes wrong, the songwriter can easily come across as twee or predictable – both cardinal sins of popular music.

Monochrome in atmosphere, the opening bars of 'Ev'ry time we say goodbye' restrict the melody to one note. Immediately the patience of the listener, encultured to anticipate a tune, is tested. Still it works as a prosodic gesture – the numb sadness of parting reflected in the absence of musical metaphor. To test the sensibility of the listener further, breaking a further taboo in the received theory of song composition, Porter then rhymes the word 'little' with 'little'. Again, the prosodic scheme works, as it seems plausible that the singer is in no mood to engage in anything as frivolous as rhyme; after all when we are saying goodbye to a loved one we tend not to think in rhyme.

As the verse progresses, in line three of the lyric Porter prosodically reserves the highest sung note for the phrase imploring the *Gods*, and to prove this is no accident, in verse two he applies the same musical gesture to the line featuring the word *love*. Leaving us with a sense of the spiritual chasm between solace and embrace, from the most mundane of initial expressions spring the most exalted.

Finally, playful and clever in the extreme, the celebrated major-to-minor line, drawn over the inevitably prosodic equivalent chord types, is the fourth example of prosody within the composition.

In the mid-sixties, The Kinks recorded 'You really got me', a Ray Davies song in which the singer is not only captured by the object of his affection, but also by the two chords that restrict and restrain the verse. Sensing the opportunity to add more drama, Dave Davies' claustrophobic, violent guitar solo further emphasizes the compositional sense of restriction. A year later The Kinks recorded another Ray Davies tune 'Tired of waiting for you', which uses similarly uses chordal repetition to emphasize what it feels like to be tired of waiting. While Ray waits impatiently for his girl to arrive, like him we glance at our watch and wait for the chords to change. Seeming to indicate that the songwriter is too tired to think of anything fresh or original, in 'Tired of waiting for you' the chord sequence is unadventurous, and the ensemble performance, which is delightfully nonchalant, further emphasizes this.

In modern times, relatively few songwriters seem to evoke prosody, although on The Streets' 2002 recording 'The irony of it all' Mike Skinner uses a fractured musical collage to project the disjointed character of Terry the lager lout, and muzak to represent the calm and reasoned cannabis connoisseur Tim. Projecting each conversationalist as a caricature and using affected accents to differentiate the two voices, Skinner overtly presents the lyric as a conversation between Terry and Tim. Many of Cole Porter's songs were relayed by others, and similarly in 'The irony of it all', the voices and their musical accompaniment make a statement *for*, rather than *by* the songwriter. 'The irony of it all' works in part because of the liberal dose of humour instilled in each character's narrative; the music quickly becoming relegated to background noise as the prosodic gesture gives way to compelling argumentative voices. Using prosody, Skinner is able to make his own comment on the values attached by twenty-first-century society to those who imbibe and inhale.

2.13 David Bowie

Prosody may help the intended meaning become more trans-parent, but what if neither the words nor the music make any conventional sense? When, in 2014, I played around 100 popular music students 'Fantastic voyage' by David Bowie, their responses were informative. As the song drew to its close, my first question to the group was 'How many of you liked that?' Almost every hand in the room was raised. When I asked 'Who can tell me what that song was about?' there was not a single hand to be seen. The polarized response evidences how it might be possible to like a song without knowing what it means. As the group discussion unfolded, it became apparent that the students had been enjoying the production, the instrumentation, the melody, the texture, the dynamic contour, the voice, and the word sounds. There were plenty of places for the ear to go to. From the perspective of the songwriter who elects not to rely upon the traditional founda-tions of song text, what can be done to captivate?

Paul Statham is a Warner Chappell songwriter who has written hits for Dido, Kylie and many others. Also a vastly experienced producer, live performer and writer of music for installations, Paul's career fully encompasses the theatrical aspect of songwriting. He has been a fan of Bowie for over four decades. 'The record I got into was "Aladdin Sane": "Panic in Detroit", "Jean Genie" and all those tunes. I was a Bolan fan and then got into Bowie', he recalls. While Paul cites Bowie as his favourite musician, he senses something missing from the art. 'He is directing the vision', explains Paul 'but unfortunately it's so beautifully calculated and managed that you are never sure if the passion is real or not.' Bowie's songs are elusive; knowing his strengths and weaknesses, he attends to some aspects of his work in extreme detail yet has little patience for others. It is a calibrated art. 'I adore the baritone, the tenor, the falsetto and his tone is left field, he can sing anything and it sounds interesting and deep', says Paul. 'But

has he ever written a "Dock of the bay"? Something without a
tinge of artifice?' Perhaps it is this measured lack of disclosure
that keeps us listening.

Having cut our teeth on the Crew Cuts' 'Sh-Boom' and The
Crystals' 1963 hit 'Da doo ron ron', us listeners have been
partial to the large-scale use of word sounds in song ever since
Jimmy Webb visited MacArthur Park in 1967 and left his
cake out in the rain. In that instance, and in the more recent
work of arch melodicists the Gibb Brothers, Finn Brothers,
Coldplay and Keane, the creative process involves auditioning
or 'singing in' a series of lyrical yet not necessarily meaningful
words to an existing musical framework. Sensing that the
music is strong enough to appeal in its own right, many of
the draft word sounds are left as they are, creating a song that
overtly directs the listener away from the words and towards
the harmony and melody.

Significantly, in a song that successfully uses word sounds,
there is almost always a line or gesture that, within the ramble,
is unequivocally direct. Of all the introductory lines ever
written, perhaps the opening to the Gibb Brothers' 'Islands in
the stream' (1983), with its contrary references to universal
harmony and instruments designed for hair-care, is the least
likely to make the transition from the liberal school of pop to
the conservative and conversational world of country. Kenny
Rogers and Dolly Parton sang it, though, and nobody seemed
to mind. Forgiveness is close at hand because for every non
sequitur about peace on earth or a fine-tooth comb, there is an
'Island in the stream', a 'Somewhere only we know' that we
can relate to; a place where we can locate our own experience.

Like 'Fantastic voyage', Bowie's lyric for 'Life on Mars' is
such a hurricane of imagery that upon first listen it might seem
to be about nothing at all. It eclipses its surrealistic predecessor, Lennon and McCartney's 'I am the walrus' (1968),
however, by asking the big question in its refrain: is there
any escape? It is very likely that 'Life on Mars', like 'Into
temptation' by Crowded House (1988), will have been written
refrain or chorus first, that Bowie won't have sketched an

apocalyptic list of nightmare images before suddenly being hit by the inspirational climactic phrase. More likely, the central question will have precipitated a list of things that need to be escaped from. Similarly, once Neil Finn has sculpted a soaring melodic line about retribution for falling into temptation, to project the all-important chorus, the surrounding verses are merely required to tread water, to create an unassuming, low-lying sectional contrast. In this way, the chorus can emerge in relief from a contrasting melody and words that barely orbit the same musical galaxy.

In the early years of the twenty-first century, Coldplay were lambasted by critics including the *Guardian*'s Alexis Petridis (2005) for writing apparently nonsensical lyrics that tended to infuriate those on the lookout for 'meaningful' narrative. Skilfully, like many of their hits, 'The scientist' is hung together with very direct and communicative hook lines that act as a thread within the word sounds. For many listeners – much like my audience of students – the remainder of the listening experience is happily spent traversing the melodic contour, the sonic texture and, of course, the word sounds.

2.14 Amy Winehouse

Canadian songwriter Ralph Murphy has a theory that contemporary songwriters are no longer willing to portray themselves in anything other than a positive light. Speaking in 2007, when Amy Winehouse was at her brief creative zenith, Ralph suggested that radio listeners would rather be stuck in a traffic jam with the autotuned voice of an airbrushed mannequin who would love them forever, than with somebody singing about having recently defaulted on a mortgage payment. As Ralph argues, chart analysis bears this out; losers are infinitely more popular in film or literature than they are in popular song. It wasn't always the case though; back in the twentieth century John Lennon sang about being a loser and Thom Yorke about being a creep, and despite possessing lyrics unequivocally negative in self-expression, both songs maintained a certain cultural and commercial notoriety.

In 2006, when Amy Winehouse delivered 'Back To Black' to Island Records, hopes may not have been high for stratospheric success. In liner notes for an Island Records label retrospective, Salewicz (2009) recalls how the label had grown accustomed to her volatile personality, food disorders, propensity to self-harm and monumental weed habit. Knowing the stakes were high after the mediocre success of her debut LP, Amy had arrived at producer Mark Ronson's studio a few months earlier with a hopeful selection of reference discs recorded by The Specials, The Ronettes and the legendary girl group The Shangri La's. Despite having signed and championed such noted purveyors of the groove as The Wailers, Traffic and Grace Jones, the label will have been aware that records layered with retro sounds and laden with narratives of fallibility had long since been absent from high end success. 'Back To Black', however, had many things going for it, not least a highly individual artist lost in love, and lost in music. As Lucy O'Brien (1995: 176) writes: 'Women have always written to make sense of their world. To clear an enviable space that is theirs rather than the possession of a man.' This record, with its relentlessly autobiographical tone, reflects that observation well.

Writing long before the grip of postmodernism took hold, Hall and Whannel (1964: 66) defined popular art as 'essentially a conventional art which restates in an intense form values and attitudes already known, which measures and reaffirms but brings to this something of the surprise of art as well as the shock of recognition'. For years, commercial audiences had been unwilling to allow an artist to shine the spotlight on their inadequacies, yet here on 'Back To Black' was someone announcing to the world across the distance of a full-length record that she was a failure in sobriety and in relationships. Significantly like fellow English agitators The Jam and The Smiths in earlier decades, Amy Winehouse seems to have checked which way the wind was blowing and deliberately set sail against it.

As Longhurst (2007: 103–4) says, 'Postmodernism entails a new fluidity between culture and society', and while 'Back To Black' is in some ways revivalist, it also reflects a contemporary social phenomenon. On this record Amy Winehouse effectively puts her tastes and flaws out there for all to see; as such, it is part of the great social grasp towards digital humanity as personified by Twitter and Facebook. In a 2009 interview with John Harris of the *Guardian*, Ralf Hutter of Kraftwerk describes the early twenty-first century as the ultimate critical leveller, an age where everyone is looking at each other. 'Everybody is becoming like a Stasi agent,' Hutter says, 'constantly observing himself or his friends.' What elevates 'Back to Black' above chatter, lifts it far beyond other contemporary confessional works, is the spectacularly forthright and assured style in which the songs are presented. Writing on the question of cultural identity, Hall (1992: 273–325) describes how the postmodern subject has no fixed or essential identity, and this theory can be linked to the individual voice and familiar music within the text. On 'Back To Black', while the sound screams 'Copy!' the expression of the artist on the face of the sleeve and the voice that fronts it are entirely unique, impossible to predicate or replicate.

As it rolls back and forth between major and minor sections with consummate defiance, the opening song on the record, 'Rehab' has all the performative joy of Ray Charles in his prime. Desperately sad lines about depression and loss are drowned out not once but twice: first by the beat and secondly by the knowing nonchalance of the vocal performance that persuades us not to worry. Rarely has catharsis sounded so confident. Following 'Rehab', taking care to stop en route to place the narrative in its authentic geographic location courtesy of references to James Bond and imported beer, 'You know I'm no good' shifts the musical landscape from America to Europe. Here, as in

'Rehab', the verses circle the core statement; we hear the slogan on repeat and in the poetry that surrounds it we enter the world of the singer.

Extending the thematic penchant for directness, and reflecting an essential quality for anyone talking about themselves and fearful not to outstay their welcome, the songs on 'Back To Black' don't hang around, and the album is relatively short. After the brisk intimacy of 'Me and Mr Jones' and the mildly unassuming 'Just friends', the title track, with its bleak impending sense of tragedy half borrowed from The Shirelles and half drawn from the well of personal experience, serves as the dramatic peak of the record. Written years before Amy rose to prominence, there is an eerie prescience in the words of O'Brien (1995: 66). 'Girl groups from the Shirelles to the Supremes have mythic status', she writes. 'As with anyone who dies young and leaves a shimmering corpse there is a fascination about the genre that has lasted decades after its death.' Years after Amy's passing in 2011, the mythology surrounding her continues to gather; while sales remain buoyant, visitors to the Camden borough of North London are confronted by her glamorous, haunted image at every street corner.

Five songs into 'Back To Black', we are entrusted with and confronted by the mortal seriousness of the singer's emotional dynamic, and this gravitas informs our listening for the rest of the album. With its rootless AAA structure, 'Love is a losing game' resembles two songs that inhabit a similarly reflective dream world: Jimmy Webb's transitory 'By the time I get to Phoenix' and The Stranglers' narcotic meditation 'Golden brown'. Devoid of a chorus or bridge, these are structures with no anchor, songs that float with a mysterious lightness characteristic of the remainder of 'Back To Black'. Side two revisits lyric themes and scenarios established on side one in bleaker, more withdrawn musical settings that gradually earth the restless narrative. As it fades away, 'Back To Black' never loses or lowers its artistic level by pretending to be anything it is not.

2.15 Bob Dylan

Born into a divided world, Bob Dylan has since worn and discarded a number of disguises: reactionary folksinger; weary sage; incurable romantic; soothsayer of the century's demise; phantom engineer; endless traveller; fearless chronicler of the awakening; political animal; believer; unbeliever; and, rewinding to the start of his recording career, the young man with the old man's voice who looked deep and unflinching into a troubled collective psyche and sang back what he saw. If any songwriter could be said to have forged their life into song it is Bob Dylan; for sheer depth of adventure and force of creative will, in the culture of songwriting he is without peer.

Slowly bending a sonic facsimile of Woody Guthrie until it began to project his own finely honed beat poetry, Dylan at the outset of the sixties is a work in progress, initially trading as much on his unique vocal tone as his ideas. Performed with voice and guitar, Dylan's early songs have nothing to hide behind. The melodies are simple and familiar, the textures limited, and the words refracted through the lens of a wide-eyed mid-Westerner with a big imagination. Moving with a newly found verve through the hitherto uncharted territories of commercial protest and ambivalent love, his second album 'The Freewheelin' Bob Dylan' illustrates the metamorphosis, capturing multiple forks of lightning in a bottle. While this record and the ones that immediately follow it have long been celebrated as examples of great, often groundbreaking songwriting, the performances are equally striking, particularly the vocal takes, which use timing and phrasing to devastating effect. Not anywhere near his most popular and feted works from this era, as examples of humour, vitriol and yearning, 'Talking World War Three blues', 'The lonesome death of Hattie Carroll' and 'Ballad in plain D' saw off his contemporaries with elan.

'The lonesome death of Hattie Carroll' is a fine example of Dylan as social commentator, a role he was quick to abdicate once reluctantly nominated as the spokesperson for the newly radicalized views of young America. The song, included on 'The Times They Are a-Changin'', is based upon a real event: the acquittal of wealthy socialite William Zanzinger for the felony of having killed a black servant, Hattie Carroll, with a single blow of his cane. Ostensibly, Dylan wants to convey his feelings on the matter; that he is overwhelmingly sickened by the injustice of it. Aware, however, that the story of the incident is fresh in the public consciousness, he knows that a simple expression of his disgust will amount to adding just one more voice in the crowd. Ingeniously, Dylan elects to involve us, not just as bystanders, but as the highest of authorities, the moral judge of events. Sculpting his feelings into accessible art, he sketches the trial and acquittal across a series of compelling chapters, leaving us to decide for ourselves how we feel.

Inevitably, the reportage of the lyric is not without heavy persuasion: Dylan uses alliteration to cast Zanzinger as a snarling, snake-like figure, phrasing the verse dedicated to this low character as if he cannot wait to banish the thought of him from his mind. Accorded a spotlight in song if not in life, Hattie Carroll is given her own descriptive verse. In the recorded performance Dylan amplifies the compassion of the lyric text in Hattie's verse by extending vocal pauses to allow her more space, more time, a small gesture intended to pay the respect the victim didn't get during her lifetime. In this way, Dylan guides us towards what he thinks our final judgement *should* be.

Elsewhere, Dylan's lyric narratives are so complex, so demanding of the solo performer that they require a bespoke compositional strategy to frame them. 'A hard rain's a-gonna fall' articulates its apocalyptic warning by using the title to precipitate a list of examples in response. Once Dylan has the title, the verses spiral explosively away from it, covering every ounce of expression in metered, alliterative and phonetically measured phrases. A similar strategy is used in 'Forever young' and 'Gotta serve somebody', the first of which draws up a list of wishes for a newborn child, while the second delivers an exhaustive roll call of those obliged to serve. From a lyric writing perspective, the composition is constructed in two steps; initially the title springs to mind and then the songwriter brainstorms phrases or ideas in relation to the title, keeping only those that feel linguistically authentic, illuminate or in some way provide balance.

With his ingenious list of wise folk through history, Ian Dury does a similar thing in 'There ain't half been some clever bastards' and repeats the trick in 'Reasons to be cheerful, Part 3'. While Dury's songs are unique and hugely entertaining, in Dylan's 'list' songs there are spiritual dimensions of poignancy and prophecy for those who remember childhood but are no longer children, who live in fear of imminent doom, or who are willing to contemplate the notion that God created all men equal. Dylan's songs demand to be taken seriously, and the weightier the subject, the more of a high-wire act it is: one slip and belief is suspended.

Returning to the mid-sixties, the late acoustic phase of songs included on 'The Times They Are a-Changin', 'Another Side of Bob Dylan' and 'Bringing It All Back Home' is effervescent and increasingly less invested in popular realism. The idea of the romantic narrator as careless lover is initiated in 'Don't think twice' and revisited, much as a master painter might revisit an elusive theme, in 'Boots of Spanish leather'. Marking his withdrawal from the unsolicited role of protest singer, other love songs, like 'Love minus zero/no limit' and 'It's all over now baby blue' are couched in poetic code, or given surreal settings that make them seem intensely personal. As a notorious CBS promotional campaign once claimed 'No one sings Dylan like Dylan' (cited by Meacham, 2007), and with the exception of The Byrds, who spirited a lively quarter of 'Mr Tambourine Man' away to the West Coast, those who dared to reinterpret his songs from this era came out a distant second best.

After his 1966 motorbike accident and subsequent period of recovery, Dylan changed tack, forgoing many of his early trademarks and turning his hand instead to writing relatively mysterious, meditative and poetic songs, often with AAA structures. On the 1967 album 'John Wesley Harding' the emphasis of the expression is again to involve the listener, this time not through performance or compositional ingenuity, but instead by inviting us to fill the spaces left unexplored by the words and music. In this collection of songs, the impetus to resolve is almost absent, the zeal and romance of yore only fleetingly glimpsed through smoke and mirrors.

The country-flavoured 'Nashville Skyline' introduced elements of traditionalism, notably in the standard structure of 'I'll be your baby tonight', a strategy revisited in 1989 for the standout ballad 'Where teardrops fall'. In these masterfully simple songs it is near impossible to identify the wordsmith of 'Desolation Row'; the artist leaves no fingerprint, rather a series of fingerprints, some of which dissolve while others can be glimpsed in the shadows of other songs. For every elliptical and dense 'Jokerman', there is a straightforward and forceful 'Everything is broken'. For every confused and disorientated Dylan 'Standing in the doorway', there is a clear-eyed Dylan reporting the injustice of the 'Hurricane'.

Multidimensional, unpredictable and equipped with an unparalleled literary and emotional grasp of storytelling and character projection, Dylan is the Picasso, the Shakespeare of his art, a pioneer who invented and set the standard for numerous ways of expressing song. Almost 800 songs after 'Blowin' in the Wind', having withstood commercial and artistic trials and tribulations that would have seen off less hardy souls, Dylan continues to re-examine assumptions, to re-evaluate truths, to seek the answer.

2.16 Ulvaeus and Andersson

Few contemporary observers thought – or think – of ABBA as political reactionaries, but history records that the band, who in the seventies lorded it commercially over all and sundry, didn't always have it so easy. At the time Agnetha, Frida, Benny and Bjorn got together, Swedish society was highly politicized, its music scene beholden to an 'anyone can play' ethos directly at odds with the musical and aesthetic sophistication of the legendary quartet. As the 2013 BBC documentary *The Joy of ABBA* reveals, from the perspective of legions of scruffy lads and lasses democratically strumming away in dimly lit bars across Scandinavia, ABBA were the rebellious ones, their glamour portraying a Sweden whose cultural legacy was questioned and whose identity was contested. While the UK public, dulled by strikes and power failures and ready for music from another planet, readily embraced the sparkly-suited Bowie and Bolan, the Swedes considered ABBA's extroverted overtures to commerce a misrepresentation bordering on the sinister.

Echoing the international success of ABBA, in the present century Sweden regularly produces an extraordinary number of successful musicians. Swedish songwriter David Myhr, leader of the Stockholm-based band The Merrymakers, points out that – incredibly for a population of its humble size – Sweden is the third biggest music exporter in the world (Feeney, 2013). Inevitably, many of Sweden's most exceptional artists and songwriters, including ABBA and latterly Max Martin, had to relocate to find global recognition. Musing on the source of all this talent, the roots of Swedish songwriting greatness can be located, David claims, in the way young Swedes discover music:

> Unlike cultures who read about or listen to music, Swedes learn drums, take turns. They hear and play music from numerous perspectives. Max Martin came to it through heavy metal, Benny through folk. You are encouraged to express yourself.

While this eclectic, inclusive and exploratory approach to music and words evidently benefits the Swedish songwriter, there may also be other advantages unique to this part of

Scandinavia. 'Also, we're better at English than a lot of
other countries', observes David, 'and maybe it's easier for
us to write lyrics because we don't see the traps and the
pitfalls.'

In the capital of a country at the forefront of technology,
where the global giants Spotify and Skype started, the
Stockholm music scene, says David is 'a small community,
where everyone knows each other and works together'.
Like ABBA, his band The Merrymakers were primarily
successful overseas. David recalls how Swedish audiences can
be prescriptive in their tastes. 'We made this Merrymakers
record in ABBA's old studio,' he says, 'music that we intended
to be popular in Japan! Nobody liked us in Sweden. It
was a period when you had to look down at your shoes,
and we were too happy.' From a domestic perspective, like
ABBA, The Merrymakers were a case of right time, wrong
place. Unabashed, David proudly claims: 'We represent the
power-pop genre, which since 1971 has been a genre of losers;
part of this obscure genre that nobody buys!' Fortunately, in
the late nineties The Merrymakers were championed by one
of their heroes, Andy Sturmer from Jellyfish. 'Andy recommended us to EMI Virgin Japan and they took us on as their
mascots', David explains, 'to show Europe and America they
didn't have to work with The Rolling Stones or Janet Jackson.
We took ourselves more seriously once we knew someone,
somewhere, liked our music.'

While Andy Sturmer turned out to be The Merrymakers'
conduit to the outside world, ABBA's equivalent figure, the
man responsible for shaping the sound of Benny, Bjorn,
Agnetha and Frida and making it universal and timeless, is
somewhat less of a household name. Like Wilco, who built
the Loft in Chicago to ensure control over their recordings,
ABBA left nothing to chance, employing Michael B. Tretow to
capture the sound at their Polar studio in central Stockholm.
In an interview with *Sounds* international magazine in 1980,
Tretow talks of using ambience microphones and separating
amps very carefully, to create a clear picture of all the sounds

being generated in the studio. Seeking to avoid what he terms an 'apologetic sound', he would allow each instrumentalist to play as loud as they wished. For Michael, it was less about dealing with volume and more about the amount of control he was able to exert over each sound. This method, ideal for a band and engineer working in a fixed space, was aligned to Michael's philosophy that recorded takes should not be excessively treated or fixed after the fact; they should sound right before they go to tape. To broaden the sound Phil Spector style, Michael would ask each player to overdub their performance, or record it for a second time, and then change the speed of the second track to achieve a subtle pitch deviation.

Prior to this phase of recording, ABBA would try out songs in different tempos, switching instrumentation to audition different moods. Once they had found the right combination, one member of the group would sing a nonsensical guide vocal as a melody for the session instrumentalists to build upon and work around. Using an approach calculated to allow the music, not the lyric, to be the metaphor, it seems that ABBA wanted the musicians to know the tune, but not to form a responsive interpretation of the meaning of the words. For one vocal to spill onto another vocal track would compromise the producer's ability to mix the sounds, and as Agnetha and Anni-Frid's exact vocal timing required them to face each other at close proximity, a great deal of 'limiting' was needed to minimize the amount of leakage. In effect, the vocal recording technique used by Tretow sacrifices some sonic quality to allow the singers to be comfortable singing. In all, he reveals, ABBA would typically spend five days on a track, during which time Michael would spend as much time on the vocals as he would on all the other instruments combined.

Tretow's attention to vocal detail is shared by his modern-day equivalent, recording engineer, mix engineer, music producer and vocal producer Will Hicks. Production, says Will, is about 'trying to get the message of the song across to the listener in the best way you possibly can. That involves mostly listening to the lyric and the melody of the song and working out how you can enhance them.' Although he now works with Ed Sheeran, One Direction, Lily Allen and Elton John, at the beginning of his career, Will says, 'I would record anyone for free, and learned through trial and error and from other people'. Like Tretow, Will developed a method of recording capable of capturing songs as effectively and as durably as possible. Interestingly, parts of his method differ from those used by Tretow and ABBA. More suited to the transitory nature of his practice which can find him working anywhere in the world, Will is confronted with new sonic and acoustic challenges on a daily basis, while ABBA are concerned with adapting sound to song in a factory environment where each variable is known.

When Will works with an artist, the relationship is always collaborative: 'We always discuss who they like; who they want to sound like, or maybe a mix of sounds', he says. Analysis plays a role too: 'When people can identify drum sounds they like, or records they like, it's very helpful because engineers can find those sounds and try to approximate and even better them. There is nothing so new that you can't get a sense of how people want to sound.' While Will's technical skills are essential to his ability to navigate sound issues and solve problems, he considers much of the production task to require an understanding of the performer's psychology. Echoing Tretow's work with Agnetha and Frida, he explains:

The skill is in making sure you make the singers feel good. Get the takes, and then compile the takes. You've got to get it sounding good before they put the headphones on. You've got maybe five opportunities to capture it. The difference between songs you buy and songs you don't is the vocal; how relaxed the singer is. It's the way the vocal is delivered. If you can make it sound like it was fun, like taking a walk in the park, that is what people subconsciously respond to.

While there are some key principles Will adheres to, depending upon the musical context and the personalities involved, he anticipates needing to adapt. 'No one will care what the drums sound like,' he reiterates, 'it's the vocals that sell recordings.' Having the sound exactly right in the headphones, he explains, makes the singer sing differently:

> With full Adele-type arrangements you get the singer further away from the microphone, a few feet back. With spare arrangements, or an intimate lyric theme, closer. However close you want it to sound in the mix, the further back you record it. On an Elton John vocal I leave some breaths, on a David Guetta one there are none. If it's an intimate piano ballad I'll leave the breaths in; if the song sounds like it's meant for a nightclub, there won't be.

To add a further layer of mediation to the process, artists project songs in different ways. 'Doing a vocal take with Ed Sheeran is not really work, because he is such a good singer', says Will. 'He'll stop a vocal take he doesn't like and go again. His ear is so good, he will hear things as he's going along and correct them, His ear is as good as mine, if not better. I don't think he knows how good he is! With "Don't" he sang it four times and that was it. Music just pours out of him. With him, you are robbing him if you take any credit.'

While Ed Sheeran typically sings his own songs and in that sense enjoys a direct relationship with the song text, others come to the song as interpreters. When this is the case, Will alters his approach accordingly:

> With a boy band it's a lot different. One Direction are really good singers, some better than others! Technology can help some people but you don't sell that many records if you can't sing. When the artists didn't write the song, as the producer you have to know the song inside out. I'll listen to it loads of times and check the lyrics are exactly as they should be. I'll work out where all the breaths are, musically

notate how the melody goes, musically notate the length of the notes for when they are drawn out and when notes are short for the ending, including what beat they finish on, so that when you start recording you can say to them, with impunity, this goes *here*, that goes *there*. With someone who didn't write the song you are trying to transfer how the original songwriter wrote it and get the best performance you possibly can out of them.

Agnetha and Anni-Frid's vocals were recorded 'as is' in the days before auto-tuning, a discipline almost unheard of nowadays. 'Alicia Keys doesn't have her vocals tuned, but everything else is made perfect after the fact', Will explains. 'I can't think of anyone else who doesn't tune vocals. Pop production has Melodyne and Autotune to make the vocal nailed in tune at all times. They do create a falseness, but on a Katy Perry record, the drums are obviously not real. The guitars are real, but the bass isn't and the strings aren't, so it's whatever sits at home with what is going on behind it. And if the sounds are synthetic, the vocal will need to be too.'

As Benny admits, all ABBA were trying to do was write songs with endless hooks; to enrich mankind with perfect pop (BBC 2013). Any place you lowered the needle on an ABBA record, he claimed, you should be able to find a memorable musical phrase, a line or motif you would find impossible to resist. Global sales indicate they did a fine job, although unlike many of today's melodically condensed and repetitive chart hits, most of ABBA's tunes are musically and performatively complex. This historical predilection for unpredictability is predictable enough, as Ball (2010: 100) writes:

If music was simply a matter of following gravity-like attractions from note to note, there would be nothing for a composer to do: a melody would be as inevitable as the path of water rushing down a mountainside. The key to music is that these pulls can be resisted. It is the job of the musician to know when and how to do so.

In the present century, Ball argues (2010: 121, 125), we have a better memory for music with small interval steps and therefore repetition makes songs more coherent and satisfying. This being the case, the question emerges: what has happened to our ears since the buccaneering, soaring days of ABBA? First, those classic ABBA singles were produced for radio and made for the home stereo; sufficient sonic information was included to make the songs project from the transistor and to live multiple lives in the living room of the *attentive* listener. The listener of the seventies was comparatively conditioned to keep up with, and to be willing to return to the adventure and individuality of the voices and instruments. When ABBA came out of the radio, there was so much going on that we'd have to buy it and listen again.

The modern chart equivalent is rarely, if ever such a multiplicitious proposition. The guitar solo, a mainstay for connecting verses and choruses during the final quarter of the twentieth century, is virtually redundant; instead the less improvisatory and more melodically and lyrically repetitive voice features more prominently. Changes in the way we make and listen to music have led us to expect a broader, more programmed and texture-driven spectrum of sound, with synthetic textures and voices clearly audible wherever they find themselves in the mix. While ABBA's 'Waterloo' selects from an instrumental palette of piano, keyboards, moog synthesizer, mellotron, acoustic and electric guitars, bass, drums and percussion, Katy Perry's 2013 hit 'Roar' states its musical case with relatively simple clarity, relying upon the programming skills of Greg Wells to create revolving chord sequences and melodies more easily acquired by the listener-as-singer. In this way, the modern song is more accessible, more a part of the people.

While ABBA would never dream of writing a single based on a chordal loop, with 'Royals' Lorde did so almost as a matter of modern tradition. For the makers of modern-day chart music, much of the focus is on the development of sound textures that will work with the artist's voice;

once a combination of sounds is in place, the song, usually memorable through repetition, can follow. Consequently, as listeners we are no longer tied to the composition, drawn to each new daring melodic phrase; instead our attention spans are free to drift, to get lost in the sound world of whatever environment we find ourselves in. As a collective, we are less likely to think 'what an interesting person' and more likely to think 'that sounds like me'; while it used to be *them* making the music, now it is them *and* us.

2.17 Morrissey and Marr

According to Janiszewski (1988, 1990), 'Consumers can attend to something in their peripheral vision, even though they may not be aware of it ... When a stimulus is in peripheral vision, it is processed by the opposite hemisphere; right hemisphere is suited for holistic, inferential processing, i.e. music. Left hemisphere for analytic, sequential and repetitive processing, i.e. words.'

Working-class northerners of Irish decent, the Smiths come from families and cultures used to dealing in the currency of emotion, and as musicians true to their heritage they want us to be emotionally involved. While the bass of Andy Rourke and the drums of Mike Joyce are integral to the musicality and force of the band, when listening to The Smiths there are two immediately appealing places for the ear to go; the relentlessly playful, mischievous and often dark voice of Morrissey and the shimmering, uplifting guitar music of Johnny Marr. Making us fleetingly yet acutely aware of the bleakness and ecstasy of our existence, The Smiths invite us to experience a sound operating somewhere between these two extremes. The vastness of scope for our involvement, the huge gulf between Marr's optimism and Morrissey's pessimism, is part of what makes the work so durable. In the mid eighties, The Smiths' records were so definitively expressive they were borderline elitist; while Aztec Camera, Prefab Sprout and others had moments of illumination, the Smiths were one long luminous and untouchable phenomenon. Listening to 'The Smiths', 'Meat is Murder', 'The Queen is Dead' or 'Strangeways Here We Come', or any of a number of singles recorded between 1983 and 1987, whatever frame of mind we find ourselves in, there is inevitably somewhere in the emotional spectrum of the sound for us to drift, to wander.

Of Liberian descent, Manchester resident and Sony recording artist Josephine Oniyama senses a link between the songs of Morrissey and Marr and the city where they originated: 'There is a real distinct feeling about Manchester music', says Josephine, 'and I think it's reflective of the city. There are a lot of mid-tempo sombre things that actually sound more energetic than they are.' These contrasting characteristics could perhaps be said to reflect the past and the present; in the Smiths' case, the dour odour of adolescence and the thrill of sudden stardom. Josephine perceives further dualities in the lyric writing and music of the band:

> Morrissey bridges a divide between being very regional in the way he expresses his lyrics, yet the things he is saying are actually very universal. He knows how to capture a moment or theme so well, and he doesn't back away from it. The structure of the words is quite northern. 'Please, please, please let me get what I want' is a wonderful song; I don't find it depressing. I think the chord progressions and the melodies are actually quite uplifting.

As Josephine points out, leading a double life as a tale of woe and an infectious hi-life groove, 'This charming man' is a nightclub classic.

This authenticity of expression, or ability to project personal experience is, claims Josephine, near impossible to manufacture: 'You do feel it when somebody hasn't experienced or seen something. Everybody understands what is possible; we're all in the here and now and if you haven't

experienced things, then people feel it. Only Van Morrison
or Aretha Franklin could interpret it so you wouldn't know
that the experience wasn't theirs.' Attention to detail, she says,
marks the best lyric work: 'Morrissey does this thing where
his songs are so specific; they are just about one incident that
happens in one person's life on one day, and once you can do
that you can write songs like that for the rest of your life.'

'Rusholme ruffians', the second track on the 1985 LP 'Meat
is Murder', finds Morrissey and Marr at their stylistic and
expressive peak. Using circularity as an overarching theme,
the Ferris wheel chord structure borrowed from Leiber and
Stoller's 'His latest flame' has no particular place to go, its
brisk, repetitive shuffle evoking the mood of a mid-century
Manchester fair, where whatever ghastly incident, permanent
or passing is destined by fate and immune to intervention. A
charged mosaic of frivolity and implied violence, locked in
the revolving sound, Morrissey's lyric immediately places us
at the scene.

To impress a palpable sense of danger, Morrissey uses
a surprise of scale by suddenly and startlingly evoking the
prospect of mortality in a schoolgirl's musing. This effect, used
previously by Morrissey in the impossibly dark 'This night has
opened my eyes' and elsewhere by David Bowie in 'The man
who sold the world' and Thom Yorke in 'Black star', both of
which generate surprise by introducing aliens into domestic
scenes, is encouraged by the strident nature of the music.
When the surprise of scale happens, it raises the affective level
of the narrative from passive to precarious; we are no longer
in the realm of genteel observation, instead we find ourselves
in the company of the unknown.

With this lyric development, the song now has gravitas, and
as the lyric develops we are given passing glimpses of love and
loneliness, shrouded spectres that increasingly tilt the song
towards drama and away from mere occurrence. Forcing us
to look twice, the repetition of verses hems us in, blocking
all exits. In acknowledgement of the suggestive nature of the
lyric, the music sustains a simple naturalistic texture that

never interferes with the voice; the sound holds us down while the words land their punches.

Elsewhere in The Smiths' canon, the opposite effect is achieved; on 'William, it was really nothing', Morrissey and Marr pin a dour narrative to a shimmering, restless soundtrack. Helping to create a breadth and depth across The Smiths' canon, the balance between light and shade is sometimes heavily tilted one way or the other; 'How soon is now' and 'Death of a disco dancer' are brooding and deliberate in all aspects of expression, while 'Cemetery gates' and 'Vicar in a tutu' roll along merrily in both narrative and musical senses.

As John Peel noted, humour, often of the most mordant kind, is a constant theme in The Smiths' work, frequently offering a salve to help heal the hard times. Sometimes the protagonist is Morrissey, booking himself in at the YWCA in hope there will be a vacancy for a back scrubber; at other times it is the 'Sweet and tender hooligan' clearly not to be trusted with a three-bar fire. Shoplifters are encouraged to unite, Joan of Arc wears a Walkman and, as the title declares, 'Some girls are bigger than others'. For every Morrissey haunted by a ghoulish headmaster ritual there is another one singing recklessly and hilariously out of tune in 'Shakespeare's sister', the coda of which comedically features possibly the most inaccurately executed sung note in the history of popular music. This shifting and repositioning of emotional definition, an opening up of emotional spaces, is what propels The Smiths, a band unfamiliar with middle ground.

2.18 Bruce Springsteen

Playing with our traditional notions of chronology, in the masterful 'Highway patrolman' Bruce Springsteen begins his narrative not at the start, but at the end of the story. In character as Sargent Joe Roberts and speaking in the present moment, the narrator tells us his fictional name and rank;

we are invited to make up the rest of what we know about
Joe Roberts from his accent, his tone of delivery and from
the barren wasteland of the accompanying musical track.
During 'Highway patrolman' we are in Nebraska, the state
after which Springsteen chose to name his 1982 album. A
solitary and stark collection of songs, 'Nebraska' was initially
rehearsed with the E Street Band but ultimately reduced down
to guitar and vocal arrangements by their author, keen to
capture a sense of desolation, of a spiritually isolated people.
To capture the mood, Springsteen recorded on Teac 4 porta-
studio track tape, a medium that effectively stripped the sound
of all modern studio pretence. As Frankl (1994: 102) describes
it: 'Springsteen's examination of the broken lives on Nebraska
went deeper than superficial political issues, probing instead
the spiritual crisis of a society in which the bonds that held the
community together were all dissolving.'

In the last line of verse one, immediately inferring that
he considers him to be of low character, Joe introduces his
brother Frankie. Why is Frankie no good? Having spent three
lines hearing about the stoic Joe, we instinctively feel we
need to know more about the potentially dramatic Frankie.
Springsteen is directing us to listen on, and in the following
verse we are granted our wish. Creating a sense of history, of
an arc of events, the first half of the second verse narrative
transports us back to the brothers' childhood, to the root of
Frankie's misbehaviour. Then, for the second half of verse
two, to regain a sense of immediacy, of current relevance, we
are drawn back to the recent past where we learn that Joe,
in his capacity as an officer of the law, is inclined to show
his brother undue favouritism and lenience. Again, questions
begin to form in our minds. What did Frankie do? Why does
Joe allow him to break the law with impunity? If we want
these questions answered, we must listen on.

Rising a fourth, the chorus again stretches time, first
returning years earlier to the memory of a celebration at which
both brothers were temporarily joined as equals. Quickly the
chorus sobers up to deliver the moral judgement that lies at

the heart of Joe's narrative: blood, and not the judicial code to which he is sworn, is the law. With consummate storytelling skill, Springsteen is able to create a multidimensional image of who each character was and who each character is.

Going back in history for a third time, in verse three Joe recalls a happier time before circumstances beyond their control caught up with the two brothers. Frankie, it transpires, was conscripted to Vietnam, while Joe stayed behind to live a difficult, yet relatively stable married life on a farm. As the tale unravels, it transpires that while Frankie had been a bad apple since the days of their youth, the fateful trajectory of the brothers' respective paths had led Joe to develop a sense of guilt, to acquire a moralistic notion that no matter what crime he might commit, Frankie had been punished enough.

Chronologically, Springsteen tells Joe's story in: the present, thirty years earlier, the present, fifteen years earlier, the present, ten years earlier, and finally in the immediate past, as we are told of Frankie's ultimate reprieve. Moving back and forth in time, within the detail of their travails and shared histories, each chapter moves us closer to the Roberts brothers. Creating a sense of authenticity, of believability in the characters and their behaviours, the storytelling method removes any sense that we are being led by Springsteen; rather it projects the lives of Joe and Frankie as a flawed and fractured mosaic, like real life.

2.19 Paul Weller

Matching The Who and Bowie for quintessential Englishness, while simultaneously acquiring a unique, pan-generational place within the British popular consciousness during the past four decades, Paul Weller has, at the time of writing, racked up 67 top 40 UK hit singles. Released in 1978, 'All Mod Cons' was Weller's third album with his band The Jam, a trio formed with Rick Buckler and Bruce Foxton four years earlier. Initially lambasted by reactionary sections of the UK music press for their revivalist style which, at a surface level, went entirely against the grain of the prevailing punk ethos, The Jam had made two albums for Polydor, one good and one indifferent, and by 1978 they found themselves under considerable corporate and public pressure to deliver on the promise of their earliest recordings. In essence, at the tender age of 19, as the main songwriter in the unit, Weller had no choice but to rewrite the identity of the band, to make a clean break with the past. Rising to the challenge, 'All Mod Cons' never rests on its laurels. Instead, it uses subtle thematic, narrative and metaphorical shifts to encircle us in its bleak and dream-filled universe.

Opening up the world that exists between what is and what might one day be, in the opening sequence that binds the tracks 'All mod cons' and 'To be someone' Weller introduces us to the far corners of the reality and the dream. A dramatic blast of anger that serves notice on the listener, the song 'All mod cons' is immediately blunt and accusatory, making its point without embellishment. Its angular brevity permits no chorus and the musical language, like the words, is concrete grey. In many ways, it sets out not to impress but to startle – a splash of cold water.

While the opening track immediately brings Weller face to face with the as yet unfocused object of his vitriol, the narrator of the following song 'To be someone' seems to be daydreaming, lost in a wistful inner dialogue. With the compositional transition the tone softens, superseding the militaristic rattle of the opening track and ushering in a gentle major to minor descent and the odd spatial interlude. In under five minutes, Weller tells us a number of things: that the narrator of the record is both angry and self-indulgent, a realist and a dreamer – in other words, someone who might have an interesting story to tell.

In both 'All mod cons' and 'To be someone', the music reflects or accentuates the lyric, and in this sense, both are unequivocal. Consolidating the hitherto conflicting emotional language of the record so far, track three 'Mr Clean', however, juxtaposes the literal and metaphorical inferences of the tracks that precede it to create a track with subtext, an altogether more involved piece of work. Mr Clean, we learn, is Weller's nemesis, a representative of social and moral decay. To make sure we get close enough to see for ourselves exactly what he means, in verse one of 'Mr Clean' Weller projects reality through the unreality of omnipresence. How could Weller be in the kitchen? How could he be unnoticed in their bedroom? How could he, or we, know what Mr Clean is thinking?

As the record gains in songwriting complexity, it refines its established thread. The antithesis of Mr Clean, 'David Watts' flips the coin, seamlessly introducing a character invented in a bygone era by Ray Davies to illustrate the nobility of aspiration. Appropriately, given the character of its fictional teenage narrator, the musical aspect of the dream is texturally and melodically simple, emotionally pure. Following 'David Watts', the unabashedly romantic 'English rose' warns us not to become complacent in our expectations; that the parameters of beauty and anger to be explored know no bounds. Later, when the record finally concludes with a violent and unforgiving flourish, the mind is cast back to 'English rose', whose pastoral optimism creates a sense of stillness that allows the nightmarish scenes of "'A' bomb in Wardour Street' and 'Down in the tube station at midnight' to thrive in sharp relief. Again, the dream and the reality are implied, but 'English rose' and 'Down in the tube station at midnight' are a different, new kind of dream and reality, the former filtered through the mist of folk tradition and the latter viewed through the bloodied lens of the urban victim. In this visceral sense, the two songs offer the most extreme evocations of the idyll and the apocalypse.

While the five tracks that lead 'English rose' to the record's conclusive denouement roam lyrically, they frequently touch base with the established theme of aspiration, deftly adding in other counterpart themes and never entirely breaking free of the core concept of what it is to be young in England. Identity, a thematic undercurrent throughout is foregrounded by 'In the crowd', love resurfaces in 'Fly' and 'It's too bad', the echo of 'David Watts' is refracted through the mind of the disgruntled teenager 'Billy Hunt', and the notion of escape first introduced in 'To be someone' returns in 'The place I love'. By the time the major chord slab of the apocalyptic "A' bomb in Wardour Street' and its bottomless, swirling, minor chord counterpart, 'Down in the tube station at midnight' resolve the album, we feel as if we have visited and revisited themes in a number of different ways from a number of different angles.

After the retrospective feel of the first album and the searching aesthetic of the second, for the first of many times we see the real Paul Weller through the multiple prism of identity, fear, romance, aspiration, dream and reality. While it is decisive as a means of introducing Weller as a truly great songwriter, critical to its immersive effect is the sequential placement of tracks, which like The Beatles' White Album could be re-ordered to create a very different listening experience. Never putting a step wrong, 'All Mod Cons' moves with thoroughbred ease, as if catching English life and distilling it onto two sides of plastic was a walk in the park.

2.20 Hank Williams

Still a young man when he passed away in 1952, Hank Williams had already surpassed the folk songwriters of his time with the haunted reverie of his conversational tales of heartbreak and euphoria. Humbly poetic and sincere, his songs mirrored the lives of those caught in the headlights of post-depression America and gave the working people a form of representation in a world without reward. One of the truly wondrous things about Hank Williams' music is that, in the words of his ex-wife Billie Jean (cited in Escott, 2004), 'You wonder how such a simple man with no education could throw that out of his brain. He projected. He lived what he sang. He put everything he had into it.' Later in the same text, Billie Jean talks about how thrilled Hank was to have one of his songs covered by the contemporary country star Tommy Edwards and had fate been kinder to Hank and had he lived to see 1960, no doubt he would have been heartened to hear that Mercury Recording artist George Jones was set to enter Nashville's Bradley Barn with producer Pappy Dailey to record a set of Hank's originals for commercial release later that year.

Within the George Jones camp, however, the question hanging heavy in the air in the days leading up to the sessions must have been how to do these songs – already cornerstones of American music – the requisite justice. Even taking into account technological advances in sound recording since Williams and his band The Drifting Cowboys laid down the templates for country music in the original Castle Studio in the Tulane Hotel on nearby 8th Avenue North, how could this singer, or any singer, hope a decade later to bring something new to the work of the master?

By 1960, George Jones had been a country star for five years. Although he had recently become a father again, a role that had helped domesticate his life to a degree, his touring schedule was hectic and his wife disapproved of his act. Plenty of reasons for George to be apprehensive perhaps, but as a song interpreter, his experience as a young man schooled in hardships akin to those endured by characters in Hank's songs certainly stood him in good stead. The Jones family, recalls Carlisle (1984: 25–31), avoided famine by growing their own food on land owned by oil companies drawn to Saratoga, Texas by the spindle top oil discovery of 1901. 'Back in those days, the streets stunk of petroleum,' says Carlisle, and 'gamblers and whores descended, drawn by the sudden flood of wealth.' George's mother made clothes from flour sacks for George and his five older sisters, and his father either broke or delivered ice, was a pipe fitter or a bootlegger, depending on whose story you believe.

Jones was, and remained, steeped in the culture and behavioural codes of the environment in which he was raised, an area known as 'Big Thicket'. Jones' biographer Bob Allen (1984) describes the Big Thicket in deceptively poetic terms as 'tall long leaf pines, cane breaks, palmetto and wild honeysuckle, mostly populated by cottonmouth moccasins'. In this rural backwater populated in significant numbers by criminals who had come to hide in the lawless swamps of South East Texas, 'the music of the town comprised old world folk ballads,' opines Allen, 'sacred heart songs and eighteenth-century English hymns'. Almost beguiling – yet it transpires that these cultural possessions were counterbalanced by a range of unsavoury pastimes including incest, wife beating, knife fighting, cock fighting and gambling. In response to this environment, Jones adopted behavioural codes that were virtually inadaptable to the outside. Singular in taste, he avoided unfamiliar lifestyles and perspectives, a behavioural trait he carried with him into his adulthood. True to the Big Thicket code, George grew up despising the rich; as Dolly Carlisle puts it, 'He did not want nobody to think he was better than them'. By extension, we might infer that George would be disinclined to compete with the Hank Williams originals, that he might instead be driven by reverence to deliver an understated reading.

Back in his adolescent years, George developed a love of Hank Williams' tunes, which he played on the porch at the behest of his insistent drunken father. Later on, he took his renditions out on to the streets of Beaumont, eventually playing them night after night on the touring circuit. Over the years, the songs he was about to record for Mercury had entered his bloodstream, had become second nature. As Carlisle (ibid.) points out, Jones liked to do only what he wanted to do, and grew to hate unfamiliarity or change. How, under the circumstances, could Jones make a record capable of reinvention, of stepping out of the shadows of his idol?

While the songbook of Hank Williams is predominantly lonesome in tone, the ten Hank Williams' originals selected for 'George Jones Salutes Hank Williams' tilt heavily towards the bright side. Even morose titles like 'Nobody's lonesome for me' and 'Why don't you love me (like you used to do)?' are propped up by jaunty musical threads. The choice of song speaks of a need to provide the audience with an *entertaining* more than a *listening* record. In keeping with the original recordings, the instrumentation is very similar. Guitars, pedal steels and fiddles are at the forefront, providing a patented texture that would have appealed to George's predilection for keeping things the same, keeping things simple. Given the permanence of sounds used on country recordings at the time, it seems unlikely that anything too outlandish would have been considered, and the main concession to the contemporary sound of 1960 is the addition, typically once the lyric theme has been established, of a high-pitched piano. This sound, entirely absent from Williams' recordings, doesn't necessarily help to improve the songs, but it brightens the spectrum of sound, brings an element of continuity and offers somewhere for the listener's ear to go. While Jones is clearly technically the equal of any other country singer, including Williams, with the insertion of this distractingly jaunty and sugary piano, the capacity of the listener to focus on the voice alone is greeted with suspicion.

Interestingly, it seems the contemporary attention span, mythically thought to have deteriorated to coincide with the rise of MTV, had already diminished by the late fifties. Further evidence of this lies in the treatment of solos on the album, which are often halved, as in 'Hey, good lookin'' or shortened, as in 'Why don't you love me?' By comparison with Hank's relatively meditative originals, there is little room for lyric meaning to be absorbed. Paradoxically, as a result of the distracting piano and decreased absorption time, while Jones' voice takes up more of the track, the lyric is, in a comparative sense, heard less.

The producer Pappy Daily seems to have paid plenty of attention to the instrumentation of the original solos, a number of which use identical arrangements and even alternate in the same order. In this subtle way, homage is paid. Less focus seems to have been paid to the direction of tempo;

some are slightly quicker, some a little slower, and some match the originals. In all likelihood, the song tempo would have been driven not by the producer or the band, but by the instinctive way Jones will have chosen to sing and play them; the pace at which, from the perspective of a singer who has sung them many times before, the melody is not compromised, the diction not threatened, and the singer's own expressive metre not tested.

For the most part, the original recording keys are raised by a tone, i.e. from D to E in 'Howlin' at the moon' and 'Half as much', or from C to D for 'Jambalaya' and 'Hey, good lookin''. This not only gives the new versions a relative brightness by comparison, but will also have been calibrated to suit Jones' voice. A consummate and versatile singer, George sounds as comfortable in the same key as Hank on 'Nobody's lonesome for me' and 'I can't help it (if I'm still in love with you)', as he does when required to raise each note by a fourth, as he does throughout 'Honky tonkin''.

The avoidance of sharp and flat keys on both the original and cover versions tells us two things: first, that country musicians rarely opt to play in keys that are difficult to navigate for the fingers or the mind. Secondly, it also probably reflects the keys in which both Williams and Jones chose to perform the songs, as Powell (2010: 170) observes: 'A lot of pop songs and most classical guitar pieces are written in the keys of C, G, D, A and E because these are the easiest keys to play on a guitar.' Across the duration of the album, Jones' familiarity with the tunes born from years of performance, both formal and informal, is almost enough to persuade us, if we did not know better, that he wrote the songs himself. Yet somehow, George seems to feel more authentically tied to the songs of loss than he does to the songs of joy. On the evidence of the album, Jones' love of the tunes comes across throughout and at no time does he sound out of his depth. Evidencing his facility to refract the emotional highs and lows of his idol, this adherence of spirit may have been down to years of rehearsal as much as the kinship of lifestyle. As George himself said, in his autobiography: 'If you are going to sing a country song, you are going to have to have lived it yourself.'

Truth be told, an album full of heartbreak ballads such as 'Take these chains from my heart' and 'You win again' would probably have been more to George's taste, but may not have satisfied the legions of country followers unprepared for the country equivalent of Sinatra's mournful 'Only the lonely'. Sure enough, two and a half years later, George was back in the studio, this time to record an album of Hank's more lonesome repertoire for United Artists. Its title? 'My Favorites of Hank Williams'.

2.21 Gillian Welch and David Rawlings

A graduate of the Berklee College of Music in Boston, where she met her musical partner David Rawlings, Gillian Welch has been based in Nashville for over two decades. Between their debut album 'Revival' and the sophomore 'Hell Among The Yearlings', the duo discovered an identity that has deepened and intensified over the three records they have made since. A revered live act, Gillian and David have played at festivals and in concert halls around the world, bringing their roots music to enthusiastic audiences everywhere. Live performances, with their inherent sense of occasion, can offer electrifying introductions to songs. By any standard, the virtuosic Leeds-based pianist and Leaf Records recording artist Matthew Bourne has an open mind to new music, devouring musical encounters with the same exploratory vigour he reserves for his mesmerizing, and often unpredictable, concert performances. A Perrier Jazz Award winner at the tender age of twenty-three, Matthew worked with broken and neglected pianos for his 'Songs From a Lost Piano' project, recorded the sublime and minimal 'Montauk Variations' in 2012 and has recently been preparing 'Memorymoog', a homage to analogue synthesizer.

Having never heard any of Gillian's records, when the duo visited Sheffield City Hall Matthew went along as an inquisitive observer, hoping but not expecting to encounter something revelatory. His experience on that evening not only redefined his impression of country music, it also led him to alter his approach to his art. Recounting the City Hall concert and detouring into other avenues of discussion via the performative approaches of Elton John and Bill Callahan, in the following narrative Matt touches on a series of key issues relating to live performance. Recast as a soliloquy to allow for the essence of a performer talking about performers to emerge, here is Matthew's story.

It brought a different focus to listening to the album after I'd seen them live. I came to the album via a friend, Jonny, and he was more into country, and I was just exploring some experimental stuff. So he always had it on, and I never really zoned in on the words. I just thought, 'Yes, it's *okay*'. Then he said, 'I've got a ticket. Do you want to come?' I went, and I had all these preconceived ideas that I might be bored by two guitars and two voices for a whole gig, especially with an interval. I thought, 'I don't know how I'm going to cope with this'. I looked at the set-up: two chairs, two microphones, and thought, 'I wonder...' Anyway, as the first set ended, I realized that I'd been sitting there for 40 minutes and I'd been transfixed. And then there was the interval. I remember saying to Jonny, 'That was incredible. I can't wait to go back and see the second set.'

After the second set they did three encores, and the third one, they stepped out in front of the microphone set-up, and they sang acoustically. This was in Sheffield City Hall, and it was packed. They didn't sing out into the hall; they sang as if they were playing in a small room by themselves, or in their home or something. They just sang, and you could hear a pin drop. It was as if all the other sounds in the room had been sucked out, and you could almost *hear* everyone listening. It was stunning.

It was so electrifying that when we tried to get out of Sheffield we got lost, because we were in this trance. I couldn't get over it. The week before, I'd bought some MIDI control pads – I was using a lot of samples at the time – a MIDI keyboard, and I'd bought Logic. I'd bought all this stuff to try to get into that whole thing. The very next day, I put adverts online and sold everything because that gig made me think, 'Well, hang on. These guys have just got a guitar, their instrument and their voice. I've got a piano. Why do I need to be worried about getting into computer music?' I'd spent so much time trying to get the software to work and function and working on a screen, and I thought, 'Well, what am I doing? I need to be sitting at the piano, not sitting at a computer', so I sold everything. I didn't sell the computer, but I sold all the other stuff that I'd bought, because after seeing that gig, I thought, 'This is all a waste of time. I should just be focusing on my instrument.'

So that gig was probably one of the best gigs I've ever seen, or it had the biggest impact. It was just simple and honest and it was acoustic. The balance of the voices, that was one thing that came across live. Obviously, you just assume, in recordings, that the balance is okay, because it's in the studio, but live his supporting harmonizing was never above the level of her main vocal; it always seemed slightly under. It was perfect. It was skilful, but they wouldn't *know* they were being skilful; they were just doing what they do. That's what I think is magic. With those two musicians, I think there's a modesty, a strength in modesty, if that makes any sense. They're not trying to be anything, and I think that's what probably came across and blew me away more than anything. Rawlings' guitar playing and the little solos that he takes, they're not shredding, but there is a lot of technique in them, when you saw that. He just plays only the notes that are needed. You think, 'Wow, this is simple', but then you try doing that. I have a friend of mine, called Mark Cresswell; he's an amazing guitarist, and he loves Dave Rawlings. He was in a band called The Bronte Brothers years ago, and his guitar skills are insane, but he's never shouted about it. He's that kind of player; he likes duff, old instruments, and he can just make them sound really good. He's played with all sorts of people, but he would never admit to it.

My mum's second husband used to buy country music tapes from the market, and they were shit. I can't remember who they were. You'd go to the markets and there's a whole stall of these ten-a-penny artists ... so I think I developed this negative view of country and western music because of this guy. It was with that music that I developed a strong hatred of lap steel guitar. I hated it. Then I went to see a gig with Bill Frisell and Greg Leisz playing the lap steel, and that changed it. I'm like, 'Okay, it is a beautiful instrument, kind of. I'm coming round to it.'

Before the Gillian Welch gig the only songwriting I really paid attention to was somebody like Joni Mitchell or even Carole King, and it was more the musical settings that drew me in. But after this gig ... it was one of the first acts that made me focus in on the lyrics. Then I bought a copy of 'Time (The Revelator)', and I remember playing it in the car over and over and over and over and over again, and listening to the lyrics and thinking, 'Wow, what are these songs about?' The last track on there, 'I dream a highway', that's 14 minutes long, and it gets slower. Sometimes I'd put that on repeat and by the time you got to the end of it, you didn't get the sense that it was a long track. The control, the feel. It's immense.

It's funny, because I've listened to a Gillian Welch album produced with a band, and I didn't like it as much. I don't know why that is. I think because for me, the other instruments get in the way of the purity. I feel the same way about a lot of singer songwriters. Elton John on *The Old Grey Whistle Test*, where he's just sitting at the piano and singing 'Rocket man' or 'Tiny dancer', or whatever it is, there's a rawness there; there's such power, control, and there's a purity about it. It's just them and the song.

But then, when I saw Bill Callahan, he was with a band, and that was phenomenal. What a band. He had this guy called Matt Kinsey on the guitar. He just had a guitar and an amp. He certainly didn't have pedals; he just used the natural resonance of what his guitar was. He used a lot of feedback in various places. They would extend whatever they were doing and pull it around as a group, so it wouldn't be like, 'Now, you do a solo', it was as if Matt Kinsey's solo just emerged out of what they were all doing anyway. The drummer, instead of a bass drum, he'd substituted parts of his kit. It was more like a percussion kit, and that was total economy. That was a great band. So it depends. It's mysterious in that it won't be the same for somebody else, but I'm fascinated by why some of those settings work and some don't.

It didn't seem contrived in any way. None of the Bill Callahan thing did, because none of it *was* contrived. But that's the thing. I would imagine that if you're doing those songs on a big tour each song will just grow into this ever-changing, morphing thing ... He gave the band no cues at all. I watched them. I just thought, 'They just know what they're doing'. The only cues he'd give, at the end of some of the songs, he'd stand slightly in front of the band, and then when he wanted the band to stop, he'd take a step back. It was such a small movement, but noticeable, but not anything like a big deal. Then they would wind it down within eight bars or whatever, or four bars, and they'd just bring it to a halt. But all he had to do was just step out and then step back.

For the first four songs, I think, he didn't say a word to the audience. He came out, the band started, and he stood there. He's quite a tall bloke, isn't he? He stood there, and I think the first song ('The sing') the lyrics were something like, 'I like beer. Thank you. I like beer. Thank you,' like that, and it was just funny. Then he did the next song, and then he did 'You dressed sexy at my funeral for the first time in your life', which is amazing. It's a great lyric. I think he spoke after that, but didn't say much. It was sold out. It was the Festival Hall, and he was there for two nights. I didn't realize he was so big. I had no idea. Again, that was another surprise, in that when I went to see the Gillian Welch gig, Sheffield City Hall was packed, and I had no idea that they would pull such a big crowd, because I didn't know anything about that scene. I kind of still don't, actually. There are a lot of people I probably haven't checked out. Maybe I should tap your record collection?'

2.22 Kanye West

Blasphemy, desperation, angst, repulsion, heart-crushing, supreme beauty, braggadocio, perverse, fantastic, fascinating, obsessive compulsive, jarring, elegantly wasted and just plain mad; all descriptors from reviews published in online and print music journals for Kanye West's 2013 album 'Yeesus'. A leading figure in the hip hop community since the turn of the century, Kanye's often controversial persona continues to divide opinion, yet if there is one thing reviewers from all corners agree upon, it is his ability to make great records.

What is it about Kanye's songwriting that elevates it above its field, that routinely accords it such a level of critical unanimity? To paraphrase a lyric from 'Yeesus', what makes him a leader, not a follower?

Upon first listen, led by familiar vocal patterns and distinctive lyric imagery, many of the concepts brought by Kanye to the writing and recording of 'Yeesus' appear to have their roots deep in the culture of the hip-hop idiom. Emphasizing the historical importance of the lyric text within black culture, in her book *Rap Music and Street Consciousness*, Cheryl Keyes (2002: 18–21) explains how West African communities would hold in high regard the storyteller or bard, whose role it was to create inventive performances through the use of verbal images. Seeking to identify a line of heritage, Keyes hypothesizes that the West African bardic tradition is linked to modern African American music by public performances given by griots, who, particularly in the second half of the twentieth century, travelled the world transmitting their spoken word. 'While performing, a bard makes use of formulaic expressions, poetic abstractions and rhythmic speech,' writes Keyes, 'all recited in a childlike fashion that prefigures rap' (ibid.: 20). On a related note, as Ryan Dombel (2013) observes in his contemporary review of 'Yeesus' for *Pitchfork*: 'Here, Kanye raps about loyalty, respect, threesomes and, yes, croissants with the urgency of someone being chased by a 30 ton steamroller.' Mixing and matching images and points of reference with seemingly random elan, Kanye appears to extend a storytelling lineage that stretches through and beyond the roots of the hip-hop movement.

Writing a decade prior to the release of 'Yeesus', Watkins elaborates: 'By insisting on borrowing from various cultural, musical, aesthetic and political traditions, hip-hop became an incredibly rich fountainhead of youth creativity and expression' (2005: 150). Adopting a similar perspective, in the 14 June 2003 edition of *Rolling Stone*, record reviewer Jon Dolan perceives the presence of 'Bunker-club hipster dance music, ring the alarm Jamaican dance hall, forlorn autotune soul, crackling old soul samples and downcast techno-rap'. Evidently, in the making of the album, like the West African griot before him, Kanye had his mind open to a broad range of influences. Within the maelstrom of influences audible on the record, the only perceivable 'anchor' is the texture of his voice; everything woven around it corresponds to an established cultural code that embraces the scattergun. If the thread is the vocal delivery, the construction of the sounds that surround it is a deliberate tangle; in this sense, by reflecting the practice of his forebears and contemporaries, Kanye seems to be observing, rather than reinventing tradition.

Inevitably, this songwriting method, which pairs taciturn and often unforeseeable combinations of words and music, occasionally generates a compositional soundscape that exists at the outposts of unpredictability. Moved to comment at length in *Rolling Stone* on the album two weeks after its release, legendary Velvet Underground founder member and main songwriter Lou Reed (2013) not only observes the capacity of 'Yeesus' to unbalance the listener through the use of what Reed calls 'sucker punches', but also insightfully perceives that what Kanye *says* and what he *does* are two different things. Investigating this dichotomy further, *Pitchfork* reviewer Dombel (2013) identifies the capacity of the artist to suddenly switch from sorrowful to furious, from dark to angelic, while fellow journalist Jon Dolan illustrates the extreme or surreal nature of the songwriting, observing how 'only Kanye West would take an American masterpiece ('Strange fruit') and use it to back a song about what a drag it is to have to attend basketball games with a girl you knocked up sitting across the court' (ibid.). On a similar theme, in her analytical essay on conflicting representations of black masculinity in 50 Cent's 'Candy shop', Djupvik (2014: 214) notes how the musical detail threatens to undermine the lyric imagery of the song. On 'Yeesus' a similar tension, involving the knowing compositional placement of juxtaposed ideas, often occurs.

Elsewhere, on numerous occasions 'Yeesus' conveys messages that seek to provoke. In *Billboard*, the reviewer reaches the startling conclusion that, in a musical sense, seven songs into the record, there is 'still no sign of traditional hip-hop' (2013). Openly defying what most consider the rules of the genre, from a creative perspective it is here that the songwriting is at its most subversive. However, as Watkins (2005: 149–51) asserts, such cleavages mirror the multiracial, multicultural and multilingual nature of hip-hop, a genre in which artists such as Kanye and the equally incendiary Public Enemy and Queen Latifah seek to 'defy all attempts to impose the strict racial definitions and caricatures that endeavour to limit its potential reach and influence' (ibid.: 150).

Writing in the *Guardian* (2013), Alexis Petridis perceptively infers that 'from its title down "Yeesus" is intended as a deliberately contrary, ambiguous act of provocation in a musical world where provocation is in pretty short supply'. In other words, the songwriting both extends a pivotal tradition of the genre and, by dint of its individuality of character it similarly appeals to the mainstream. Petridis also notes the funny side of 'Yeesus', and while the record has distinct moments of intentional humour, within the review media these lighter touches are not to everyone's taste. Considering it to be aimed primarily at teenagers, guest reviewer Lou Reed is, for instance, particularly dismissive of Kanye's use of sexual innuendo. Ultimately, it could be argued that, in its quest to portray a grown man still in thrall to sophomore appetites, and in its subsequent will to appeal to audiences both young and old, 'Yeesus' perhaps at times overstretches itself. This impulse to impress is hardly new to the genre, however, as Dery (2004: 410) points out:

> In the final analysis it is important to remember that while rap is political, rappers are not politicians. Like callow young men of all races, they often fall prey to macho posturing, misogyny and xenophobia.

Somewhat unusually for modern times, in a move that seems to undermine its commercial potential, 'Yeesus' is prone to lament the failings of the songwriter himself. The *Billboard* review of 14 June 2013 identifies 'Hold my liquor', 'Blood on the leaves' and 'Guilt trip' as tracks during which self-doubt prevails, and *Pitchfork*'s Dombal (ibid.) also hears confessional overtones of ineptitude and insecurity. Adopting a more expansive perspective, Lou Reed's narrative pinpoints Kanye's willingness to project himself as both great and terrible (ibid.). Perhaps this highly contrary mode of self-perception helps to make the record so compelling, so demanding of our attention. As Petridis (2013) notes:

> The lyrics seem to sound like a kind of unfiltered, instinctual vomiting forth of thoughts in a world of PR control and damage limitation. They're variously shocking, funny, thought provoking, nonsensical, contradictory and occasionally reprehensible, the only consistent thing about them being how inconsistent they are.

These qualities, most of which go against our perception of the traditional commercial mainstream, combine to give 'Yeesus' a second life, as a work not just for contemplation, but also for discussion. Indeed, from the perspective of the artist, the temptation to provoke through the use of flawed or questionable sentiment is welcome, as it is likely to promote discourse within the community. As Uberg Naerland (2014: 486–9) argues, hip-hop is a 'potentially vital supplementary vehicle for democratic political communication' in the sense that:

> First, the song facilitates public discourse by commanding public attention through the use of hyperbolic language … Secondly … the song employs lyrical and musical devices in order to effectively engage and address the audience … it potentially fosters emphatic imaginings crucial in moderating as well as strengthening the quality of public deliberations.

Seemingly random yet somehow coherent, 'Yeesus' has little of the early twenty-first-century music industry mainstream in its sonic appearance, but plenty relating to the broader, extra-musical mainstream in its realization. Kanye West understands the value of social media to record and ticket sales, and on numerous levels the album generates that most prevalent of contemporary social concepts, debate. Is it a hip-hop record or not? Does he take racial inequality seriously, or is he too far removed, by wealth and privilege, from the victims and agitators of Ferguson to care? Does he have a messiah complex or is he painfully insecure? Can he write good tunes or are they merely a mishmash of pre-existing sounds? Is he an adult or an overgrown teenager? Does he represent the mainstream or the alternative? Is he an innovator or an imitator? The real thing or a fake? Like all great and enduring modern works, 'Yeesus' asks more questions than it answers.

At heart, the artist knows that in the temporary, ever-shifting world of modern entertainment, the statement likely to burn brightest and last longest is the one that polarizes. For every Lou Reed apparently unconcerned by Kanye's decision to include a provocative lyric reference to civil rights, five others are ready to take umbrage, and while purists every-where cringe at the use of 'Strange fruit' as a backdrop to a personal domestic crisis, others applaud the sheer audacity of the gesture. Like viewers of Picasso's ambitious and moving 1937 painting 'Guernica', we are repulsed, yet profoundly intrigued by the ability of the artist to convey it. As listeners caught in the complex crossfire of the twenty-first century, we acknowledge the madness and the complexity of the expression, and ultimately understand it to be a truth.

2.23 Alex Turner

More impatient than his fellow storyteller Bruce Springsteen, in 'When the sun goes down', Arctic Monkeys songwriter Alex

Turner wastes no time involving us in his drama, immediately confronting us with a question. While Springsteen's Joe Roberts seems to be lost in reflective reverie, Turner's narrative is insistent from the first note, initially introducing us to the cast of characters, and later involving us in the drama. While we view 'Highway patrolman' from afar, in the latter phase of 'When the sun goes down' we find ourselves in a questionable part of the north of England. It is not a screen we are invited to look at; the action is all around us.

Indelibly tied to the Sheffield region, the specific sense of place is predominantly created by Turner's accent. On this subject, author, songwriter, producer and course leader at Southampton Solent University Professor Paul Rutter (2015) notes how, through the dialect in his vocal delivery, the singer effectively helps to sell the distinctive and idiosyncratic persona of UK music culture to the wider world. As Paul observes, this tradition goes back via Scottish duo The Proclaimers, whose accent added a steely resolve to their music, and The Small Faces, whose 'Lazy Sunday afternoon' could not be located anywhere other than London, all the way to George Formby, whose charming and comedic recordings of the thirties relied heavily upon a northern brogue.

Like 'Highway patrolman', 'When the sun goes down' uses verses as short chapters, and, after an opening verse that sketches a female character, by the beginning of the second verse our attention is diverted away from the girl towards a male figure. While Springsteen uses a complex chronological strategy to allow the story of Joe Roberts to unfold, Alex Turner uses chapters to surround us with sights and sounds that trade in anticipation and foreboding in equal measure; that place us in a netherworld between the present and future. As listening participants shorn of any contextual reference to the past, our response is less intellectual, more sensory.

As the lyric focus moves from female to male in the second chapter, the musical backdrop of a single angular 'cheap' electric guitar remains the same. Like Springsteen, careful not to distract by using additional instrumentation, Turner wants us to hear everything he has to say about both characters. With its vivid depiction of illegal trade and playful overtones of exotica, the opening sections bring to mind Picasso's 1907 painting 'Les Demoiselles d'Avignon', the clandestine sparkle and threat of the chief protagonists waiting and threatening to act.

By the end of the second chapter we have heard the verse music twice, enough times for the songwriter to be wary of it becoming overly repetitive. We have also met two new fictional characters, each brought to life within the space of half a minute, both of whom are fresh in our minds. If the music repeats, we may become irritated. If a new character is introduced, we may struggle to remember what we know about the other two. To resolve the compositional issue, Turner begins a new chapter by bringing the two figures together, first in physical proximity, and then more dramatically, through a perceived sense of injustice. Having made the necessary introductions and forged a dramatic dynamic, at this moment the expressive pulse of the song, the message its author seeks to convey, is first felt.

By the end of verse three, something is still missing, though. While we understand what is happening, there is a nagging chance that the characters may not be real; they may be figments of Alex Turner's imagination, and if so, why should we care about their fate? Brilliantly, by using the prefix 'you're' at this juncture, Turner brings *us*, the audience trying not to listen, into the action. Instead of watching from the comfort of a remote listening location, we are now *there*. Here, the musical pulse also quickens, the implication being that now we have arrived on the scene things will start to happen. In verse four, the net closes as the narrative involves you (us), the girl, the man and Turner himself, the proximity between each character reduced to within speaking distance. Gradually, over the course of sixteen lines of skilfully crafted narrative, we have been drawn in. With typical subtlety, Arctic Monkeys use a motley choir of backing vocalists to attribute the chorus slogan to a collective, thereby adding a further layer of communal involvement.

The dense activity of the opening five chapters places a significant demand upon the listener's attention; to keep up, we have been obliged to follow numerous musical and lyrical twists. When the title arrives, its undemanding repetition allows the listener's mind to rest (Braheny, 2007: 96). Perhaps upon first listen we will not be able to absorb it all, but it is likely that the various compositional cues and directions will have been persuasive in telling us that we are hearing a song that will, over time, continue to reward our attention.

2.24 Lennon and McCartney

Songs with two choruses: 'She loves you', 'Can't buy me love'; two bridges: 'I'll be back'; four unrepeated sections: 'Happiness is a warm gun', 'A day in the life', 'You never give me your money'; unorthodox chord changes: 'Julia', 'Two of us'; impenetrable poetry: 'I am the walrus', 'Strawberry Fields forever'; and mantra-like simplicity: 'Hello goodbye' – when it comes to songwriting innovation, The Beatles' sense of adventure is boundless in its ambition. Plenty of their original ideas have since been refracted by a generation of younger songwriters into new, inventive compositional shapes, including one of their less-celebrated innovations which can be found in a trio of observational songs about women from a male perspective. Like Ray Davies' agora-phobic voyeur in 'Waterloo sunset', the voices who watch in 'Eleanor Rigby', 'She's leaving home' and 'Lady Madonna' do so from afar, but unlike The Kinks' protagonist, these observers have no location, and as a consequence take on a quality of omnipresence.

Written in the golden recording period of 1966–68, all three songs are to some extent underpinned by the authors' shared childhood loss of matriarchal figures in the late fifties. Given the imminent arrival of Lennon's 'Julia' and McCartney's elegiac 'Let it be' it seems reasonable to suggest that they were at this time exploring sensitive psychological territory, using different musical backdrops to make sense of it, or to mediate a resolution. As Reising (2002: 65) says:

> The purpose of the song 'Eleanor Rigby' is to draw attention to the lives of disconnected and lonely people. The story of the lonely spinster's demise adheres to one of the great narratives of the European tradition. Countless operas and words of literature require a woman's death to bring the drama to its climax, redeem other characters and provide closure.

Strangely for such a series of finely detailed observational studies, the characters in each song appear featureless; there is no visual description of any character. Bolstered by references to morning, noon and night, and the fleeting, yet consolidating presence of the mother, father and children, however, they *seem* real. Ultimately, from the songwriters' perspective, perhaps it matters less what Lennon or McCartney think they look like – they only exist in their imaginations after all – and more what we think they look like, who we want them to be.

Forging another link to the fast-disappearing world inhabited by their mothers, Julien (2008: 84, 116) observes: 'The classical feel of the song ("She's leaving home") would seem to be connected to the old dusty world of the parents' generation; that world from which the girl is trying to escape.' Further:

> As is the case with 'Eleanor Rigby', no Beatles play instruments on 'She's leaving home', suggesting their distance from the pathos of these dreamy domestic dramas. The Beatles visit the so-called generational gap with a tenderness perhaps unique to this song; even to the hip and the young, The Beatles put themselves in the position of somebody outside the swirl of the counterculture. (ibid.)

Equating our perception of life in general to how we view music, Meyer (1956) asserts that people are inclined to make predictions on the evidence of the past. Meyer contends that music and life are closely connected in the sense that, in both contexts, emotions are evoked by deviations from what we expect to happen. As a result, he argues, when our expectations are not met, when a melody or chord sequence meanders from its apparently inevitable shape, much like when we awake to find the winter's first snowfall, the resulting deviations of feeling – no matter how dramatic or minor – reflect our existence.

Given the emotive nature of the theme, the intricacy with which all three songs are written, arranged and performed is impressive. When fellow northerners The Smiths and Arctic Monkeys later revisited the theme of female observation with 'What she said' and 'Fluorescent adolescent', they too used the lyric subject of feminine misfortune as a counterbalance to invest the music with a spring in its step (Rogan, 1993: 221). Perhaps suggesting an undertone of a brighter past or future, a faint silver lining to contextualize or mask the implication of solitude in each case, the music pulls against the sadness of the narrative. There are some striking similarities within the three Lennon and McCartney songs – compositional elements that contribute to their lasting quality. First, questions are asked within each narrative: Where do the lonely people come from? Where does the money come from? What did we do wrong? As such, the lyric is open-ended, unresolved, inviting us to create our own answers.

Although Moore (1997: 37) considers 'Eleanor Rigby' 'rather dispassionate' and less sentimental than 'She's leaving home', one dimension of our involvement in the theme is articulated by Julien (2008: 101), who writes: 'The song is not just about a lonely old woman and her lonely pastor; rather, it is about all the lonely people in the world.' Within this trilogy of songs, McCartney has picked the front door lock of the priest, the suburban family and the single lady and is free to roam unnoticed, yet he does so not to find answers or to pass judgement; rather he invites us to step inside, take a look around and ask our own questions. What questions are we invited to ask? There is a sense that at some point in our relationship with each song we will be inclined to ask the same ones Lennon and McCartney must have asked themselves many times. What is the source, benevolent or otherwise, of the emptiness felt by these people? What and where is the spiritual force? Where do we belong? Who saves us?

3

Songwriting

3.1 Idiolect

To establish a foundation as an original songwriter, the key initial element is likely to be the discovery and exposition of an individual voice. In such a saturated and post-modernist culture, how can there be such a thing? Fortunately, from the outset all songwriters find they already have a distinctive voice shaped by accent, timbre, enculturation and limitation. As long as a conscious effort not to sound like someone else is made, there is likely to be an individuality of sound. Perhaps our individuality will come, in part, from where we live? As the Texan songwriter David Olney (2002) notes, an unusual number of songwriters were raised in Lubbock, Texas, a seemingly unspectacular part of the world that, to the outsider might not appear to be a *particularly* inspiring location. Another native Texan songwriter, Leslie Satcher, once explained to me how the wide-open spaces of rural Texas gave the imagination a clear, expansive palette upon which to paint; that the wild creativity of Janis Joplin, Ornette Coleman, Blind Lemon Jefferson and Willie Nelson is born of the barren landscape. When I mentioned this to Nanci Griffith, she looked at me as if I had lost my mind, and told me the reason so many original Texan musicians had emerged over the past few decades was that they read a lot of books.

Whatever the truth, there must be something in, or not in, rural Texas that sparks the imagination. Where we come from determines our accent, shapes the way we are heard, and helps us to form an identity. Some songwriters draw more upon this than others. Alex Turner of Artic Monkeys leans heavily upon his Yorkshire accent; without it the unique character of Arctic Monkeys would be transformed. Writing on the capacity of song to link individuality to identity, Shuker (2001: 102) recalls how young songwriters working in New York's Brill Building in the early 1960s such as Carole King, Gerry Goffin, Ellie Greenwich and Jeff Barry were able to use their own experiences of teenage life in the United States to write songs that resonated with a contemporary teenage audience. Grammy award-winning songwriter Jimmy Webb (1998: 17) further emphasizes that 'it is the intensity of experience that marks us with knowledge and intuition, not longevity and repetition'. Rather than hiding on an un-thumbed page of a secretive theoretical manual waiting for us to find it, our songwriting fingerprint already exists.

Few know more about songwriting than Bob Dylan, who voices the opinion that there are already enough conventional songs in the public domain (cited in Zollo, 2003: 72). Dismissing the idea of writing songs that conform to popular expectation as a meaningless pursuit, Dylan insists that songs should possess 'a pure heart' and have 'something to say'. If we feel ownership of the sounds we make, they are already worth something to us. If they also happen to mean something in their unaltered, unedited state to others, then all well and good; we have a communicative premise; someone is talking and someone is listening. One potential problem with trying to come across as the kind of character we *think* people will want to hear from is that it requires us to project a character we don't know to an audience we have never met. What is the likelihood that an audience in possession of an instinctive understanding of the nuances of music and language will be diverted by our smokescreen, fall for a fabricated voice?

Secondly, if we write about what we know, we have control over our art. No artist is obliged to make a full disclosure of what excites or troubles them; that would leave little room for interpretation, for the imagination of the listener to roam. All we need as songwriters is a sense that we might be able to capture something that is real to us, and to feel confident in our ability to refract that fleeting impetus as an expression in music and words. Essentially, in seeking to establish a compositional identity, we transpose feeling and not invention into composition.

Echoing Hennessey's (2003: 253) observation that intrinsic motivation, or engagement with tasks for enjoyment rather than to achieve an external goal, is key to artistic development, songwriter Dolly Parton (in DeMain, 2004: 38) advises that adherence to formulaic types of practice is likely to prevent the songwriter from being a 'true' songwriter, that the individual should instead follow his or her own instincts and feel no pressure to conform to expectation. Further, David Byrne (in Zollo, 2003: 496) asserts that a songwriter gains knowledge of what he or she is doing by following his or her own instincts. Acknowledging the importance of emotion and self-identity in the creative process, Powell-Jones (1972: 14) argues that creative potential can best be realized through a clearer understanding of the self, or a 'crystallisation of self-image'. The songwriter needs to know what he or she stands for, what they believe in and what makes them tick. If we don't understand who we are, how can we expect others to understand us? Such a definitive crystallization of self-image does not remain static, as Nick Lowe truthfully sang in 2006: 'People change, they always have, they always will.' As a consequence, from time to time our notion of self needs to be re-evaluated. What are the sights and sounds that appeal to us today? What moves us right now?

Logically, and in accordance with the way we acquire most skills, it is tempting to learn the craft of songwriting according to the rules; to build a perfectly liveable house of song, with double-glazed windows, a sturdy roof that keeps the rain out, running hot and cold water and a neatly tended lawn. Technically, it is an achievement to be able to build such a house; the process requires a significant amount of understanding, concentration and application, not to mention knowing when to stop. But how many of us want to read a book with a familiar plot? When was the last time we rushed out to see a movie that had reviewers gushing over its conformist quality?

For reasons steeped in historical and psychological enculturation and tradition, the song listener would rather travel somewhere new. As progressive consumers of sound, when we turn on the radio or access a playlist, we are, for the most part, hoping to meet a songwriter we haven't met before. Problematically, there isn't enough time to meet every one, and not every one is somebody we would want to meet. With the need to project accessible and compelling work in mind, once the songwriter has had his or her unedited compositional say, the next phase tends to involve shaping those outbursts into a structural form that preserves the individuality of expression, but increasingly acknowledges our shared cultural and critical understanding of what we hope song *might be*. The initial expression may come easily; the rewriting is often the lion's share of the task.

Gruber (1980) asserts that the quality of artistic work is dependent upon generative ideas that, after a series of false starts and incorrect pathways, gradually evolve over a significant period. This theory seems to imply that in songwriting, progress may be linked to attrition. There are always exceptions to the rule though; David Byrne, Tina Weymouth and Chris Frantz's first-ever song 'Psycho killer' was an enduring critical and commercial success for Talking Heads (Jackson, 2002). Although on rare occasions the expression might not need to be edited, it would be presumptuous to imagine that musical ideas direct from the soul will necessarily need alteration. Mostly though, the editorial phase requires the development of the skill of being able to sift good ideas – those that audiences will most likely want to hear – from bad ideas that would be less likely to be of interest. In this way, we shift from being the creator to being the sensor.

Arieti (1976) observes that creativity requires a tertiary phase in which these two processes, generating and shaping, combine to yield effective novelty – an idea echoed by Ruggiero (1988), who claims that critical thinking and creative thinking are mutually beneficial in the sense that both are needed for solving problems. Critical thinking, Ruggiero argues, saves creative thinking from the pursuit of novelty for its own sake while creative thinking saves critical thinking from being merely reactive; as a consequence an holistic model which incorporates a balance of principles and strategies from both types of thought is said to be conducive to successful art.

Hallam (2001: 69–70) offers an alternate theory that understanding is developed through absorption rather than conscious awareness, and that it primarily involves the inter-nalization of musical structures and characteristic sounds. Generative processes are developed simultaneously, claims Hallam, by creating music through performance, improvi-sation or composition. With practice, argues Hallam, musicians develop an automaticity of skills that at some stage enable technical aspects of musical cognition to be attended to without conscious consideration. Once acquired, these automatic skills 'free up' the songwriter to concentrate on communicating the music to the audience. In this way, argues Hallam we *fall* into songwriting.

Time flies when the uncritical mind is in flow, and an hour can seem like a minute. For many, the initial writing of the music and lyric text is a blurred, almost imperceptible phase of the work. Finding the textures, shaping the structure and devel-oping a sense of lyric continuity, sculpting the song until it has a compelling feel, is often the most intensive and rewarding phase of the process. Again, as Sondheim (2010) says, content dictates form, and to do ourselves justice as songwriters, we need to think laterally about the possibilities open to us. Does the introduction captivate? If not, how can we make it so? Are any words or phrases linguistically disconnected or too challenging to interpret? What alternatives are there? Do the music and words coexist as threads? How can they be made to work together? Do the sounds made by the instruments accentuate the voice? What are the options?

All of this presumes that the initial impetus for the song is a good one, that it has the potential to acquire traction. Is a good idea one that reflects or conveys the feelings of the songwriter we might ask, or is it one that has the potential to resonate with an audience? It could be argued that all song ideas are authentic; after all they come from the imagination of the individual or individuals who wrote them. When Adele sings about her own life in 'Someone like you' (2010), although the song was co-written with Dan Wilson, it is widely perceived to be a genuine form of expression – the transmission of genuine feeling. By comparison, when The Crystals sing the immortal words 'Da do ron ron', we may be inclined to hear this as a relatively contrived expression. Alternatively, if by listening to 'Da do ron ron' we are fondly reminded of a particular time and place, or a certain feeling, in a communicative sense it could be argued that both tracks offer a moment of affective recognition. In both instances, the instinct of the songwriter, the inclination to trust the creative impetus was right.

While we sometimes think we know what makes a songwriter tick, in truth we can only ever guess at what it is they have in mind when writing a song. The only true critical judgement we can make involves how authentic the song seems to us as individual listeners, how involved we are in the sounds being made. In updating the text from draft to artefact, songwriters include us by creating things we recognize as song-like by singing in tune, applying contour and structure, using familiar instrumentation and then taking deliberate steps to subvert these conventions in a way that takes us on a journey of recognition *and* exploration. When it is working well, this journey, infinitesimal in scope yet somehow tangible in form, involves both the experiences of the listener and those of the songwriter.

Songwriting might then be said to consist of two phases: the generation of a link between the song and the songwriter and the generation of a seperate link between the song and the listener. Considering it an act of solipsism, Dewey (1958) describes self-expression as the simple disclosure of character to others, a purely cathartic activity lacking in communicative dimension; when only the initial link exists, there is a risk that the song will lack communicative emphasis and come across as an overly introspective note to self. A composition that exclusively forges a bond between the song and its author can have value however, as an authentic reflection of our thoughts and feelings at a given time. It is often important in a cathartic sense, for these personal and individual feelings and thoughts to be captured. To be authentic, therefore, we must first enter the realm of self-reference or anti-creative solipsism. The implication from a songwriting perspective is that, for a period of time during the creative process we should ignore the outside world, set aside what we imagine to be the tastes and preferences of the listening audience and focus solely on the indiscriminate generation of ideas.

Should we choose, alternatively, to overlook the solipsistic generation of a link between the song and the songwriter, we risk trading that inherent authenticity for commercial guesswork. Without the stamp of individuality that can only come from our personality, we enter the field of generic gesture, where whatever we sing might sound like something already said. If the audience responds unfavourably to our inauthentic work, we are left with music neither the audience nor us can relate to. If, on the other hand, even a small number respond favourably to our authentic work, at least we have a record of our own condition, and a community that relate to it; a shared journal that tells us something of value about our lives and of those around us.

Having been authentically generative, how do we refine that material for the audience? In seeking to generate a link between the song and the listener, knowledge of the history of communicative, i.e. known songs, acquires increasing importance; an interpretative understanding of how communicative songs are constructed and how, within the context of our original practice, they can be made to work. Analytical skills involving attentive listening become a key part of the songwriter's methodology.

In this way, songwriting encompasses a communicative framework wherein the artist uses metaphor in tandem with more immediately recognizable signifiers. To transmit messages that balance the predictable and the unpredictable in ways that evoke recognition and intrigue in those who encounter them, in song those signifiers need to be evident. As Beall (2009: 1) argues:

> Any work of art requires a proper balance between the comfort of the predictable and the surprise of the unexpected ... If there is too much that is unpredictable, the audience will find only chaos, if the audience gets what they expect, they will be bored ... The challenge lies in striking the balance.

Anything too predictable will be considered passé, anything too left field could defy classification and be rendered remote, almost anti-creative.

3.2 Methodology

On finding a creative process we identify as one we can trust to project our expressive ideas as we would wish them to be heard, Braheny (2006: 20) advises:

> Every writer eventually finds her own process (or more than one) for creating. So it's a good idea to explore many. Your own unique personality will determine an approach that is comfortable and productive for you.

It is worth noting that Braheny stresses methods in the plural; while many songwriters rely upon one process to enable ideas to emerge and take shape, there is no prescriptive reason to be confined. Although it seems reasonable that songwriters may be disinclined to discuss their working methods, perhaps for fear of dissipating the magic or compromising their creative myth, it seems hard to imagine that a songwriter has no inkling of the process that works for them. By writing songs and linking the processes to the outcomes, the songwriter will be able to create a roadmap specific to the development of his or her own creativity. To be oblivious to method, infers Webb (1998), is to leave the process open to chance.

To progress as a songwriter, the individual is said to need an understanding of lyric, melody, harmony, rhythm, arrangement and performance (Bradford, 2005: 38), a list which overlooks Moore's (2004) earlier inclusion of production skills. While the constituent elements identified seem comprehensive in scope, the form of this 'understanding' is subject to debate. While Webb (1998) argues that to have the necessary control over the musical elements of the composition, the songwriter should be able to read music, Baroni (1999) observes that, in music composition the ability to solve problems requires the composer to have informal rather than notational knowledge of the musical generative grammar. Through a process of enculturation, Green (2002: 66, 76, 96) writes, musicians who have never been taught formally or encouraged to employ a conscious or systematic approach to playing are able to reproduce music and improvise with high levels of technical proficiency. In her study of popular musicians, Green (ibid.) observed that they often taught themselves to play music they identified with, the music within which they were encultured. They appeared to acquire skills both consciously and unconsciously, often listening attentively and sometimes distractedly, leading to a tendency to imitate and improvise. Notation books were occasionally used, but the written word was always secondary to sound and they often learned from each other by exchanging musical ideas and views.

Translating these findings to incorporate a global perspective, Schippers (2009: 68) refers to this as 'tacit' knowledge, or knowledge that implicitly informs the act of making music. As a consequence, while musicians of all kinds are often unable to name technical musical procedures, they invariably have 'tacit' knowledge of them. Offering an example of tacit learning in action, in Schippers' discussion of how drummers learn to play djembe within the West African percussion tradition of Mandinka, the author observes how the players have no formal description of what is right or wrong, yet have a clear idea of what is acceptable or not within the tradition (ibid.).

Considered by Webster (1996) to be largely innate, 'musical aptitude' refers to convergent thinking skills related to the recognition of the rhythmic and tonal patterns that make up the musical whole. Also innate, according to Webster, is our ability to recognize dynamic flexibility in music, and to identify originality or unusualness of expression. The songwriter, in Webster's view, actively acquires 'the knowledge of facts' related to musical composition, before applying 'craftsmanship', or the ability to apply those facts to the creation of original musical composition. Finally, argues Webster, the songwriter acquires 'aesthetic sensitivity', or the ability to shape sound structures to capture personal feeling in the form of idiolect.

Cook (1998) considers notation to be primarily useful in the conservation of music, an opinion to which Shippers (2009: 221) adds that a reliance upon symbols often seems to invite atrophy of the musical memory. Arguing that musicians should think in sound, imagine sound, construct possible sounds 'in the head' and improvise music before learning symbols, Odam (1995) claims that over-reliance on a notation system can hinder the development of aural skills. Suggesting a methodological approach, Durrant and Welch (1995: 19, 22) assert that music is primarily aural rather than written and that the exploration of sound need not refer to the written symbol, or notation; a musical composition is created, they argue, when the composer selects sounds and places them in a sequence in relation to other sounds. In support of this theory, they contend that it is not necessary for those who write moving poetry to be moved by a poem *and* to know what it is about the poem that was moving. Similarly, they argue, it is not necessary to be a composer to know what makes a good piece of music. Such knowledge, they argue, is often instinctive or tacit.

While songwriters are likely to be better at writing songs than those unpractised in the art, they do not necessarily have greater powers of critical judgement when it comes to evaluating song quality. Over time, analysis may enable a songwriter to become more discerning as a creator of music, but those who have never played a musical instrument yet have experienced a similar process of enculturation, will be equally able to tell a good song from a bad one. Perhaps this ubiquitous familiarity with sound environments helps to explain why experts with little or no songwriting experience are able to make consistently accurate judgements on how popular music is likely to be received.

Many songwriters, including Irving Berlin and Paul McCartney, had no knowledge of notation at the time of writing widely acclaimed compositions (MacDonald, 1994: 9). The famous Bing Crosby and Beatles recordings of 'White Christmas' and 'Yesterday' with which we are most familiar were, however, interpreted by musicians using notated scores prepared by skilled arrangers. While the writing of the text required no formal music reading skills, the recordings did. As musical interpretations often rely upon orchestration to achieve expressive effect, to be self-sufficient, perhaps it could be argued that some songwriters need notational knowledge and some don't.

Characterizing the songwriter as one who is able to suspend individuality of expression to a degree needed to meet the specific demands of established genre-types, Webb (1998: 3) asserts that a good songwriter should be adaptable to the degree that he or she should be able to write a song in any genre for any purpose. At the same time, stresses Frith (1988: 174), it is hard to overestimate the importance of originality in songwriting. Perhaps the two perspectives are not irreconcilable; the approach forwarded by Webb does not exclude the songwriter from bringing an element of original personality into a range of compositional fields.

While it happens frequently, songwriters do not necessarily form musical skills in tandem with lyric writing skills. For example, Michelle Escoffery (in Bradford, 2005: 60) began as a poet, later adding music to her words. While the presence of a poetic quality in a lyric is important to songwriter Andy Partridge (Harris, 2005), others are less concerned with the appearance of words on the page and more focused upon how musical they sound when sung (Woolf in Bradford, 2005: 202; Sondheim, 2010). American songwriters Leonard Cohen and Jewel (in Zollo, 2003: 335; DeMain, 2004: 202) characterize the process of songwriting as mysterious, claiming to have little idea of where song ideas come from or what is happening while a song is being written. Alternatively, songwriting partners Bacharach and David (in DeMain, 2004: 1–17), who traditionally divide the responsibility for music and lyric writing, reflect at length upon their respective songwriting processes, characterizing the activity as repetitive, predictable and sequential.

As previously mentioned Webb (1998) considers the development and conscious awareness of a methodology, including a critical awareness of the sequence of compositional activities and the surrounding environmental effects, to be closely linked to the ability to control craft. In support of this idea, fellow songwriters Graham Nash and Lindsay Buckingham (in Zollo, 2003: 365, 467) descriptively link specific processes to successful outcomes. Within the realm of methodology, there is plenty of room for argument. Davis (1988: 7) advises the reader to make a series of key decisions prior to disembarking on the writing process:

> Choose the gender, select the viewpoint, decide the voice, decide the timeframe, set the scene, identify the tone, pick the diction, determine the song form, become a character, know your audience.

Conversely, songwriters Kim Richey (2009) and Lindsay Buckingham (cited in Zollo, 2003: 467) have found that they write most effectively when they begin the songwriting process by playing an instrument and later exploring, through verbal audition, lyric themes suggested by the initial instrumental phrases. Similarly, as Jeremy Lascelles (2014) notes: 'U2 would record a 90 minute jam, record it and pick a couple of minutes from it. It's whatever works for the artist.' On the genesis of songs, Bradford (2005: 53) says:

> Inspiration is something that can rarely be forced or controlled … The best songs or ideas are often not the result of routine of structure but the happy coincidence of accidents.

While this undoubtedly true for some, Lennon and McCartney, like Holland, Dozier and Holland (cited in Zollo, 2003: 150), wrote many of their most successful songs while working to a structured routine (MacDonald, 1994: 196). Codes of practice vary and are specific to each individual. Just as there is no right or wrong song to write, there is no right or wrong way to write a song; the key for the songwriter is to find a method that works for them.

With the honourable exception of Adele (2015), few songwriters begin the writing process at the beginning, with the opening words and chords of the song. The majority will begin with an idea – perhaps a title or chorus that sounds good, and seems to evoke the possibility for further detailed exploration. Like most authors and film makers with some honourable exceptions, most songwriters will not begin work until they have an idea of what they intend to say. Giving impetus to the imagination and allowing the songwriter to feel and visualize the emotional core around which a framework of ideas can be built, themes have the capacity to focus the mind.

The satellites that orbit the far reaches of the framework are often what gives the song its narrative fingerprint; the original images that invite the songwriter to revisit familiar territory with fresh intent. Some of these verbal satellites may orbit close to the title, giving the expression at the core of the lyric text an added intensity; the singer can't help but explore the inner reaches of the theme. At other times, evoking a playful sense of distraction and inviting the listener to sense authenticity in the form of individual personality, the words may seem relatively removed from what we understand the central meaning to be. If the composition is not relatable as sound or meaning, the risk is to bewilder the listener. By beginning with a title, the songwriter effectively controls the expression, auditioning further aspects of meaning and metaphor that might live alongside the title and expand the initial idea; for the songwriter this is often a fascinating process that brings hitherto unforeseen perspectives into being and invites previously uncharted areas of the imagination to the forefront.

Gestalt Theory (Duncker, 1945) contends that there are no discrete stages involved in the creative process, merely a gathering and restructuring of sub-elements that have not been connected before until a moment of insight, when the constituent parts become organized, or fit together. On the subject of timescale, both Duncker and Gruber's theories imply that, to allow the artistic creative process to operate optimally, sufficient time should be allowed for ideas to form.

In his seminal text *Creativity: Flow and the Psychology of Discovery and Invention*, Csikszentmihalyi (1996) argues that the traditional perspective on the creative process as described by Wallas (1926) and others as a series of stages (preparation, incubation, insight, evaluation and elaboration) should not be taken literally; that the prescribed phases are often interspersed with periods that elude the strict character of the phase in question. He agrees that immersion in a domain or field of interest is a necessary initial form of engagement, followed by a phase of 'incubation' in which conscious and unconscious connections are made. How long this period requires, Csikszentmihalyi states, is dictated by the nature of the problem and by facilitative routines imposed by the individual. Insights, however, are often numerous and punctuated by immersion, evaluation and elaboration. During a fourth phase of evaluation, the creative individual references the 'internalised criteria of the domain, and the internalised opinion of the field' (Csikszentmihalyi, 1996: 80). Finally, a potentially lengthy process of elaboration occurs in which the idea is translated for presentation to the outside world. Returning to his initial argument Csikszentmihalyi suggests that the process of elaboration is also interrupted by periods of incubation and insight in the form of finishing touches.

Creative people, Csikszentmihalyi argues (ibid.: 52), possess a genetic disposition for a given domain. This genetic advantage is then augmented by an early interest in the domain, a condition that requires access to the domain in question. For creativity to flourish, it follows that the involvement of those who raise the individual is critically important during these early developmental phases. Finally, in order to communicate productively with peers whose opinions and attentions matter within the community at large, a person must have access to a comparative field. The creative process is said to become enjoyable when the individual has clear goals every step of the way and there is a certainty of purpose. In what Csikszentmihalyi calls a 'flow experience' (ibid.: 111), the creative thinker knows how well he or she is doing and senses possession of the skills needed to meet the challenge. As a condition of being creative, he argues, the individual needs to able to focus and concentrate and to suspend any fear of failure.

Csikszentmihalyi claims that those who have been acknowledged to be highly creative are remarkable for their apparently paradoxical character traits. They are often alternately energetic and restful, smart yet naive, playful yet disciplined, imaginative yet realistic, extroverted yet introspective, competitive yet cooperative, passionate yet objective. To remain creative, Csikszentmihalyi argues, the individual needs to take charge of his or her schedule by working at the most efficient times in the most productive environments. Time should be made for reflection and relaxation, because 'once you know what your daily life is like and how you experience it, it is easier to begin getting control over it' (ibid.: 358). The individual should make a record of the feelings they have about what they are doing, it is argued, and then internalize this self-knowledge by acting upon it.

Once a song has been written in its draft form, states Webb (1998), the songwriter should reflect upon what has been written with a view to making further edits and amendments. Often this process is overlooked and the songwriter is left with what he or she believes to be a bad song. Lateral thinking is useful here as a means of exploring the possibilities for how the song, or certain elements of it, might form the basis of a successful reconstruction. And why rewrite once? Why not twice?

Chomsky (1971: 7) argues that a 'distinction must be made between what the speaker of a language knows implicitly (what we may call his competence) and what he does (his performance)'. Concurring that understanding and producing language are separate skills, Swain (1985) argues that skills in language production can only be developed through talking and writing. In practical terms, her theory of 'comprehensible output' requires the learner to formulate hypotheses about the rules of the language, test them out by producing his or her own language and then revise or refine as necessary once feedback has been received.

Similarly, Long's (1983) 'Interaction Hypothesis' claims that language acquisition occurs when creative individuals share ideas with others, a process referred to as 'negotiation of meaning' – an activity designed to enable the learner to make his or her output more comprehensible. Ellis (1997: 141) defines this as 'the interactive work that takes place between speakers when some misunderstanding occurs'. During the process, we are said to be developing an inter-language by making sense of the language and imposing a structure upon it (Hedge, 2000: 11). Any songwriting method should, it is implied, involve both doing and hypothesizing. While some songwriters consciously edit songs to try and make them as universally open for contemplation as possible (Maher in DeMain, 2004: 15; Hatch and Millward, 1987: 141), others believe it is impossible to second-guess what an audience will want to hear (Dido in Bradford, 2005: 209).

Jackson and Sinclair (2006: 114) assert that intuition and critical thinking often occur in balance and that it is not necessarily a case of either/or. For songwriters who write better songs by uncritically committing ideas to paper and applying a critical-editorial process when the song has been written in draft form, committing critical information to memory for use during the creative process may be problematic, introducing what Amabile (cited in Braheny, 2006: 17) calls an inhibiting sense of 'surveillance'. The emotions of the songwriter are conveyed through creative activity, sometimes in a cathartic sense. It would seem to follow that in actuality songwriters might not be exclusively seeking to communicate, but also to express emotion.

In terms of creative origination, AABA songs will often begin with refrains or title lines. George and Ira Gershwin's 'They can't take that away from me', for instance, will have started life as a sung refrain. Two things need to follow for the song to emerge: a melodic and chordal verse framework for the music leading up to the refrain, and a list of things that can't be taken away from the singer. When the list of things that can't be taken away is sung, it will need to sound good *and* fit the melodic metre of the verse. Perhaps the music was written prior to the list. If so, the addition and insertion of words will have resembled a crossword puzzle with the Gershwins obliged to fill in the blank spaces. Alternatively, if the title had immediately suggested a stream of connected words, the impetus may have been for the composers to sketch the remaining words first, adding music later.

Almost certainly a great many lyric false starts will have taken place, with only the finest, most consistent or authentic lines making the final cut. Once three verses had been written, each of which in this song deal with memories recalled by the singer in the past and present tenses, the Gershwins would have needed to have added a further compositional element, a bridge, to provide relief from the musical repetition of the A sections. Here the music changes character from the relaxed major chordal flow of the verse to a more solemn, even foreboding minor key setting. In doing so the song acquires its gravitas. No longer a simple and light meditation, the song acquires a hitherto unforeseen dramatic dimension.

To add further dimension, in the bridge the composers alter the past tense narrative to encompass the future tense. Equally critically the metre of the vocal is altered, and notes are held for longer than in the verses. This provides not only variation, but also a subtle dramatic rise to indicate the depth of the singer's feeling towards the subject.

Having written a first draft of a song with verses and choruses, the song may seem incomplete, perhaps more plain than it should be. To allow the song to breathe, often what is required is an instrumental riff. In songs like 'I heard it through the grapevine', instrumental motifs are often written last and auditioned as new musical sections to follow the chorus, to allow the listener time to reflect on what has been heard. Once this post-chorus instrumental melody has been formed it may then double as an intro-duction or a coda.

AB songs that sound too sweet and somehow fail to convey intent may benefit from the addition of a pre-chorus to break the melodic flow and ramp up anticipation levels. Exemplified earlier in the sub-chapter on structure, pre-choruses are typically simple or repetitive, testing the patience of the listener before dissolving as they reach the chorus. In a creative sense, these tension-inducing sections are counter-intuitive anomalies in that they require the songwriter not to engage, but to frustrate the listener.

The wisdom of setting out to achieve this delicate balance during the initial writing phase when the word sounds lexicon and meaning are of primary importance is negligible. If, halfway through the compositional process, you happen to have written a past tense and a future tense verse, and still need a third verse, why not try to sketch something in the present tense? There's a good chance it will add to the communicative nature of the song. Of course, not all songs use all three tenses from a narrative perspective, and the song may be completed using a different strategy. The mindset needs to be open, and the methodology of the songwriter flexible enough to allow for a range of eventualities. In the mediation of structure it is often important to think laterally and to audition and critically review variations.

In the late nineties, as a staff writer at Warner Chappell Nashville, I developed a songwriting methodology that allowed me to identify relatively quickly the potential of an idea, preserve and expand the essence of the idea during the writing process and to convey the idea, to the best of my ability, in communicative terms. This methodological framework remained constant for the majority of my years as a songwriter, but changed as I got older, as I shall try to explain.

Essentially, I used to shape the lyric and music to reflect the sights, sounds, characters and emotional tones I felt and visualized. The central idea would typically revolve around a phrase, until the finished composition was recognizable to me as a dimensional embodiment of the initial concept, or spark. As the originator of the idea, the songs invariably had, and still have meaning to me, a factor that ensures a greater sense of ownership and hopefully for the listener a more tangible authenticity.

Each song began with a written title. Once the title had been written at the top of the page, to constantly remind me of what it was, words and phrases that related to the title were then sketched in an area at the foot of the page reserved for provisional ideas. At that stage of the process, it was possible to gauge whether there would be enough connected material to sustain a song and make the lyric vivid to me;

my initial line of critical questioning, before launching into the full scale compositional process of realizing the song would therefore involve asking if the images were recognizable. Did the words and phrases possess an identifiable language that could lead to the development of a distinctive, or compelling overall plot or set of characters? Occasionally, a title that initially seemed to have the potential to lead the lyric towards a number of interesting scenarios did the opposite, and at this point in the process it would be wiser to temporarily or permanently abandon the idea. The more songs I wrote – the better I got at evaluating the potential of title ideas.

In the initial compositional phase, to generate provisional ideas I would effectively look 'behind' the title, asking questions about its potential storyline. For example, the title 'Only the heart can see' would prompt questions such as: What is it that the heart can see that the eyes can't? Why can only the heart see it? Who is making this statement? Who are they making it to? Where is it being made? Is it really a statement or is it an inner thought? The answers to these and other questions may suggest character types, vivid phrases, narrative shapes and maybe elicit an idiolect, real or fictional. In turn, these characteristics may suggest a type of music. At the back of my mind I would know that while these characteristics were themselves not musical, they would require a musical subtext that did not detract from their ability to convey their expression; that swam downstream rather than upstream. Specifically, from my perspective, the music should not detract from the lyric text by creating a distraction for the listener in the form of a contradictory or bland subtext.

Having created a musical template, the next task was to set the title within a melody that corresponded to the relevant part of that template. Often, if not always, the aim was to make the title 'sing' memorably, as this would avoid the relatively exacting and unpredictable task of struggling to 'crowbar' the title into the song at a later stage. I would then write a number of new sections of music around the section that harboured the title, keeping the ones felt to be closest to the initial feel. This decision making process was more instinctive than analytical in the sense that no thought was given to how the piece would be received, rather the focus was on how the music related to the initial idea. For me, the constructive process of writing new pieces of music that contrast with each other seemed to be based upon a reaction to the pieces of music that already exist. Writing with guitar and voice simultaneously, the aim would be to write new sections that both characteristically reflect and provide musical variation upon the established mood.

The following writing phase required a provisional estimate to be made, based on the content so far gathered, of the likely eventual musical structure of the song. Usually quite quickly, a decision was made using what might be called embedded taste: the evocation of a critical preference generated through prior listening and songwriting. At this point for one brief moment the potential involvement of the listener enters the conscious awareness, while a quick check is made to ensure that the idea is not too similar to another one.

With the title, melody and harmony elements in place, a large number of compositional 'spaces' that still need to be filled by lyric and arrangement ideas were created. Referring back to the initial brainstormed provisional lyric sketches, I would experiment with a view to discovering which words and phrases might be effective as lyrics within the musical framework. Perhaps unsurprisingly, these initial word sketches often needed to be rephrased to sit comfortably and coherently as lyrics within the established musical setting. As a part of my methodology, to enable the best chance of capturing elements of the composition directly related to the initial idea, the finalized lyrics were added during the session in which the music was written.

During the process of attaching lyric to music, I was less mindful of the way the structural, melodic and lyric elements interacted, instead I was more engaged with the notion of capturing the spirit of the initial impetus. The final process of editing required a step back to be taken, to look at the song from an 'outside' perspective. If I were approaching the song as a listener, would the music and lyric content be sufficiently engaging? Overall, to consider the wishes of the audience during the writing process was considered to be a negative activity likely to obstruct the process of capturing the initial emphasis. As argued earlier in the book, at first, a link between the song and the songwriter needed to be developed, and later a link between the song and the listener.

Finally, the song was recorded with guitar and voice, and listening back I could imaginatively audition ways in which the song might be instrumentally expanded. Philosophically, the aim was to try to ensure that the attention of the listener would be focused on either the music, the melody or the lyric at any one time. The element at the forefront may alternate during specific parts of the song, but, mindful of the risk of demanding too much of the listener, in the editing process a conscious effort was made not to present 'competing' elements. Typically, if a lyric was particularly involved or told a story over a number of chapters, in anticipation that the listener, once familiar with the melodic section, would find it easier to focus upon the development of the lyric, I would seek to construct a relatively repetitive melodic structure. Alternatively, more implicitly inviting the listener instead towards the instrumental or musical dimension, an adventurous melody or structure might be accompanied by a less demanding lyric.

The production and performance of the song sought to add further emphasis to the expressive quality of the melody and lyric. As such, they constituted a 'prism' through which I intended the song to be heard. Occasionally, songs would need 'breathing space' to allow the listener respite from the 'demand' of having to follow the lyric; this type of editorial consideration was made entirely with the listener in mind. How should the song be sung? Should the instrumentation enhance the song in a way that might be anticipated by the listener, or, if a more duplicitous mode is needed, what kind of unorthodox strategy should be adopted? Essentially, the aim is for the listener to be compelled by at least one element of the song upon first listen; then, so the theory went, maybe the song would be worth revisiting.

Fifteen years later, my method is very different. I would add that there was no transition or gradient involved – merely that from my perspective, one method enabled me to authentically convey my ideas, and then another approach allowed me to do the same. This account seeks to illustrate how the means of expression can change over time; that any assumption concerning the infallibility of an established method may be worth revision.

Each of my recent original songs has originated in short bursts, typically with sung melodies using word sounds and chord sequences composed in tandem at the piano. Clearly the cue is metaphorical. Rather than seek a literal meaning to expand upon, I am searching for music to suggest what might be said by the voice. This opens up the field of possibility for a lyric theme, and consequently the lyric could be about almost anything.

Perhaps this approach indicates how, at this point in time, I want to capture and convey how I *feel* about things more than what I *think* about them. If I like the short musical sketch at first review, confident that it has my being at its source, I resolve to use it as the foundation to develop a song. Having made an initial instinctive judgement on whether the sketch is a verse, chorus or other section, I then build the remaining musical sections, again in chord, melody and word sound form, around it. At this point, I search for a title – some words that sound good to me when sung into the existing compositional framework. Once I have a title, for instance 'The whisperers' or 'The way the morning breaks', I leave the song to settle, returning to it over the following days to evaluate and re-evaluate its potential qualities as a vehicle for a lyric.

Contrary to my original method, which involves writing one song at a time, this method allows me to generate multiple miniature musical sketches in one sitting. Using the sketches, a metaphorical thread is created in response to my mood at the time. Subsequently, I will record each foundational musical framework and hang them, in a manner of speaking, up on the wall, and add phrases one by one. Significantly, the words must continue to appeal as word sounds for the lyric to be sung with a freedom reflective of the instinctive method used in the original generation of the music. Once the words or phrases are written, for evidence that some instinctive thread has been at work in the construction, I will run an editorial check for meaning.

While the literal communicative focus and intent of my earlier songwriting method required me to make very few, if any, changes, this new approach often requires rewriting, particularly if the tangent between title and surrounding lyric is too obtuse. The method also requires fine-tuning to ensure word sounds sing as fluently as I am able to make them. It takes longer to finish songs, perhaps a period of weeks rather than a few hours, but the new process is more consciously involved, more playful and less clinical than the early one. Importantly, I enjoy it more. As the songwriter Iain Archer says: 'With the amount of writing I do, I find myself working intuitively and cerebrally, which a lot of people I work with find a bit confusing at times.' With this I can empathize entirely.

Offering an alternative songwriting method, collaborating with other songwriters can broaden an individual's understanding of how songs might potentially be constructed (Tennant in Bradford, 2005: 234). The relatively increased rate at which ideas are usually generated means that, in collaborative paradigms, productivity rates tend to increase (Seskin in Tucker, 2003: 153). Further, the activity typically provides an immediate source of feedback for the songwriter to critically review and reflect upon, gradually enabling the songwriter to develop critical thinking skills (Blume, 2003: 15).

Bacharach and David, Morrissey and Marr, Goffin and King, Lennon and McCartney: some of the finest pop songs in history have been written by duos. But why do songwriters collaborate when so few authors write books together, and why – give or take the odd Gilbert and George – do so few visual artists choose to share the creative burden? Sometimes it is because songwriting tends to require two discrete skills, one involving the relatively literal world of lyric and one concerning the predominantly metaphorical universe of music. A Burt Bacharach or a Johnny Marr might use their talents to create a metaphorical landscape without necessarily imagining how a lyricist will forge their music into a more definitively communicative gesture.

At the 2012 Leeds International Songwriting Festival I discussed a process used by Iain Archer as a means of collaborating with eight undergraduate songwriters at Leeds College of Music. The eight songs premiered at the festival each possessed a thread of uniqueness while also equally representing the diverse characters of Iain's collaborators. In an interview conducted as part of the conference presentation, one of the students who collaborated with Iain described the process as follows:

> He spent quite a lot of time working on concept and sort of creating the world the song would be about, which is something I had touched upon before but I'd always written chords and harmony and everything together and kind of let them figure each other out rather than coming up with the concept completely separately.

In addition to having songs recorded by Snow Patrol, Example and Leona Lewis, Iain has co-written a string of hit singles with Jake Bugg. On the initiation of his collaborative relationship with Jake, Iain recalls: 'My publishers, Kobalt were aware of Jake; he'd just signed his deal with Mercury and he had already written plenty of great songs. Kobalt had an intuitive idea we would connect, and I got put with

Jake for an afternoon.' Fortunately, as Iain remembers, 'On every level it worked'. Such intuitive plans can go wrong, but on this occasion the creative chemistry was well judged. 'A lot of the time it can feel unnatural for the artist' Iain admits, 'but the whole idea is that the relationship becomes something a lot more than something put together by some money-oriented human beings'. When writing with talented performers relatively new to the craft of songwriting, Iain says:

> I try and get a sense of who somebody is and then try and magnify it through the song. If you can tell people who you are in the song, you don't need a billboard to tell the world who you are.

While Kobalt are constantly looking for new artists to work with him, there are certain qualities Iain looks for in a collaborator. 'What sets new songwriting apart is a sense of boldness', he says. 'It has to be innovative or convincing. If they are communicating really well with their voice, you get a sense that they are going to communicate really well in general. If there is an inherent message, something being articulated, that's a place to start. That presence of a driving force in the voice is instantly recognizable. Some artists have no social confidence but plenty of artistic confidence.' Iain adds: 'And it's wonderful that they have that root, it underpins what they do.'

While his track record dictates that he is almost always the senior partner in the room, Iain acknowledges that co-writing is a two-way street, and that his strengths as a collaborator should be visible to his opposite number: 'The person who reflects back has to be someone you respect, someone who has earned your respect on some level. And it takes time to earn somebody's trust', he says. Experience has a further benefit: 'Once you have taken all the wrong turns, like I have earlier in my career, that helps you spot the wrong turns others might be about to take.'

Sean Devine, vice president of the London wing of ASCAP (American Society of Performers, Composers and Authors), describes the arc of collaborative evolution: 'In the time of Tin Pan Alley they'd all go to the pub together and play each other songs, and that network was really important because writers would think "I've got to write a better chorus than that".' In the present era, says Sean, 'Songwriters know their strengths and weaknesses, and their drive is that they need other cogs in the wheel. There has been a rise in groups or teams of songwriters because people have found they can work better with others. Bacharach and David's roles were very defined, but these days you get writers describing themselves as "an all rounder but mainly a lyric guy".'

Some things remain constant, however, as producer Will Hicks observes:

> The London session community is a small one, and if you are a pain in the arse you would not get any work. You get thrown into a dark cave and you've got to be friendly; musicians are always friendly. If you ever ask them to do something in a different way they are always open to it. It's the same with assistants and engineers. Nobody falls out with anyone over an idea.

In recent times, the role of the songwriter, once confined to the structuring of words, melody and harmony, has expanded to incorporate elements that elevate the properties of the simple text to those of a record. The reasons for this shift are connected to a cultural switch in thinking. Increasingly accustomed to the high quality production and arrangement values awarded by pro tools and logic, producers are inevitably more inclined to be involved in the songwriting process. Consequently, in some fields the lines between songwriting and production are increasingly blurred.

For a variety of reasons, the roles are not always porous. While they are skilled performers, artists do not always have the aptitude or patience to write songs capable of connecting with an audience. Similarly, not all songwriters are able to sing and play at a level required to be an artist. Those who perform all functions – the Princes and Stevie Wonders of the world – are few and far between and, inevitably, songwriting has become an increasingly collaborative culture. To thrive, modern songwriters need not be masters of all trades, but need at least a critical, if not technical, awareness of what their collaborators bring to the table.

Whoever writes words to music is creating a subtext, a layer of meaning that must to some extent contradict, reinforce or exist harmoniously within its musical surroundings. To do this, the lyricist has to be able to mediate, or interpret the potential scope of the music, to know where the words *cannot* go. The degree of precision involved means that such partnerships often work well for those who create on an asynchronous basis, away from one another and in their own time. Morrissey, for instance, would spend days or weeks absorbing the musical fragments given to him by Johnny Marr, a co-writing method that served both very well; almost every song The Smiths recorded remains critically revered.

Creating music and words face to face, songwriters working in Manhattan's Brill Building in the fifties and sixties would collaborate very differently. Requiring both writers to make immediate critical judgements with little time for reflection, in this reflexive mode, ideas are bounced back and forth on the spot. Creatively energized by the immediacy of the experience and perhaps by the speed at which ideas quickly became songs these songwriters were able to construct ideas almost instinctively, without losing sight of the composition as a whole.

Not all collaborators have the luxury of time, and while Csikszentmihalyi argues for levity in allowing creativity to flourish, songwriter Martin Brammer, perhaps best known for his work with James Morrison, Tina Turner and The Lighthouse Family, doesn't mind working to the clock. He explains: 'It's an interesting mind game. Having only one or

two days allows you to make quicker decisions; forces you
to embrace things and make them as good as you can. And
sometimes that's better than having two days.' A balance
needs to be struck, however, as being able to adapt, while
retaining your own preferred method of working or creative
temperament, is key:

> Some people will have lots of ideas and not be inclined to
> make any of them great. I don't like sitting in silence for
> half an hour thinking about the next thing, but if you just
> have the confidence to say 'everybody calm down, we're
> going to think of something in a minute', maybe something
> good will come.

Like Iain Archer, Martin emphasizes the value of building the
collaboration at a social level: 'Getting to know the artist is a
much better way of collaborating than saying "Hey, I've got a
great song for you". You adopt the role of the person you're
writing for, and they'll let you know if you're capturing their
voice or not.' Competition is fierce and individuality of voice
is integral for performing songwriters who want to succeed in
commercial markets. As Martin observes:

> The artists who survive the development process have
> really got to have something, not to get crushed. They'll
> have to come up with 60 songs and that will be soul-
> destroying for anyone who chooses not to go with what
> they're feeling.

Even if the songwriters have written for some of the biggest
acts in the world, Martin says, the artist has to come first.
As he recalls: 'Me and Steve Robson [songwriter of hits for
Christina Aguilera, Carrie Underwood and Paloma Faith]
were writing with John Newman, and threw about fifteen
great ideas at him. John went over to the piano and started
playing something we'd heard a million times and we thought
"Oh no!" But, it was real for *him*, and our ideas weren't

real to him. And to his credit, he is single-minded in what he wants to do. He collaborates well with people who do what *he* wants to do. You put all your experience in to it, but the artist has to be at the centre.'

Fellow collaborator Josephine Oniyama agrees: 'The person whose project it is has to have the final say, and the other person has to respect that.' Just because it is a collaboration doesn't necessarily mean the song will exceed the sum of its parts. Sean Devine notes that songwriters who are too familiar in style often struggle to write together, as they find little new in the creative capacity of their opposite number. Much depends on the attitude or mindset of those involved; if this is not right, the issue of talent is academic. As Josephine says:

> When you find the collaborators that work fantastically, it's better than anything you can do alone. The worst collaborators are the ones who want to get something done at any cost. And then it doesn't belong to anybody.

Adapting a systematic process, Jez Ashurst encourages collaborators to consider and outline their respective roles in advance of disembarking on the co-writing process. Patience, or a willingness to accept that some songs take longer to write than others, is also cited by Jez as a virtue, as is a willingness to have an open mind to unfamiliar themes: 'Adapting an idea you're not keen on can often get the ball rolling', he says. 'Often I've really disliked an idea because it wasn't something "that I do", but I've since realized that this is the point of collaboration and often the blending of these ideas makes the song stand out and have more interest.'

As a collaborator, Ivor Novello award-winner Simon Aldred works with Sam Smith, Lianne La Havas and Qwabs, among others. Simon agrees with Martin and Josephine. 'You've got to be a master of communication really. You've got to remove yourself from it; you've got to help them say what they want to say', he reasons. 'You've got to try and move it in the right direction. Qwabs is introverted and Sam Smith is quite extroverted. They've got to start singing about their feelings, which is a bit like taking their clothes off.' In tandem with his solo songwriting for Cherry Ghost, the collaborative process has many advantages for Simon, as he explains: 'It teaches you to work really quickly; you're obliged to work. I generally swan about thinking about a song for two weeks, but co-writing helps to write songs that don't sound laboured, and it's nice to listen to someone else's singing voice.'

Ideally and perhaps eventually, as Iain Archer observes, a songwriter is able to discern good or bad ideas as they emerge, shaping the material that survives into successful art. It doesn't always happen this way though; some songwriters uncritically generate all of their ideas before stepping back and making any necessary critical decisions. The process is commonly threefold: first a moment of impetus or feeling that a concept worthy of expression and reception might exist; secondly, an uncritical flow of ideas, virtually a stream of consciousness that exemplifies and expands upon the original concept; and finally, an editorial phase in which ideas are sifted and selected for inclusion.

3.3 Criticality

Acknowledging the crucial missing element in the pursuit of learning songwriting by reading books, Braheny (2006: 29) identifies what the ambitious reader-songwriter really needs:

> I'm not saying that every song you write must appeal to a mass audience ... You should write everything and anything your creative impulses trigger. At some point, though, if you want to make a living at songwriting, you've got to develop some perspective on your songs.

Echoing the notion that the more one writes, the more critical one is likely to become, Powell-Jones (1972: 15–17) argues that creative learners need to be taught how to apply considerable thought to problems or tasks by securing all the information available prior to attempting to solve the problem. The original ideas may never improve, the theory implies, but the knowledge acquired in selecting and shaping them will add critical and editorial muscle.

Group critical feedback can inform the learner on aspects of practice that are non-textual. Similarly, as music is metaphorical, the critical feedback of others can inform the songwriter on the directness or ambiguity of meaning within the musical element of the developing songwriter's practice. As music appeals to the emotional world of the listener and individuality of practice is broadly considered desirable, similar advantages apply to the discussion and evaluation of the affective nature of the work.

Self-taught songwriters are independently able to acquire theoretical knowledge; consider expert opinion; analyse existing works; write songs and formulate critical judgements of original and established works. However, those who learn alone lack the significant advantage of being able to reflect upon and critically discuss completed songs and work in progress with others. Given the importance of critical discussion and reflection in learning, it would appear that environments involving these activities have the capacity to accelerate, and add further dimension to the learning process.

How can the songwriter develop? Bloom (1985) and Csikszentmihalyi (1988) stress the importance of 'social support networks' involving mentors and colleagues in enabling the creative individual to sustain a high level of motivation. Clearly, having a group to play and discuss works in progress and finished songs with has the potential to be beneficial. However, the role of each member of the community in providing encouragement may be decisive in terms of whether the creative individual is able to achieve to his or her potential (Foster, 1967: 88; Sarsani, 2005: 5).

Ground rules for such a critical community may need to be established from the outset. Seeking to define accuracy in the use of language, Canale and Swain (1980) identify four dimensions of competence: 'grammatical competence', or lexical and grammatical capacity; 'sociolinguistic competence', or an understanding of the social context in which the communication occurs; 'discourse competence', or an understanding of the broader context of how messages are conveyed and interpreted; and 'strategic competence', with reference to strategies employed by communicators to initiate, terminate and repair language communication. Similarly, Raimes (1985: 229) notes how writers of language initially consider their purpose and audience, a characteristic further emphasized in subsequent studies of writers by Mount (1988: 64) and Hedge (2000: 305). In keeping with the likely expectations of the receiver, structure and content should be shaped according to the genre of the discourse community in question; members of the discourse community should share a set of communicative purposes, and a rationale for the genre recognizable by the community should shape and influence the content and style of the communicative interaction (Swales, 1990: 58). Communication can only be considered meaningful when the recipient interprets the message (Wilkinson, 1975: 5) and to maintain social interaction those involved often need to establish meanings both can accept.

Transposed from the communicative context in which they originally emerged, these theories appear to imply that learners should share a common purpose; that a creative community should agree the parameters or types of creative work it will or will not support. Perhaps, to gauge progress in acquiring discourse competence, a songwriter might pre-empt the performance with an outline of its expressive intention; a contextual summary that allows the listening audience to compare the success of the songwriter in matching expressive intent to meaning.

Developing Csikszentmihalyi's (1996) concept of a 'congenial' environment, Cropley (2001: 6) sees creativity as an interactive pursuit that occurs within an environmental framework shaped by the degree of risk taking that will be tolerated and the rewards that will be offered to those who take risks. Arguing that there is little incentive to produce novelty that is not supported by those in the audience, Cropley sees the environment as a critical factor in the development of the individual as an innovator. Reflecting the creative trait identified by Csikszentmihalyi, risk taking and exploration are encouraged, with acceptance and acknowledgement of errors seen as a sign of learning (Richards and Rogers, 2001: 109–10). In her study of the techniques or devices a learner may use to acquire knowledge, Rubin (1975: 43) found that 'good language learners' are keen to guess, intend to communicate and are willing to do so at the risk of appearing foolish. It is often the quirks or eccentricities of songwriting that elevate it above the mundane, and the guidance of a critical community would be helpful in aiding the songwriter to identify and sift these characteristics.

Through talking, it is argued, learners can engage in cognitive rehearsal, effectively re-shaping ideas previously held in a vague way (Yager, Johnson and Johnson, 1985). Similarly, in the process of learning communicative competence, engagement in dialogue with other group members, communicating one's own individual viewpoint and considering the viewpoints of others can help clarify existing understandings and facilitate the development of new ones (Barnes and Todd, 1994: 11, 21).

To improvise a hierarchy based upon the hegemony of the songwriter as expert may be ill-advised. Jackson and Shaw (2006: 102) state that 'when working with problems that society is interested in, practitioners must communicate with people outside their discipline'. This would imply that listeners as well as musicians should be included in the critical community. Further, there is a need for critical voices to be drawn from across the social spectrum. Francis (1977: 18) asserts that the analytical knowledge offered should be rooted not only in the values and beliefs of a mentor or expert, but also in 'a selection of intelligent and artistic works by representatives of communities which have valued them in some other time or place'. As noted earlier, musicians not only learn from listening to each other but also by watching each other play and discussing musical ideas (Green, 2002: 82). There often seems to be a sense of caution attached to the critical discussion of other songwriters' work, however (West, 2006) and those developing songwriting skills often seem inclined to be more objective when discussing songs written by those they do not interact with on a social basis.

Being able to communicate requires more than linguistic competence (Widdowson, 1978), it requires an understanding of the social context in which the communication occurs (Hymes, 1971; Wilkins, 1976). Markova (1979: 15) defines communication as 'activity directed towards resolving the tasks of social intercourse' and communication is commonly classified as dynamic rather than static, relying upon a negotiation of meaning between two or more individuals who share some common knowledge of the language (Oxford, 1990: 7). Further, the communication of experience requires generalization, or the relation of content to a known group of phenomena or class (Vygotsky, 1956: 51). As we are all born with the facility to create and interpret music and language, there seems no reason to exclude non-songwriters from an effective and representative critical community. While a critique offered by a non-musician *may* be limited in technical language, by being free of knowing the technical processes and parameters of doing, the critic may actually be more capable of hearing and identifying significant flaws than the musician.

Wilkinson (1975) also argues that, in a communicative interaction, the speaker not only gives but also receives his or her own message. Further, Johnson (2001: 92) states that the learner who is attending to his or her own language as it is being produced is more alert and has his or her 'internal monitoring device' at its highest setting. On a related note, discussing the value of communicative paradigms, Swain (1995: 125) hypothesizes that 'output' can enhance accuracy by enabling learners to notice a gap between what they want to express and what they can express. Songwriters who share works in progress with audiences are able, in Swain's view, to make more precise critical links between what they are trying to convey and the forms they use to communicate their ideas. When the learner performs original work to the group he or she experiences a heightened sense of self-criticality often not experienced during the preparation of the performance. In turn, this sharper critical perspective can inform the development of the work by eliciting areas where corrections need to be made.

In a study of creative learners, Oliver et al. (2006: 44–58) concluded that when learners were anxious or depressed they felt less likely to be creative. Dialogic environments that gave learners scope to try out new ideas without fear of negative peer assessment were favoured. A productive critical community perhaps needs to be a supportive one; a mutually supportive space that takes account of the psychological dimension of the practice. Few songwriters benefit from negative criticism of new original work. An asynchronous critiquing environment in which the listening audience can forward their thoughts on an anonymous basis, perhaps through a neutral conduit, might allow for feedback to be absorbed and considered over time.

Littlewood (1981: 4) asserts that the most efficient communicator is not always the best at manipulating its structures, but is often the person most skilled at processing the complete situation, taking into account the knowledge shared among those involved and selecting items appropriately. The constructive criticism, forwarded anonymously by other members of the group, could eventually form the basis of a response from the songwriter in the form of a rewrite. The rewritten song could then be brought back to the community for further review, creating a cycle in which the songwriter uses inductive critique to continually refine song ideas over time.

In the critical community, the songwriter might expect to encounter numerous disparate perspectives. For instance, in his discussion of compositional balance, Beall (2009: 103) says that:

> Too many words detract from the emotion ... melodies that are too busy will pull the listener out of the rhythmic groove. Harmonic progressions full of dense, complex chords will detract from the melody.

Bob Dylan's 'Like a rolling stone' is six minutes long, however, with four relatively lengthy verses and four choruses, but still it was voted the best song of all time by *Rolling Stone* in 2004. Similarly, 'Bohemian rhapsody' by Queen, a melodically, rhythmically and harmonically complex song considered subversive within its genre (Periano, 2005: 232), was voted by the best British Single released between 1952 and 1977 by the British Phonographic Industry in 2002. From the perspective of the songwriter, who will need to weigh the critical evidence carefully, a rational argument could be made that some songs require many words to communicate emotional expression appropriately, whereas others require less, and that on a song-by-song basis, a balance between expression, music content and lyric content is what needs to be struck.

Elsewhere, Rodgers (2003: 65) advises: 'The chorus melody should rise higher than the verse.' Again, the prescription is argumentative; there are no primary hook-related high notes in New Order's 'Blue Monday', which was a top ten international hit upon release and has sold over one million copies in the UK alone. Elsewhere, on the subject of complexity in songwriting, Beall (2009: 102) states that 'Simplicity builds trust in the listener'. While it may build trust in the listener who enjoys relatively simple song recordings, it could be less true for the listener who is drawn to the complex melodic structures of progressive rock, intricate jazz arrangements, or the metaphysical symbolism and wordplay found in the lyrics of Van Morrison (Mills, 2010: 151) or Elvis Costello (Smith, 2004: 156). Again, the fledgling songwriter will need to negotiate and absorb such crossfire. From the perspective of the songwriter, if two or three, or even a majority of the members of the critical group should identify an identical flaw, perhaps the motivation to review the flaw will be greater than if only one had identified it. Either way, while it makes little sense to ignore the singular and triangulated critical responses of others, at times it is necessary to assert integrity on the basis of self-understanding by opting not to respond by making a change.

What kinds of questions might a songwriter ask themselves prior to presenting a song to the critical community?

Is it a good idea for a song?
Is the subject matter likely to be of sufficient intrigue?
Does it work best as autobiography or should I adopt a fictional character?
Am I the right singer to convey the idea or expression?
Is the instrumentation right for the song?
Is the performance I intend to present sympathetic to the expression of the song?
Is the instrumentation right for the singer?
Do the music and lyrics clash?
Are the musical ideas or sections effectively structured?
Does the lyric have or require continuity?
Are there times when it is likely the listener's ear will not be engaged? Does the arrangement of the recording require a more pronounced dynamic?
Does the song possess an element of originality or surprise?
How does the song compare to those that already exist?

Urban (1996) proposes the following conditions for fostering creativity: an atmosphere free of stress, anxiety or sanction, a climate that is cooperative rather than competitive and an environment that discourages negative reactions. Sufficient time to reflect, investigate, question and challenge is also advised. In the process, the songwriter should seek to discover the strategies that lead to error and to become sensitive to the effects of environmental stimuli. Through the discussion of how songs relate to their writing processes, we can begin to make connections between our working environments or methods that work, or enable us to convey what we intend to express, and those that don't.

Larsen-Freeman (2003: 129) suggests that, without feedback from the listener, there is no way for a speaker to evaluate the degree to which his or her communicative attempt has achieved its purpose and that in such instances, the exchange cannot be called communicative. Audiences who applaud might be doing so as a point of convention, merely doing what is expected of a bystander. A communicator can only guess how much of an intended meaning has got across (Hodge, 1981: 7) and communication involves a number of stages, each of which could potentially cause a communicative gesture to fail. In depth analysis, or the critical unpicking of each element of a song could prove to be potentially rewarding. As Urban (1996) suggests, sufficient time for this to occur is crucial, as without sufficient time, key aspects may be overlooked.

Swanwick (1999: 73) suggests that a performance of a relatively simple piece should not necessarily be accorded less musical value than the performance of a more complex one. Rather, he advises critics to 'stay close to the idea of music as metaphor and concentrate on the visible external layers on either side of each metaphorical transformation'. These observable layers he suggests, consist of materials, expression, form and value. Each of these values could be perceived to be equally accessible to songwriters and non-songwriters; in this context, it is again clear to see how the critical perspective of a non-musician would add quality.

Try listening to some songs which have recently been released commercially but have not yet become successful, and ask yourself these questions:

Are you listening to the words or the music? Why?
Across the breadth of the tracks are there any recurring themes or patterns in the production, arrangement or songwriting?
What might these relate to in terms of current cultural tastes?
Is it original?
Who does it sound like?
Is it likely to be successful and why?

The contemplation of original works in progress might be the primary feature of a critical community, but the investigation of existing works in the field may add a valuable context within which to locate the original work. Placing our own acquired sensibilities at the core, for Swanwick (ibid.) the genuine aesthetic experience occurs when the past experience of the listener aligns with the feeling gestures implied by the work. Problematically for the songwriter, the majority of the listening audience will be an unknown entity; the songwriter is obliged to guess how best to 'infect' a mystery populace. It seems possible, if not likely, that this guesswork can to some degree be informed by acquiring an understanding of how listening groups have been 'infected' by modes of expression in the past; if an audience responded positively to a particular chord sequence or texture, or were moved en masse to dance to a particular rhythm, perhaps they will again?

Analysis, practice and imitation each have a role in enabling the songwriter to develop. Discussing levels of analysis used by musical practitioners, Campbell (2004) describes three different types of listening that bring about the development of musical knowledge and skills: 'attentive listening' or directed listening focused on musical elements and structures; 'engaged listening', which involves the songwriter actively participating in music making; and 'enactive listening', which involves listening attentively to every musical aspect and nuance of a piece with the intention of recreating a performance of it as accurately as possible.

With further reference to the perceived presence of structural predictability in the listening experience, Blacking (1987) notes that:

> In so far as music is a cultural tradition that can be shared and transmitted, it cannot exist unless at least some human beings possess, or have developed, a capacity for structured listening. Musical performance, as distinct from the production of noise, is inconceivable without the perception of order in sound.

Citing Beethoven as an example of a notable composer who mastered the existing forms of musical harmony in his youth, Powell-Jones (1972) observes how exceptional inventors are able to achieve novelty within the bounds of certainty, and Ireson et al. (1999: 23) concur that the learner needs a knowledge base in order to be creative. Being aware of our field, and in particular our distinctive place within it, becomes important.

Webb (1998) argues that to possess the ability to write great songs, a songwriter needs to have heard great songs. Harlan Howard (in DeMain, 2004: 24) advises attentive listening as a means of informing practice and similarly, fellow songwriter Barry Gibb (in Bradford, 2005: 371) advises songwriters who want their work to appeal to a broad range of listeners to identify and analyse resonances between old and new songs to develop an interpretative knowledge of popular nuances and techniques. With reference to such a technique, author Sheila Davis (1988: 45) identifies a number of musical structures that she claims have proven consistently popular among listening audiences over a number of decades.

In addition to preparing songs for critique, to develop at a greater speed the songwriter should also reflect upon practice away from the critical forum. Metacognition refers to the ability to manage, plan and evaluate self-learning (Hallam, 2001: 64). Metacognitive strategies, it is argued, enable us to become consciously aware of strengths and weaknesses, select appropriate strategies for particular tasks, plan and monitor progress towards a goal, develop problem-solving skills and reflect upon and evaluate final outcomes. The acquisition of such skills is thought particularly apposite for musicians in the sense that they often benefit from acquiring rational strategies to compose, improvise and perform. Metacognition, therefore, enables learners to become aware of conditions in which they can work effectively.

In a social learning environment, the analysis of songs, or the critical negotiation of elements that are argued to have been involved in the structuring of communicative compositions, may be helpful in enabling songwriters to acquire knowledge of frameworks that may be adapted to original works to add communicative emphasis. Wary of encouraging songwriters to look in too great a depth into the mechanisms of song, Gass (1991: 731) is concerned that technical analysis threatens to absorb the excitement of the initial encounter that takes place between the listener and the music. Perhaps, to a degree, there is something to be said for knowing how songs work without necessarily using them as a directive point of reference.

With particular reference to the study of the literature on communication, Moffatt (1978: 208) states that there is no evidence that asking a student to analyse how a famous writer solved a problem will enable the student to solve his or her own writing problems. The author asserts that analytical exercises are more likely to intimidate learners by implying their involvement in a competition they are destined to lose. In response, it may be beneficial to focus in part on the analysis of songs that have recently been released and have not yet received critical or commercial acclaim; in these instances learners may feel relatively inclined to confidently specify areas of songwriting they perceive to be insufficiently communicative. Similarly, as many developing songwriters have yet to publish songs, the analysis of unpublished songs may help to avoid a situation in which the songwriter feels unable to compete. Through listening and questioning, the thoughts of the songwriter can, at an intuitive more than an imitative level, inform the shaping of original work.

In reflecting upon your own practice, the following questions might be indicative:

- Within the context of your repertoire, how good is your most recent song?
- What makes it different?
- Who are the bands or artists with whom the song shares a genre?
- What were the main challenges in writing the song and how did you overcome them?
- How are you improving as a songwriter?
- What advice would you give to fellow songwriters attempting to write to a similar theme or in a similar way?
- What will you do next?

Alternatively, if someone other than the songwriter is the singer:

- On the evidence of existing recordings, what notes does the singer typically sing?
- What is their preferred range?
- With reference to the above questions, what key should I set my recording in?
- What words or syntax do they use?
- What themes do they tend to gravitate towards?

- What is their phonetic style?
- How long do they like to remain quiet?
- What are the verses, choruses etc., and where do they tend to happen?
- What are the differences between singles and album tracks by the artist?
- What instruments and sounds are used on their successful recordings?
- Who do I know who can sing like them?
- What communicative strategies does the artist favour?
- How will I record this song and who will play on it?
- How will I make it different from what they have done before?

If the intention is to co-write:

- Why collaborate?
- Asynchronous or reflexive co-writing, which one is likely to work best? What are my strengths?
- Who should I write with?
- How can we begin?
- If neither of the collaborators, what is the narrative identity of the singer? Who is the singer singing to?
- What does the singer want?
- How should the song be structured and arranged?

Generally useful questions

How will I write the song?
What will it be about?

What is the method that enables me to capture and convey ideas?
What are the major song types?
What chords will I use?
How can I make it sound like me?
Who will play on the recording and how will I make it?
How will I make the song as communicative as possible?

3.4 Reception

'There is very little knowledge which we can consider to exist in isolation from other knowledge' (Fautley, 2010: 119), and no musician is ever isolated from the culture in which his or her own musical playing style is situated (Green, 2002: 77). From the postmodernist perspective, music has no self-contained meaning but is a form of discourse to be valued and interpreted by its sponsors (Allsup, 2009: 54). As a consequence, argues Regelski (1998), the quality of types or genres of different forms of music cannot be measured by the same criteria, rather the value of each piece should be determined by the role its particular culture has created for it. The meaningful reception of songwriting is not, and never has been limited to charts or physical sales. Many successful songwriters, including those who write for children, film and advertisement purposes, rarely or never have their work played on the radio (MacLean, 2010: 111–12).

On a similar note, Nettl (2002) considers music to be inseparable from its surrounding culture and Small (1998: 8) believes that the meaning of music lies within the precise set of social relationships formed wherever it is performed. Pre-empting Nettl and Small, Shepherd et al. (1977) adopted the position that the meaning of music can only be truly understood by the society from which it originates. These are complex arguments, however, in a world where music has few boundaries. Because popular songs are typically distributed physically and digitally as recordings, they need to be portable. While the environment in which a live performance is given can to some extent be controlled by the performer who can to some degree actively adapt a performance mode to the venue, once the recorded song has been recorded, released, streamed and purchased, the songwriter has no control over the setting in which it is experienced.

In a chapter on assessing creativity, Cowan (2006: 156–65) argues that, because the process is unpredictable, difficult to describe and creative people find their route to solutions in so many different ways, creativity is the most difficult cognitive ability to assess. Further, the dimensions of creativity vary from challenge to challenge and for this reason it is problematic to judge one creative act against another. Cowan (ibid.) is concerned that creative work tends to be assessed within the context of what is socially commendable and that examples of apparently good creative work may be recycled, and not as innovative as it first appears. From the perspective of the songwriter it makes sense to seek potentially enthusiastic markets; to be strategic in the timing and distribution of releases.

Discussing the psychological aspect of songwriting, Bradford (2005: 15) advises: 'It's important to take a risk with songwriting. Don't be afraid to write a song.' Bradford's comment is supportive of intrinsic motivation, encouraging the songwriter to allow him or herself the freedom to experiment without being conscious of the requirements of the audience. In seeking to unravel the issue, Blake (in Braheny, 2006: 52–9) uses neurobiological evidence to enable the reader to know something of what is happening when the listener interprets creative work:

> The imagination is literally wild and has no discipline to it. You, the writer, must realize that you set off the same crazy process in the listeners head with every word you write; and

it is you who must bring discipline to the listener's imagination. You need to impose controls on it in order to keep
it somewhere in the domain in which you intend it to be.

The subject of whether a song can be heard with an instrument
and vocal arrangement or whether it needs to be heard fully
arranged has been a topic of debate among publishers and
songwriters for quite some time. It seems reasonable to
anticipate that a songwriter should present a song as he or she
would wish it to be heard; if the song can be structured and
performed as an instrument/vocal piece and still sufficiently
convey expression, then fine. In most instances, however, the
listener will expect to hear an arrangement when listening
to a song, and as a consequence the vast majority of song is
produced and arranged.

The argument that the quality of the song can be heard
beneath its arrangement seems an odd one – a bit like trying
to judge what a painting that is in colour would look like
in black and white. Likewise, the songwriter should not
take for granted that the listener will be able to imagine an
arrangement for a song that may need one. Anecdotally,
songwriters occasionally deride publishers, producers and
artists who cannot imagine how a song might be arranged,
but again this is akin to showing someone a black-and-white
picture and asking them to imagine the colours. Why *should*
they imagine the colours? And, if they did imagine colours,
how likely is it that they would be the same colours as those
intended by the painter? It follows that the songwriter should
be responsible for presenting the song as he or she intends it
to be heard; only then can both the songwriter and the listener
be sure that what is intended to be heard, and what is being
heard are the same thing.

Moore (2004) argues that the songwriter's range of opportunity to communicate his or her work is determined to some
degree by the acquisition of technical skill and competence.
To be successful as a songwriting communicator, he stresses,
learners need not only the creative skill to work within their

own niche, but also the technical musical ability to enter the commercial marketplace. Reasoning that production has a significant effect on the song as a sonic artefact, Moore considers the ability to produce to be an integral part of songwriting. Mindful that some songwriters develop work for acoustic performance, Reddington (2006) advocates the development of a gradual understanding, advising songwriters not to become involved in production until they have decided it is essential to what they are doing.

While each songwriter's career trajectory is unique, the career to date of Chris Turpin and Stephanie Ward, both founder members of Warner Brothers recording artists Kill It Kid, illustrates some of the experiences and pressures that might be encountered. A highly charismatic singer and guitarist, Chris was originally influenced by the raw blues of the Reverend Gary Davis, Son House and Charley Patton. Decidedly individual in his interpretation, Chris translates the music of those inspirational pioneering figures into the sound that drives their three albums 'Kill It Kid', 'Feet Fall Heavy' and 'You Owe Nothing'.

From an entirely different musical background, Stephanie trained as a classical player and met Chris while the two were students in Bath. The music of Kill It Kid is as restless as its members, who have spent much of the past seven years on the road in England, Europe and America. Over the years their sound has evolved, as Chris recalls: 'When we started out we were a weird alt-country band being compared to Anthony and the Johnsons and Johnny Cash.' Stephanie takes up the story: 'The second record was garage blues and now we're grunge rock blues; everybody strings a few words together. We must be hard to describe!'

While legend has it that the band were signed almost immediately after a legion of Artist and Repertoire folk descended upon one of their early hometown shows, that myth doesn't quite tell the whole truth. 'We planned a 35-date tour up and down the country', says Chris. 'I was calling up venues lying and pretending to be a booking agent saying "I've got this band who are the next new hot thing, and they've just won this award" and so on. That, alongside an EP we recorded with John Parish, led to One Little Indian calling us. We didn't take them seriously when they called,' Chris remembers, 'it was a crazy Italian woman and it turned out they looked after Bjork and Skunk Anansie and all sorts of things.' From Chris's perspective, the band's independently energetic and imaginative approach to publicity paid off: 'We knocked on everyone's door; they thought we were really proactive and that's really what a record company wants.'

Once the label had made their initial approach, the pressure was on Kill It Kid to live up to the hype. 'We did a very late night show in London at about three o'clock in the morning,' continues Stephanie, 'then we met with them really early in the morning. In One Little Indian's London office they had dogs with their legs missing and a Tae Kwando machine upstairs', she recalls. 'I didn't even know what a record label was! I had no idea what anyone was talking about. Derek Birkett, the managing director of the label said "You're a third album band", which is something you would never hear now.' Chris explains further:

> It's getting harder and harder for the record industry to support bands. To support five people across the cycle of an album for eighteen months and also the video costs, press teams and actual recording and mastering costs is huge. We were talking to Warner Brothers and they were saying how they are now signing artists like Robin Shultz for single song deals. To succeed now you need the recorded object; everything is about that.

Chris's analysis illustrates the increasing trend for major labels in some, if not all territories to favour an artist who has created one entirely finished radio-friendly song over an artist who shows promise but needs development to realize their commercial potential.

Kill It Kid's story, though, is of a band determined to remain true to a creative vision; to see where music that is real to them will take them. Their first record label, One Little Indian gave them the operational independence to match their independence of musical spirit. While Kill It Kid explored ways of differentiating their sound from that made by their contemporaries, One Little Indian trusted the band to direct their own visual and live aesthetic. Eventually, as Chris and Stephanie reflect, one drove the other, allowing them to develop a distinctive collective persona. Hundreds of live shows have led that identity to evolve, as Stephanie explains: 'Naturally our persona has changed. We've done so many gigs and so many tours now that you lose your inhibitions. You do have a persona but once you are on stage you just learn to not care.' Vast experience on the road has taught Stephanie that 'Things that feel silly on stage don't necessarily look silly to an audience. In the first videos we did I was so aware of every movement that I made, so concerned about looking cool. And then the last video we did you find yourself prancing around in front of the camera … It's like any job, you get used to it. The more you do it, you just naturally adapt.' Chris adds: 'When you're not trying to please tastemakers, that when your persona comes through.'

Placing the songs in new settings on tour has allowed the band to experience their songs in new ways, the type of audience being instrumental in shaping the experience. 'Slovenia was one of the best gigs', remembers Chris. 'An old cinema in the middle of nowhere, 500 hundred people, it was like the Rolling Stones or something!' Of another memorable performance, Stephanie says: 'When the crowd knows the words its definitely different. We did a Scandinavian tour recently and we'd never released anything there but there was this town and we were the first British band ever to play there. We had to take two planes from the mainland to get there. And the crowd went mental; they all knew the words, it was weird. And we spoke to them afterwards and they said "we saw you on the listing so we bought your album and listened to it!" It's not like London, where they are completely over-saturated with music. People [in Scandinavia] are desperate to have a good time and get everything they can out of the gig.'

Many a young songwriter's dream, for Chris the actuality of being pursued by a major label was a waking nightmare. The negotiations of such deals, even when conducted by intermediaries, are often protracted and threaten to impose conditions that rarely favour the artist. Says Chris:

> When we first started talking to major labels, which is a terrifying and heart-breaking process, we did a showcase for Atlantic in New York and it was so awkward. You have a stage, a huge PA system and monitors and three execu-tives pull up chairs and make you play three to five songs, and they don't clap or say anything. It's awful!

While America has a history of valuing tenure, of encouraging performing songwriters to build up audiences and generate radio traction prior to signing licensing or publishing agreements, as Stephanie observes, 'In England all the companies are looking for something outside of the mainstream; if you follow trends, they are always going to want something different. Everyone is looking for the next new thing, before you have any history.' As a consequence she advises: 'The more songs you can get stocked up before you emerge, the better.'

In the twenty-first century, it can be challenging for any modern act – even one signed to a major label – to subsist on the traditional streams of publishing, mechanical, touring and performance related income alone. For Kill It Kid, film and television have proven to be essential to their survival as a creative unit: 'Sync is very important', says Stephanie. 'It's one of the best ways of making money; to get your music out there, because not everyone goes to live shows but everyone is sitting at home watching TV. It exposes your music to people who would never normally seek it out.' As an example of how sync can affect the regular activity of the band, Kill It Kid recently toured Norway because their music was used in a VW car advertisement there.

Chris continues: 'In theory your publisher should be like an agent going out and getting you syncs.' The reasons are immediately evident: 'Various pitches come in from big businesses and the first one we got from Samsung was three times our first record advance.' He elaborates on the process: 'Sometimes you get the ad to see, and other times they want stuff specifically written for a concept. It makes a huge difference in terms of impact. From a Samsung ad we got loads of other syncs and songs in American dramas.' The income stream can be lucrative, as Chris explains: 'Every TV and radio station has to log everything it plays and PRS and PPL collect royalties and send them to you, so you start to get performance royalties from syncs about a year later.'

Revenues from dominant streaming sources are relatively miniscule, something the band – like many other artists around the globe – would like to see remedied. Referring to the offices of one well-known streaming company, Chris is uncharacteristically disdainful: 'Their offices were full of these coked-up drunk people on bean bags who were clueless about how revenue streams work for artists.' The streaming companies' argument, he claims, has logic but lacks empathy. 'Why would you buy something when you can get it for free? The money they pay is an absolute pittance. You want everyone to hear your music, so we've got no choice.' Picking up the theme, Stephanie adds:

> If all those people had bought the single we'd be making money. The record industry is still working like it was 25 years ago and everyone in it knows it's a complete shambles and that something will have to change. Because there is no money in the music industry, they are taking a cut of everything they can.

Both Chris and Stephanie see artists becoming increasingly creative in their bid to circumvent the injustices of existing revenue models. 'You don't have to approach A&R or play in Camden any more', says Chris. 'These days bands are signing directly to sync agencies, bypassing publishers, recording their own songs, signing to a label for a small advance but tour support instead.' Even more circuitously, 'A lot of bands these days are getting investment deals from investors; then you can do everything you want to do.'

As well as reaching out to audiences at the further geographical extremes, by working with data analysts Chris and Stephanie are able to take their music where they know it is already popular. Says Chris: 'We keep tabs on where our audience is. It's much bigger in Europe than it is here! Europe supports bands for life, the English are fickle and the Americans blow you up out of all proportion. To be an English band in Europe is a really good deal,' he claims, 'you are perceived really differently, with more artistic reverence.' To illustrate this phenomenon, Chris explains: 'A Belgian interviewer once asked me: "How did you even dare pick up a guitar and start writing songs with the legacy of English music?" I said: "I never even thought about it!".'

Songwriter and producer Steve Chrisanthou collaborates with established and new artists, using his understanding of recording technology and ear for a great tune to help them to realize the potential of their ideas. A Grammy nominee for his work with Corinne Bailey Rae, Steve combines a vast musical knowledge with a method that relies heavily on instinct. 'You've got to arm yourself to the teeth', he says. 'You've got to be the best singer you can, be the best musician, be aware of what is going on, and then forget about it all and be who you are, because ultimately, people are interested in people.' Reflecting his philosophy, his collaborative writing methods are unscientific. 'The starting point is the person in the room', he explains. 'We go through some ideas with guitars, and talk about something and try and capture the spirit in the room, without being too pushy, just waiting for an opportunity for someone to react and then you react back, and that's what is exciting about music.' Believing the right conditions to be integral to the creation of new ideas and placing formal methodology second to environment, Steve creates space for the songwriting to occur.

Operating from a home studio in Hebden Bridge and a separate studio in Tileyard, near King's Cross in central London, Steve is able to escape from and immerse himself in the industry of the UK music capital at will. Like many other songwriters, Steve is in constant dialogue with his publisher, who acts as a critical collaborator in the development of new songs. The partnership is both creative and commercially oriented, with both sides seeking to develop song recordings that have a contemporary artistic edge – that use the immediate present to predict the immediate future.

Recently, Steve has noticed an increasing emphasis on working economically, both in terms of time and sound: 'People expect more quickly; you've got to get to the point quicker. Take the Sam Smith stuff; if you break the production down, it's very simple. But he's got a great voice and when he sings you are listening to the whole thing. It's about learning to back off and not overpowering it with a million things.' Throughout the dialogue, Steve has learned to trust his own instinct:

> My publisher will say if you get halfway through a song and it's not a hit, stop doing it. How can you tell? Once you've started the process you've got to see it through. As long as there is something eclectic and different in there – it's about honesty.

Whatever collaborative scenario Steve finds himself in, the minimum requirement is to fully produce each song, even if it is not intended for release. 'It needs to sound like a record before you give it to somebody to critique', he explains. 'That's the evolution of music; back in the day, someone picks up a guitar and sings and you think "I'm moved". But then you've heard it a million times ... Technology dictates things. Will it go full circle? I don't think so.'

Manchester-based songwriter and lead singer in the band Cherry Ghost, Simon Aldred leads a dual existence as a band leader and writer for other artists. A former mathematician, he writes with a crafted precision that has led him to be held in the highest regarded by his peers. Simon's interpretation of how songwriting is received is at once mystical and matter-of-fact: 'After ten years of travelling up and down the motorway,' he remembers, 'I recorded four songs, did a gig in a Mexican themed restaurant and got offered four record deals. If you write a good song then people will hear about it', he says.

From a creative perspective, the years spent in development were far from passive. As Simon explains, his ascent as a songwriter was due to a combination of 'sheer stubbornness and determination'. There are lots of good artists about, he claims, 'but there is plenty of room for more good music. You start tailoring what you do to suit the industry and the industry moves on. If you are good at what you do, you will get there. You've got to make it impossible to ignore.' Offering sage advice to the unsigned performing songwriter, Simon warns: 'Looking like you don't care is better than looking needy. They'll come to you eventually.'

One of his finest songs, 'People help the people' has a sense of community that reflects the way he sees the cultural role of songwriting: 'You can write a song about whatever you want to write a song about,' he says, 'but it needs to unite people in some sense and resonate with a group of people in a way that brings people together.' The right approach, from Simon's perspective, is always to be authentic and project a personal voice, but also to be economical. As he explains: 'I'll try and get a sense of something I've experienced and then spin it out; extrapolate a story from a grain of truth. I've always got to have a vision in my head, and try and make it interesting; love, loss, loneliness. You don't need loads of meaningless words; say what you need to say and then hold off.'

The acquisition of a sense of authenticity needn't be over-thought: 'You should use words you would generally use,' Simon advises, 'it doesn't have to be highbrow. "Wichita lineman" isn't sentimental; its *in between* the words that the song exists.' Further – and returning to the theme of economy – there is no need to write songs for the sake of stockpiling them. As Simon argues, 'Unless it's something that needs to be said, why write a song every week? I'd rather write six good ones in a year.' The will to explore is more important: 'You have to push yourself to write in a new way, to find an interesting way of doing it. Occupying other people's lives keeps it from being just about you, and incidental things are important: shoes, cups – it doesn't have to be some grand gesture. Be vulnerable but dignified.'

For Simon, in terms of enjoyment the process and the outcome may be contrasting experiences, and this methodo-logical awareness allows him to be objective prior to offering songs for reception: 'You can enjoy writing a song and listen back and it's not that good', he explains. 'I'd give it 24 hours before listening. If you need a string section to rescue a song you should probably just forget the song, but if it still sounds good after a week then maybe it's good.' The conditions of review are critical: 'You automatically think anything new is good, but I'll hear a song differently if I'm playing it to someone.' Ultimately, Simon advises: 'If someone says they don't like it and you think it's good, then tell everyone else they don't know what they are talking about!'

From Simon's perspective, he needs to know the song is right, in part because he knows the tastemakers called upon to pass judgement will respond in ways impossible to predict. 'Radio stations dictate artistic terms more than labels do', he claims. 'If you don't make a change, the station might never play any of your tunes again. A&R people can be very up and down. Some will hear the same mix at a different level and think it's a hit!'

Having experienced the trajectory himself, Simon acknowledges the difficulties and opportunities in developing a
reputation as a songwriter within the global community: 'I
was helped by my reputation as an artist but it's quite competitive', he observes. 'The way it generally goes is that you've got
to start writing with unknown artists, or your friend's band.
And that gives you some kind of reputation. It's a lot about
working your way through the ranks really until you're at a
stage where you've got people who ask you to write for them.'

Despite the current malaise within commercial music
markets, Simon sees the pervading economic gloom as deceptively helpful to emerging artists and songwriters. He concludes:

> Major labels suddenly realized they didn't have as much
> money as they thought they did. There has never been a
> better time for making your own music and releasing it,
> and you don't have to do as much gigging as you used to.
> You need to be special and unique and interesting. People
> are more focused on making a living from doing gigs,
> which is great because people are getting better on instru-
> ments. You're less likely to be loaded, but if you can make
> a living out of doing something you love, that's a success.

As vice president of international affairs at ASCAP (American
Society of Performers, Composers and Authors), Sean Devine
occupies a mid-Atlantic role that finds him simultaneously
engaged with both US and UK markets. A former manager
and publisher, Sean has never written a song, but, as his track
record shows, he knows a good one when he hears it. As he
says: 'Most people who buy music are not musicians: they are
just passionate about music.'

At his office in Cork Street, London, Sean shares his
philosophy on the reception of songwriting: 'Being successful
anywhere is down to luck, skill and hard work', he claims.
For songwriters who are not performing artists, he says, 'the
hard work is finding the artist who wants to work with you'.
Like Simon Aldred, he considers preparation to be essential,

explaining: 'Music capitals like London can be unforgiving if a lot of the music community come to see you and it doesn't go that well. It can be very, very hard to come back from that. It's best to try and make mistakes elsewhere.'

Sean describes an influential culture within London, a discrete community of individuals whose discourse is central to aspiring songwriters: 'The tastemakers, anyone who will talk about your records, journalists, promoters, are really important', he says. 'You get a tweet from Adele saying she likes one of your records and all of a sudden everyone has to check you out.' Offering a theoretical model based on persuasion, Sean is aware that the oversaturation of the market has led to industry gatekeepers needing information other than the music to filter acts. As he explains: 'A&R people are not the same age as the listening demographic, so it's your job as the songwriter to show them that the kids like you. Major labels can no longer do a good job with your 5,000-selling album. If you can sell 50,000 without them, then they might raise their eyebrows. They think they can get you to a million; that's their job, to get you from 50,000 to a million. That's their model.'

Increasingly more important than the relationship between the label and the songwriting artist is the relationship between the artist and the fan. Sean advises: 'To give the fan that direct relationship is the new job of the music business; the music business need to find ways of communicating to people who have never heard an artist, how great that artist is.' As he observes, 'Nobody cares what label Justin Bieber is signed to, because he has that direct relationship with his fans. Labels are now just a vehicle for you to get directly in the face of your fans, and online PR who can get the right fans looking at you are really important.'

As a critical listener, Sean has developed a particular method of review: 'It's hard not to like a song after 30 seconds,' he says, 'but easy to dislike it after one minute.' Placing the emphasis upon the music to communicate to him as the listener, Sean considers the lion's share of the task is not merely to generate ideas, but to extend and expand upon them. 'It's the songwriter's job to keep me involved,' he reasons, 'because I *already* like it. You've made a level of commitment; it forces you to ask the question of what is going to happen.'

Sean perceives a contrast in what is expected of songwriters in the US and UK: 'American listeners take things more seriously because music there is around a lot longer', he explains. 'Most songs there will climb because of the enormity of the market. American hits are built to last in that way, with structures the listener will find durable. In America you've got so many heritage influences to draw upon; R'n'B, polka, blues … They can draw upon all those things, whereas we would never think of doing the equivalent with our musical past.' Recognizing a further cultural divergence, Sean says: 'In the US the spectacle is important; neutral fans all watch the Superbowl and that would never happen here. The collective makes the hit, and mythologizes it, whereas here we question it.' Further, Sean observes how, in the UK, 'There is less storytelling and detail in our songs, it is more incidental. We create things that are more oddball and creative, and because of the immediacy of those songs we can move a lot faster.' Consequently, as Sean notes, 'American songwriters like our individuality and the things we can get away with'.

Acknowledging that it is not necessarily helpful for the songwriter to over-analyse the typology of song in a targeted market, Sean cites the Grammy-winning songwriter Rick Nowels, who has had international hits with artists as diverse as Madonna, Tupac Shakur and Weezer, who claims that it doesn't matter what the market is, a great song is a great song. Consequently, Rick argues, it is impossible to write for any market on the basis that you think you know the market. Simon Aldred is of a similar mind when it comes to responding to trends, saying: 'Writing a song is like planting a seed and then forgetting about it. Then it might go off and do its own thing in Germany!'

Songwriter, producer and former singer Martin Brammer works in central London. A regular collaborator with James Morrison, the story of how Martin and James met supports Simon Aldred's earlier espoused philosophy that, if you are a good enough songwriter, someone will find you. Martin recalls: 'The first time I heard James I thought "Wow, who is this guy?" He was in Derby at the time and two days later we drove up to see him.' As a friend and collaborator, over the years Martin has witnessed James' artistic development: 'Over the four albums his songwriting has benefitted from writing with so many others', he observes. 'He is leading things with much more confidence than he used to.'

While many young artists race for recognition, Martin recognizes songwriting progression to be a long-term game:

> There is so much to learn as a songwriter. It took me ages to find my voice. Most people start by playing the songs of people they admire, and I can absolutely remember the first song I wrote, which was still an amalgamation of influences, but that sounded like *me*. Nineteen- or Twenty-year-olds say: 'What have I got to sing about?' It evolves in terms of where your ideas come from. There is a constant search to find your own voice, because the voice changes through your life experience.

Like Iain Archer, Martin works with developing artists, helping them to shape material. 'With young writers,' he says, 'you're trying to help them find their own voice, to encourage them to look for the truth, for what is believable.' This emphasis on authenticity is not limited to the traditional singer-songwriter: 'The most successful exponents of cheesy pop, who give it some longevity,' claims Martin, 'are the people who believe in it.'

Unlike songwriters who strive to iron out the impurities by critically honing the writing, production and arrangement to perfection, Martin has a different philosophy: 'The magic is often in falling short, not quite getting what you were after', he says. 'There are elements of that rawness that shouldn't be dismissed. On some of the best records you can hear the struggle to achieve something. I'm not making an argument in favour of crap songs! It helps to have some consistency of logic or emotion, but at the point where it all makes sense, it's dreadful. It's like a Janet and John book. If it's all technique, it feels like you're writing songs about writing songs.'

When not performing in the UK, Sony recording artist Josephine Oniyama tours extensively in mainland Europe. On her travels she has noticed some significant divergences in the way songs are perceived: 'Production styles are very different in Europe', she says. 'The UK focus is going back towards real instruments, while the European production style is relatively more electronic.' Consequently, Josephine says, live shows and touring are much more emergent in the UK. In different territories the local tastes for innovation and tradition can be subject to a specific balance. 'In Germany and Holland there is a big emphasis on nu soul and hip-hop, not in a pop way, but in a more classic soul way', she explains. Some aspects of music reception are universal though: 'People like live music because it is something you can't fake. You'll never be able to replicate that. The hologram thing is interesting, but it still doesn't work. What people want is a substitute for the CD or the thing you used to be able to hold in your hand.'

About to complete work on her second album, Josephine considers it essential to test material prior to release by playing it to a small audience before taking it in to the studio or on stage: 'At least get a bunch of friends in a room so that you are testing the song every time', she advises. From then onwards the process of gauging how strong the material is should continue on an inductive basis:

If you watch the audience and see how they respond, you can learn what communicates with people and there is no replacement for that. A certain amount of coaching and advice is useful, but in the end you have to try it.

Not only has BMG Chrysalis songwriter Jez Ashurst written or programmed songs for Leona Lewis, Gabrielle Aplin, Celine Dion and Imelda May, but as a founder member of Farah, a member of the *X Factor* production team and an experienced teacher, he wears a number of hats extremely well. His journey to becoming a professional songwriter required him to be open to all offers. As he recalls: 'Just saying yes to anything to do with music takes you outside of your comfort zone, and then it *becomes* your comfort zone. If it's vaguely on the road to where you're trying to go, it's worth doing.' Further, Jez adds: 'If you're too super-focused you can miss some interesting stuff. Playing on *X Factor* I'm learning something about songs by taking songs apart and arranging them.'

In his London studio Jez writes and records with promising young artists who are recommended to him by his publisher: 'If you're not going to be an artist now,' he says, 'the best thing to do is find an artist and co-write with them, help to develop them. To get a publisher to sign you, you need to be associated with an artist who is going to sell. And you might back ten horses a year and have one come in.'

Jez encourages songwriters to question their own motives as part of the creative process by asking: What do you want the song to do? What is it for? Merely writing songs for the sake of their existence, he argues, can dissipate creative energy by denying it a focus. Like many other songwriters, he considers the voice to the most critical aspect of song projection, and consequently the element most likely to influence reception: 'Is it a good vocal?' he asks. 'Does it sound committed, engaging and interesting?' For Jez, a vocal can sell a song regardless of its arrangement, although it would have to be the right kind of song and the right kind of singer: 'You can do a piano vocal demo if the song is strong and you want to show off the vocal', he explains. 'A&R can then print their imagination on that. The producer's job is to throw stuff around the vocal and see what works, otherwise you want to make it sound as much like a record as it can be.' Experience can be a hindrance,

Jez argues, and as a consequence he encourages songwriters to embrace a certain naivety: 'To be crap at technology is actually more fun than being good at it', he argues. 'You can be creative as an artist. Have fun, that's when accidents happen. It should be like play; get that glockenspiel, grab that guitar and see what happens!'

In terms of song reception, with particular reference to emerging from the field, Jez acknowledges how difficult it is to create a narrative around original music. To attempt to direct or influence tastemakers, critics and journalists, the songwriter has to trust their own use of language to define the indefinable. Alternatively, Jez recommends developing individual characteristics as a means of drawing the attention of the audience via word of mouth: 'If people talk about you in terms of specific qualities: they played didgeridoo, they dressed as moles, the show was seven minutes long … then word about you as an individual artist can spread quite effectively.'

Before he began a seventeen-year tenure as the CEO of Chrysalis UK, Jeremy Lascelles was a tour manager, an independent label owner and, for a spell, the head of Artist and Repertoire at Richard Branson's Virgin Records. Having since signed deals with such songwriting pioneers as David Grey, Fleet Foxes, Bon Iver, Laura Marling and Ray LaMontaigne, Jeremy enjoys an unparalleled reputation as a finder and developer of excellent original artists.

Initially there is a sense that, for Jeremy, song reception is not complex. 'People listen in a very simple fashion', he says. 'Does it excite, interest them, capture their imagination? Can they connect with it? Does it move them? Those are fundamental things.' Inevitably, as he goes on to explain, there is more to it than that; the songwriter's ability to create music for listening either attentively or passively plays a key role in identifying durable quality. As Jeremy says: 'People often listen to music in the background at first, and get drawn in by something that makes you ask: what's that? And you need to go back and listen more. It's a combination of refreshing what you know, and finding things you didn't find first time around; music does that in such a multi-layered way and there are so many things you can go back and find.' From Jeremy's perspective, live and recorded performances are separate entities: 'You've got to make the most of each medium. The audience don't notice the same amount of detail live as they do on record. Live music is as much about the energy as it is about the detail.'

Whatever the environment, Jeremy's vast and varied experience tells him that song quality can be predetermined by the text; that a great song will transcend any setting. 'When Tori Amos plays "Whole lotta love" and "Smells like teen spirit" they are great songs on *every* level', he argues.

As evidence of the historical advantage of working with a trusted critic, Jeremy cites the quality of 'extra' material unearthed for inclusion on expanded releases, claiming: 'The out-takes you find on box set reissues are inevitably not as good as the original tracks that were included. Ninety per cent of the time it has not made the record for a good reason.' The role of critical mentor is essential, Jeremy says, in terms of development:

> Artists are often not great judges of their own material. They find it hard to distinguish, and have odd reasons for liking some songs more than others. Sometimes they want to keep the songs that were fun to make, which is not necessarily a good reason! Novelists have editors, and songwriters need people to tell them what is working and what is not.

Ultimately, songwriters need to know which voices to trust and which ones to ignore. As Jeremy iterates: 'A&R at their most meddlesome are interfering in the process, but the most important thing you can do is be an objective listener who is prepared to say very candidly and very constructively what works and what doesn't.'

Ivor Novello award-winning songwriter Iain Archer concurs, abiding by the mantra 'Be careful what voices you listen to, within and without'. Also a performer, producer and recording artist, Iain has enjoyed critical and commercial success during his career as an artist and songwriting collaborator. Before he made a living as a musician, Iain was a social worker, and central to his progress is a heightened sense of empathy; an acquired habit of listening closely. 'I help a lot of people to make their first records,' he says, 'and I think it's important to reflect back to the artist: here is what you are telling me. Your most important asset is your intuition; if you have somebody else to help you with that and remain objective, that's a really positive thing.'

For Iain, in a psychological and affective sense, the way songs are produced has a profound influence on the way they are eventually heard. He explains: 'There should be five words for the word producer, because it is done in so many different ways. The way the work ends up depends completely upon the producer's process. Some are merchants of chaos who create tension by provoking the players and send the whole thing off on a sonic odyssey. Rick Rubin set the tone for people like Chad from the Chili Peppers to come in and start playing, and for that to seem normal, which it's really not! With Jake Bugg, he made a huge amount of space for the artist. There was this conduit between Rick and Jake, and everything was pretty much handled between Jake and Rick, who was kind of the Jedi master. That's not something that's discussed or elaborated on, it's just that Jake has a sense of himself as the centre of the process, and that's the way it should be.'

The right producer can enhance or detract from the song. As Iain explains: 'You can be dislocated from your work by some people and plugged into it by others. Rick Rubin, for instance, will let the band play the song three or four times and wait for something to happen. He will make some little changes as it goes along, and then invite everyone in to listen. Musically it's always good, but directionally for whatever reason it's not right. So we'll all reflect, listen to some tunes as a point of reference for where the energy might go, and the band goes back in and plays it six times better. That situation, where everybody is pushing for a sound or a vibe, I love.'

Other producers have different ways of facilitating atmospheric recordings: 'David Kosten can create spectral sounds, a kind of emotional fabric that can get great performances out of you', he says, adding: 'The social psychological aspect is maybe 60 per cent of the job, it's how you get what you want from the performance. How do you create an environment that allows the songs to be heard at their best?'

As the impact of social media continues to increase, audiences tend to be more inclined to use mobile devices in social settings. Existing auditorium facilities, once the exclusive preserve of the concert experience, are increasingly not the only places we might expect to hear music. Among other contested issues in the sphere of performative convention, as consumers increasingly come to expect to be active in events influential in the shaping of their culture, the lines of division between the performer on stage and the seated listener are commonly questioned. This new participatory emphasis inevitably leads to an expansion of collaborative possibilities, between musician and non-musician, songwriter and non-songwriter, offering those whose voices may not be otherwise captured in song to be heard. At the same time as this consumer-led shift from patron to contributor is happening, traditional touring models continue to exist and thrive. 'Coming together as a community', as Josephine Oniyama observes, 'seems to act as a replacement for the meta-experience.'

Crowdsourcing platforms like Detour and Indiegogo allow fans to contribute financially towards the costs of bringing a songwriter to a specific location, or to make new recordings, yet these methods, while laudably democratic, threaten to take control away from the songwriter. As traditional platforms for the performance and retail of song become increasingly marginal, the skill of being able to network within public cultural infrastructures that encourage dialogue becomes increasingly significant. Such consultative systems, the development of which relies upon investment, patronage and the will of those who wish to participate, have the facility to construct and develop settings in which songwriting and song performance can exist and thrive under negotiated conditions set by the artist and the audience. Possibilities for new and exploratory artistic collaboration will become increasingly accessible to those with the social empathy and communal vision to shape events.

In a recorded context the situation is similarly in flux, as analyst Mark Mulligan (2013) writes: 'With a streaming service the transaction is for *all* the music in the world. The brand of any individual artist is inherently diluted.' The answer, he suggests, is in the introduction of artist subscriptions within existing streaming services, since as more of consumers' music experiences occur within access-based environments, more needs to be done to build artist-specific experiences within them. This solution requires the songwriter to extend their communicative skills in a less reflexive, more asynchronous way, adding editorial stories and audiovisual content that reward the listener by adding dimension to and hence creating *value for* the music. As Mark continues:

> Such a model, an enriched experience which allows the listener to explore the music, through the people who actually make the music, based on providing the subscriber with exclusive rarities, playlists of artists' influences, remixes, acoustic sessions, concert footage and interviews, would allow the songwriter to control the brand without compromise, or dilution, to direct the interaction.

Iain Archer observes, however, how 'Some artists are relatively less compelling as personalities in a non-musical setting'. The role of the mediator in curating the content that might satisfy the subscriber, while allowing the songwriter to preserve a modicum of privacy, to retain an element of mystery, could be significant. Maybe it would be a positive thing for the mainstream to become critically aware of how songs are made, who plays on them, and how songs can radically change in different settings? While this proposition is likely to suit versatile artists who, like Iain Archer, are able to be creative and critical at the same time, others would perhaps be loathe to make works-in-progress available, viewing such an act as a dilution of the art. As Csikszentmihalyi observes, many creative individuals wish to be marginalized, and this increased emphasis on performer audience interaction makes it seem likely that there will be a prominent place for the promoter or mediator.

In full knowledge that music is now effectively free, and aware of the need to avoid making the pampered and demanding digital consumer work to find songs, major labels have responded by seeking to place an emphasis on having everything in one place: catalogue, links, tour dates, merchandise and so on. Many within and outside the music industry feel that the decline in music sales in the twenty-first century is a direct consequence of much music not being good enough to release. In turn, the theory goes, the consumer has been driven towards live music as an antidote, a phenomenon that continues to favour live musicians capable of giving compelling performances. While technological advances have created a situation in which anyone can make a record, not everyone can play live.

Rumours of the death of the traditional music industry have, however, been greatly exaggerated. The Universal label, for example, is increasingly successful as a business, and many major labels and publishers, particularly those with a vast catalogue at their disposal, continue to find ways to diversify income streams. Importantly, major labels also enjoy an ongoing and mutually beneficial relationship with radio – a medium responsible for breaking more than half of worldwide acts. Further, majors continue to play an active role in nurturing artists, in particular songwriters and performers, for success in local, international and global markets.

Wherever major labels and radio don't succeed in filtering quality, recommendation engines step in, providing a curation service for listeners who don't have time to sift the good from the bad. Playlists are about the identity of the curator; from the songwriter's perspective it is helpful to develop an awareness of who these curators are. As in a live performance context, again the emphasis for projection and reception is based upon networking, the ability to generate influential contacts. What is the best way to network? MD of Sound Diplomacy Shain Shapiro says it is about more than getting to know people; that effective networking involves knowing what you have to offer and specifically what you stand to gain from the networking opportunity. Upon such interactions, he claims, worthwhile and mutually beneficial partnerships can be built.

At a global level, many industrial anomalies exist. Streaming accounts for the vast majority of music consumption in Scandinavia, and it is nigh on impossible to make a living as a songwriter by selling CDs in Norway. Conversely, German sales are 75 per cent physical. A phenomenal number of artists have in recent times emerged from the Icelandic scene, while the music of Australia has become so diverse that much of what is released is increasingly challenging to categorize. The American mainstream market, once fiercely parochial, is increasingly open to music from other parts of the world, and in the UK, vinyl sales continue to increase. The rationale behind each trend is in part historical and, as such, can only be applied to the territory in question. As a means of generating hitherto unknown opportunities, from the perspective of the songwriter it is beneficial to have a current awareness of global market developments.

In a further technological development, increasingly sophisticated qualitative and quantitative data is now available to show how fans react to each aspect of a marketing campaign, thus providing indicators for how new and established acts can be successfully marketed. By acquiring data on where an audience is, or where a potential audience is likely to be, performing songwriters can find out where they are popular, where their music is being streamed and, importantly, respond to those areas by going there. Equally importantly, data holds the capability to connect with fans who can be kept in touch with what the songwriter is doing. As this information can be gathered and distributed in real time, independent artists can react as quickly as major label acts, in this way creating a more equal playing field. In a somewhat intrusive big brotherly fashion, this data can identify who is listening, their age and where they are.

Clearly, within all of this industrial and social stability and instability, there are numerous options open to the songwriter who wishes to operate sustainably, or even profitably, within the culture. Those most likely to benefit are those who understand what they do and what they want, and who use that knowledge to develop a commercial model suitable to their own situation.

Observing how many songwriters adopt default behavioural patterns of recording, pressing CDs and touring, label owner Ben Cottrell advises the independent musician to reflect upon why they are doing what they are doing, by asking the following questions:

- Where do I fit within the marketplace?
- Am I unique?
- Is anyone doing what I do better than me? And how?
- Is it necessary for me to record?
- Am I seeking to raise awareness of my act or am I trying to make money?

- Should I record an album, an EP or a single? Why?
- Should I only play my original material?
- Do I need a laptop or a professional studio to record my songs?
- Can I self-fund? If not, who might invest?
- Should I realize my songs on digital, CD, vinyl, or another format?
- Should any of my songs be offered free as tasters to entice?
- Is Bandcamp or CD Baby the most practical mode of distribution or do I need to hire an expensive PR company?
- Why am I playing live?
- Do I have to and what is the aim?
- What time of year should I play?
- In what cities and territories?
- Should I play festivals?
- How do my live performances tie in with my recording releases?
- How do my website and social media platforms help me project my songs?
- Why do I deserve the support of an audience?
- What is my definition of success?
- What next?

BIBLIOGRAPHY

Published sources

Abeles, H. (2010), *Critical Issues in Music Education: Contemporary Theory and Practice*. Oxford University Press.

Allsup, R. E. (2009), 'Philosophical Perspectives of Music Education', in H. Abeles and L. Custodero (eds), *Music Pedagogy: Frameworks for Practice*. New York: Oxford University Press.

Amabile, T. M. (1983), *The Social Psychology of Creativity*. New York: Springer-Verlag.

Amabile, T. M. (1996), *Creativity in Context*. Boulder, CO: Westview Press.

Andsell, G. (1995), *Music For Life*. London: Jessica Kingsley Publishers.

Arieti, S. (1976), *Creativity: The Magic Synthesis*. New York: Basic Books.

Aston, Martin (2014), 'Commentary on "The Man With The Child In His Eyes" by Kate Bush', *Mojo Magazine* 251, October 2014, 75.

Ball, P. (2010), *The Music Instinct: How Music Works and Why We Can't Do Without It*. London: Bodley Head.

Barnes, D. and Todd, F. (1994), *Communication and Learning Revisited: Making Meaning Through Talk*. Portsmouth, NH: Boynton/Cook.

Baroni, M. (1999), 'Musical Grammar and the Study of Cognitive Processes of Composition', *Musicae Scientae* 3 (1): 3–21.

Barron, F. X. (1969), *Creative Person and Creative Process*. New York: Holt, Rinehart and Winston.

Beall, E. (2009), *The Billboard Guide to Writing and Producing Songs that Sell: How to Create Hits in Today's Music Industry*. New York: Billboard Books/Watson Guptill.

Birdwhistell, R. (1972), *Kinesics and Context*. Philadelphia: University of Pennsylvania Press.

Blacking, J. (1987), *A Common Sense View of All Music*. Cambridge: Cambridge University Press.

Blake, C. (2006), in Braheny, J., *The Craft and Business of Songwriting (Third Edition)*. Cincinnatti, OH: Writer's Digest Books.

Bloom, B. S. (1985), *Developing Talent in Young People*. New York: Ballantine.

Blume, J. (2003), *Inside Songwriting – Getting to the Heart of Creativity*. New York: Billboard Books.

Boden, M. A. (2001), 'Creativity and Knowledge', in A. Craft, B. Jeffrey and M. Leibling (eds), *Creativity in Education*. London: Continuum.

Bradford, C. (2005), *Heart and Soul – Revealing the Craft of Songwriting*. London: Sanctuary.

Braheny, J. (2006), *The Craft and Business of Songwriting (Third Edition)*. Cincinnatti, OH: Writer's Digest Books.

Bunt, L. (1994), *Music Therapy: An Art Beyond Words*. London: Routledge.

Burge, C. (2013), *Taking Creativity to the Nth Degree*. Ossining, NY: TS Poetry Press.

Campbell, P. S. (2004), *Teaching Music Globally*. Oxford and New York: Oxford University Press.

Canale, M. and Swain, M. (1980), 'Theoretical Bases of Communicative Approaches to Second Language Teaching and Testing', *Applied Linguistics* 1 (1): 1–47.

Carlisle, D. (1984), *Ragged But Right: The Life and Times of George Jones*. Chicago: Contemporary Books.

Chambers, J. A. (1973), 'College Teachers: Their Effects on the Creativity of Students', *Journal of Educational Psychology* 65 (3).

Chomsky, N. (1971), *Selected Readings*. J. P. B. Allen and P. Van Buren (eds). London: Oxford University Press.

Cloonan, M. (2005), 'What is Popular Music Studies? Some Observations', *British Journal of Music Education* 22 (1): 77–93.

Cohen, C. (2006), cited in Braheny, J., *The Craft and Business of Songwriting (Third Edition)*. Cincinnatti, OH: Writer's Digest Books.

Cook, N. (1998), *Music: A Very Short Introduction*. New York: Oxford University Press.

Cooke, D. (1959), *The Language of Music*. Oxford: Oxford University Press.

Cowan, J. (2006), 'How Should I Assess Creativity?' in N. Jackson, M. Oliver, M. Shaw, and J. Wilson (eds), *Developing Creativity in Higher Education: An Imaginative Curriculum*. London: Routledge.

Craig Watkins, S. (2005), *Hip Hop Matters: Politics, Pop Culture and the Struggle for the Soul of a Movement*. Boston, MA: Beacon Press.

Craft, A. (2001), 'Little c Creativity', in A. Craft, B. Jeffrey, and M. Liebling (eds), *Creativity in Education*. London: Continuum.

Cropley, A. J. (1969), *La Creativita*. Firenze: La Nuova Italia, (Edizione Italiana).

Cropley, A. J. (2001), *Creativity in Education and Learning: A Guide For Teachers and Educators*. London: Kogan Page.

Csikszentmihalyi, M. (1996), *Creativity: Flow and the Psychology of Discovery and Invention*. New York: HarperCollins.

D'Souza, W. (1981), 'Non-Verbal Communication', in B. Hodge, *Communication and the Teacher*. Melbourne: Longman Cheshire.

Dacey, J. S. (1989), *Fundamentals of Creative Thinking*. Lexington, MA: Lexington Press.

Davis, S. (1988), *The Songwriter's Idea Book*. Milwaukee, WI: Hal Leonard.

Dellas, M. and Gaier, E. L. (1970), 'Identification of Creativity: The Individual', *Psychological Bulletin* 73: 55–73.

DeMain, B. (2004), *In Their Own Words: Songwriters Talk About the Creative Process*. Westport, CT: Praeger.

Dery, M. (2004), *That's The Joint! The Hip Hop Studies Reader*. Abingdon: Routledge.

Dettmar, K. J. H. (2009), *The Cambridge Companion to Bob Dylan*. Cambridge: Cambridge University Press.

Dewey, J. (1958), *Art as Experience*. New York: Capricorn Books.

Djupvik, M. B. (2014), 'Welcome to the Candy Shop! Conflicting Representations of Black Masculinity', *Popular Music*, 3/2. Cambridge: Cambridge University Press.

Dorment, Richard (2013), 'George Braque: How He Changed Western Painting For Ever', *The Telegraph*. 23 September 2013.

Duncker, K (1945), 'On Problem Solving', *Psychological Monographs 58*. American Psychological Association.

Dunsby, J. (1995), *Performing Music: Shared Concerns*. Oxford: Clarendon Press.

Durrant, C. and Welch, G. (1995), *Making Sense of Music: Foundations for Music Education*. London: Cassell.

Dylan, B. (2005), *Chronicles: Volume One*. New York: Pocket Books.

Elliott, D. J. (1995), *Music Matters: A New Philosophy of Music Education*. Oxford: Oxford University Press.

Ellis, R. (1997), *Second Language Acquisition*. Oxford: Oxford University Press.

Empire, Kitty (2014), 'Before The Dawn: Review of Kate Bush', *The Guardian*. 26 August 2014.

Escott, C. (2004), *Hank Williams: The Biography*. New York: Little, Brown and Company.

Ericsson, K. A. and Smith, J. (1991), *Toward a General Theory of Expertise: Prospects and Limits*. Cambridge: Cambridge University Press.

Fautley, M. (2010), *Assessment in Music Education*. Oxford: Oxford University Press.

Foster, J. (1967), *Creativity and the Teacher*. Basingstoke: Macmillan.

Francis, H. (1977), *Language in Teaching and Learning*. London: George Allen and Unwin.

Frankl, R, (1994), *Bruce Springsteen*. New York: Chelsea House Publications.

Frith, S. (1987), 'Why Do Songs Have Words?', in A. L. White, *Lost in Music*. London: Routledge and Kegan Paul.

Frith, S. (1988), *Music for Pleasure: Essays in the Sociology of Pop*. New York: Routledge.

Fromkin, V. Rodman, R. and Hyams, N. (2009), *An Introduction to Language (Ninth Edition)*. Boston, MA: Wadsworth.

Gadamer, H. G. (1975), *Truth and Method*. New York: Seabury Press.

Gardner, H. (1993), *Multiple Intelligences: The Theory in Practice*. New York: Basic Books.

Gardner, H. (1997), *Extraordinary Minds: Portraits of Four Exceptional Minds and the Extraordinary Mind in All of Us*. New York: HarperCollins.

Gass, G. (1991), 'Why Don't We Do It in the Classroom?', *South Atlantic Quarterly* 90: 729–36.

George, N. (1998), *Hip Hop America*. New York: Penguin.

Getzels, J. W. and Jackson, P. W. (1962), *Creativity and Intelligence*. New York: John Wiley & Sons.

Gillett, C. (1996), *The Sound of the City: The Rise of Rock And Roll*. Boston, MA: Da Capo Press.

Godlovitch, S. (1998), *Musical Performance: A Philosophical Study*. London: Routledge.

Goldman-Eisler, F. (1961), 'Hesitation and Information', C. Cherry (ed.), *Information Theory*. London: Butterworth.

Goldman-Eisler, F. (1968), *Psycholinguistics: Experiments in Spontaneous Speech*. London: Academic Press.

Gordon, S. (2010), *Mastering the Art of Performance: A Primer for Musicians*. Oxford and New York: Oxford University Press.

Gordon, W. J. J. (1961), *Synectics: The Development of Creative Capacity*. New York: Harper.

Gray, M. (2000), *Song and Dance Man III: The Art of Bob Dylan*. London: Continuum.

Green, L. (2002), *How Popular Musicians Learn: A Way Ahead for Music Education*. London: Ashgate.

Greyck, T. (2007), *Listening to Popular Music: Or, How I Learned to Stop Worrying and Love Led Zeppelin*. Ann Arbor, MI: University of Michigan Press.

Gruber, H. E. (1980), *Darwin on Man: A Psychological Study of Scientific Creativity*. Chicago: University of Chicago Press.

Hall, E. T. (1959), *The Silent Language*. New York: Doubleday and Co.

Hall, S. and Whannel, P. (1964), *The Popular Arts*. London: Hutchinson.

Hall, S. (1992), 'The Question of Cultural Identity', S. Hall, D. Held and T. McGrew (eds), *Modernity and its Futures*. Cambridge: Polity in association with The Open University, 273–325.

Hallam, S. (2001), 'Learning in Music: Complexity and Diversity', C. Philpott and C. Plummeridge (eds), *Issues in Music Teaching*. London: Routledge Falmer.

Halliday, M. A. K. (1976), cited in G. Kress (ed.), *System and Function in Language*. London: Oxford University Press.

Hanslick, E. (1854), *The Beautiful in Music*. New York: Liberal Arts Press [Trans. 1957].

Harris, J. (2005), 'Riddle of the Bands: Interview with Andy Partridge', *The Guardian*. June 24 2005.

Harris, J. (2009), 'Interview with Ralf Hutter', *The Guardian*. 19 June 2009.

Hatch, D. and Millward, S. (1987), *From Blues to Rock: An Analytical History of Pop Music*. Manchester: Manchester University Press.

Hedge, T. (2000), *Teaching and Learning in the Language Classroom*. Oxford and New York: Oxford University Press.

Hennessey, B. A. (2003) 'The Social Psychology of Creativity', *Scandinavian Journal of Educational Research* 47 (3).

Hills, P. J. (1986), *Teaching, Learning and Communication*. London: Croom Helm.

Hodge, B. (1981), *Communication and the Teacher*. Melbourne: Longman Cheshire.

Hymes, D. (1971), 'Competence and Performance in Linguistic Theory', R. Huxley and E. Ingram (eds), *Language Acquisition: Models and Methods*. London: Academic Press.

Ireson, J., Mortimore, P. and Hallam, S. (1999), 'The Common Strands of Pedagogy and Their Implications', P. Mortimore (ed.), *Understanding Pedagogy and its Impact on Learning*. London: Paul Chapman.

Jackson, B. (2002), 'Classic Tracks: Talking Heads 'Psycho Killer', *Mix Magazine*. 1 August 2002.

Jackson, N. (2006), 'Imagining a Different World' in N. Jackson, M. Oliver, M. Shaw and J. Wilson (eds), *Developing Creativity in Higher Education: An Imaginative Curriculum*. London: Routledge.

Jackson, N and Shaw, M. (2006), 'Developing Subject Perspectives on Creativity in Higher Education', in N. Jackson, M. Oliver, M. Shaw and J. Wilson (eds), *Developing Creativity in Higher Education: An Imaginative Curriculum*. London: Routledge.

Jackson, N. and Sinclair, C. (2006), 'Developing Students' Creativity: Searching for an Appropriate Pedagogy', in N. Jackson, M. Oliver, M. Shaw and J. Wilson (eds), *Developing Creativity in Higher Education: An Imaginative Curriculum*. London: Routledge.

Jakobson, R. (1960), 'Concluding Statement: Linguistics and Poetics', in T. A. Sebeok (ed.), *Style and Language*. Cambridge, MA: MIT Press.

Janiszewski, C. (1988), 'Preconscious Processing Effect: The Independence of Attitude Formation and Conscious Thought', *Journal of Consumer Research* 15: 199–209.

Janiszewski, C. (1990), 'The Influence of Print Advertisement Organisation on Affect Towards a Brand Name', *Journal of Consumer Research* 17: 53–65.

Johnson, K. (2001), *An Introduction to Foreign Language Teaching and Learning*. London: Longman Pearson.

Joubert, M. M. (2001), 'The Art of Creative Teaching: NACCCE and Beyond', in A. Craft, B. Jeffrey and M. Liebling, *Creativity in Education*. London: Continuum.

Julien, O. (ed.) (2008), *Sgt. Pepper and the Beatles: It Was Forty Years Ago Today*. Aldershot: Ashgate.

Kessel, C. (2009), *The Words and Music of Tom Waits*. Westport, CT: Praeger.

Keyes, C. (2004), *Rap Music And Street Consciousness*. Illinois: University of Illinois Press.

Kivy, P. (1997), *Philosophies of Arts: An Essay in Differences*. Cambridge: Cambridge University Press.

Landgraf, E. (2014), *Improvisation As Art: Conceptual Challenges, Historical Perspectives*. London: Bloomsbury Academic.

Langer, S. (1956), *Philosophy in a New Key: A Study in the Symbolism of Reason, Rite and Art (Third Edition)*. Cambridge, MA: Harvard University Press.

Langer, S. K. (1953), *Feeling and Form: A Theory of Art Developed from Philosophy in a New Key*. London: Routledge and Kegan Paul

Larsen-Freeman, D. (2003), *Techniques and Principles in Language Teaching (Second Edition)*. Oxford: Oxford University Press.

Laver, J. (1968), 'Voice Quality and Indexical Information', *British Journal of Disorders of Communication* 3: 43–54.

Littlewood, W. (1981), *Communicative Language Teaching: An Introduction*. Cambridge: Cambridge University Press.

Long, M. (1983), 'Does Second Language Instruction Make A Difference? A Review of the Research', *TESOL Quarterly* 17: 359-82.

Longhurst, B. (2007), *Popular Music and Society*. Cambridge: Polity Books.

Lydon, M. (2000), *Ray Charles: The Man and His Music*. New York: Riverhead Books.

Lyons, J. (1970), *Chomsky*. New York: Fontana/Collins.

MacDonald, I. (1994), *Revolution in the Head: The Beatles Records and the Sixties*. London: Pimlico.

Markova, A. (1979), *The Teaching and Mastery of Language*. White Plains, NY: M. E. Sharpe Inc.

McCullough, D. (1978), 'Review of "Lion Heart" by Kate Bush', *Sounds*. 25 November 1978, 37.

McLean, D. (2010), *The Songwriter's Survival Guide to Success*. Milwaukee, WI: Hal Leonard.

Meyer, L. B. (1956), *Emotion and Meaning in Music*. Chicago, IL: University of Chicago Press.

Mills, P. (2010), *Hymns to the Silence: Inside the Words and Music of Van Morrison*. London: Continuum.

Moffatt, J. (1978), *Teaching the Universe of Discourse*. Boston, HN: Houghton Mifflin Co.

Moore, A. (1997), *The Beatles: Sgt. Pepper's Lonely Hearts Club Band*. Cambridge: Cambridge University Press.

Mount, H. (1988), 'Language and Learning in English', J. Hickman and K. Kimberley, *Teachers, Language and Learning*. London: Routledge.

National Advisory Committee on Creative and Cultural Education (NACCCE) (1999), *All Our Futures: Creativity, Culture and Education*. London: DFEE.

Nettl, B. (2002), *Encounters in Ethnomusicology: A Memoir*. Warren, MI: Harmonie Park Press.

O'Brien, L. (1995), *She Bop: The Definitive History of Women in Rock, Pop and Soul*. London: Penguin.

Odam, G. (1995), *The Sounding Symbol: Music Education in Action*. Cheltenham: Stanley Thorne.

Oliver, M., Shah, B., McGoldrick, C. and Edwards, M. (2006), 'Students' Experiences of Creativity', in N. Jackson, M. Oliver, M. Shaw and J. Wilson (eds), *Developing Creativity in Higher Education: An Imaginative Curriculum*. London: Routledge.

Oxford, R. L. (1990), *Language Learning Strategies: What Every Teacher Should Know*. Boston, MA: Heinle and Heinle.

Pavilcevic, M. (1997), *Music Therapy In Context*. London: Jessica Kingsley Publishers.

Penman, I. (1978), 'Review of "Lion Heart" by Kate Bush', *NME*. 25 November 1978, 53.

Periano, J. (2005), *Listening to the Sirens: Musical Technologies and Queer Identity from Homer to Hedwig*. Oakland, CA: California University Press.

Perkins, D. N. (1981), *The Mind's Best Work*. Cambridge, MA: Harvard University Press.

Perone, J. E. (2008), *The Words and Music of Prince*. Westport, CT: Praeger.

Petridis, A. (2005), 'Review of "X and Y" by Coldplay', *The Guardian*. 27 May 2005.

Petridis, A. (2013), 'Review of "Yeesus" by Kanye West', *The Guardian*. 17 June 2013.

Philpott, C. (2001), 'Is Music a Language?', in C. Philpott and C. Plummeridge, *Issues in Music Teaching*. London: Routledge Falmer.

Pilgrim, D. and Ormrod, R. (2013), *Elvis Costello and Thatcherism: A Psycho-Social Exploration*. Aldershot: Ashgate.

Pollack, H. (2006), *George Gershwin: His Life And Work*. Berkeley, CA: University of California Press.

Powell, J. (2010), *How Music Works*. London: Particular Books.

Powell-Jones, T. (1972), *Creative Learning in Perspective*. London: University of London Press.

Raimes, A. (1985), 'What Unskilled ESL Students do when they Write: A Classroom Study of Composing', *TESOL Quarterly* 19/2: 229–55.

Regelski, T. (1998), 'The Aristotelian Bases of Praxis for Music Education and Music Education as Praxis', *Philosophy of Music Education Review* 6 (1): 22–59.

Reimer, B. (1989), *A Philosophy of Music Education (Second Edition)*. Upper Saddle River, NJ: Prentice River.

Reising, R. (ed.) (2002), *Every Sound There Is: The Beatles' Revolver and the Transformation of Rock 'n' Roll*. Aldershot: Ashgate.

Rhodes, M. (1961), 'An Analysis of Creativity', *Phi Delta Kappan* 42: 109–35.

Richards, J. C. and Rodgers, T. S. (2001), *Approaches and Methods in Language Teaching* (2nd edn). Cambridge: Cambridge University Press.

Richards, K. (1977), Interview, *Rolling Stone Magazine*. 5 May 1977.

Robertson, Sandy (1978), 'Review of "The Kick Inside" by Kate Bush', *Sounds*. 18 February 1978, 29.

Rodgers, J. P. (2003), *The Complete Singer Songwriter: A Troubadour's Guide to Writing, Performing and Recording.* Milwaukee, WI: Backbeat Books.

Rogan, J. (1993), *Morrissey and Marr: The Severed Alliance.* London: Omnibus Press.

Rogan, J. (2005), *Van Morrison: No Surrender.* London: Secker and Warburg.

Rooksby, R. (2003), *The Songwriting Sourcebook: How to Turn Chords into Great Songs.* Milwaukee, WI: Backbeat Books.

Rubin, J. (1975), 'What the 'Good Language Learner Can Teach Us', *TESOL Quarterly* 9 (1): 41–51.

Ruggiero, V. R. (1988), *Teaching Thinking Across the Curriculum.* New York: Harper and Row.

Salewicz, C. (ed.) (2009), *Keep on Running: The Story of Island Records.* Island Trading Company.

Sarsani, M. R. (2005), *Creativity in Education.* Delhi: Sarup and Sons.

Sarup, M. (1988), *An Introductory Guide to Post-Structuralism and Postmodernism.* London: Harvester Wheatsheaf.

Schafer, R. M. (1995), 'Argentinian Soundscapes', *British Journal of Music Education* 12 (2): 91–101.

Schippers, H. (2009), *Facing the Music: Shaping Music Education from a Global Perspective.* Oxford and New York: Oxford University Press.

Sheldon, D. A. (2004), 'Listener's Identification of Musical Expression through Figurative Language and Musical Terminology', *Journal of Research in Music Education* 52 (4) (Winter 2004).

Shepherd, J. (1977), 'Whose Music?', in *A Sociology of Music Languages.* London: Transaction Books.

Shilling, J. (2013), 'Interview with Lucinda Williams', *The Telegraph.* 25 May 2013.

Shuker, R. (2001), *Understanding Popular Music (Second Edition).* London: Routledge.

Sim, S. (1992) 'Structuralism and Post-Structuralism', O. Hanfling, *Philosophical Aesthetics: An Introduction.* Oxford: Blackwell/Open University.

Sloboda, J. A. (1985), *The Musical Mind.* Oxford and New York: Oxford University Press.

Small, C. (1998), *Musicking: The Meanings of Performing and Listening*. Hanover, NH: Wesleyan University Press.

Small, C. (1999), *Music of the Common Tongue: Survival and Celebration in Afro-American Music*. Hanover, NH: Wesleyan University Press.

Smith, L. D. (2004), *Elvis Costello, Joni Mitchell and the Torch Song Tradition*. Santa Barbara, CA: Praeger.

Sondheim, S. (2010), *Finishing the Hat*. London: Virgin Books.

Stravinsky, I. (1970), *Poetics of Music in the Form of Six Lessons*, trans. A. Knodel, A and I. Dahl. Cambridge, MA: Harvard University Press.

Sutcliffe, P. (2014), 'Commentary on "Feel It" by Kate Bush', *Mojo* 251. October 2014, 61.

Swain, M. (1985), 'Communicative Competence: Some Roles of Comprehensible Input and Comprehensible Output in Development', in S. Gass and C. Madden (eds), *Input in Second language Acquisition*, 235–56. Rowley, MA: Newbury House.

Swain, M. (1995), 'Three Functions of Output in Second Language Learning', in G. Cook and B. Siedlhofer (eds), *Principle and Practice In Applied Linguistics: Studies In Honour of H. G. Widdowson*. Oxford: Oxford University Press.

Swales, J. (1990), *Genre Analysis*. Cambridge: Cambridge University Press.

Swanwick, K. (1979), *A Basis for Music Education*. Slough: National Foundation for Educational Research.

Swanwick, K. (1999), *Teaching Music Musically*. London: Routledge.

Taylor, A. (1959), 'The Nature of Creative Process', in P. Smith (ed.), *Creativity*. New York: Hastings House.

Tolstoy, L. (1960), *What is Art?*', trans. A. Maude (orig. work published 1896). Indianapolis, IN: Bobbs Merrill.

Torrance, E. P. (1967), 'Creative Teaching Makes a Difference', J. Foster (1967), *Creativity and the Teacher*. Basingstoke: Macmillan.

Toynbee, J. (2000), *Making Popular Music: Music, Creativity and Institutions*. London: Arnold.

Trager, G. L. (1958), 'Paralanguage: A First Approximation', *Studies in Linguistics* 13 (138): 1–12.

Treffinger, D. J., Sortore, M. R. and Cross, J. A. (1993), 'Programs and Strategies for Nurturing Creativity', in K. Heller, F. J.

Monks and A. H. Passow (eds), *International Handbook for Research on Giftedness and Talent*, 555–67. Oxford: Pergamon.

Tricky (2014), 'Introduction to Kate Bush Retrospective', *Mojo* 251. October 2014.

Tucker, M. (1995), *The Duke Ellington Reader*. New York: Oxford University Press.

Tucker, S. (2003), *The Secrets of Songwriting: Leading Songwriters Reveal How to Find Inspiration and Success*. New York: Allworth Press.

Uberg Naerland, T. (2014), 'Rhythm, Rhyme and Reason: Hip Hop Expressivity as Political Discourse', *Popular Music* 33/3. Cambridge: Cambridge University Press.

Urban, K. K. (1996), 'Encouraging and Nurturing Creativity in School and Workplace', in U. Munander and C. Semiawan (eds), *Optimizing Excellence in Human Resource Development*, 78–97, Jakarta: University of Indonesia Press.

Vygotsky, L. S. (1956), *Selected Psychological Investigations*. Moscow: Izdatel'svo Akademiii Pedagogicheskikh Nauk.

Wallas, G. (1926), 'The Art of Thought', in P. Vernon, *Creativity*. London: Penguin.

Webb, J. (1998), *Tunesmith*. New York: Hyperion.

Webster, P. (1996), 'Creativity as Creative Thinking', in G. Spruce (ed.), *Teaching Music*. Milton Keynes: Oxford University Press.

West, A. (2006), 'An Investigation into the Epistemology and Pedagogy of Songwriting with a view to Informing the Development of a Curriculum to Support the Implementation of a Postgraduate Award'. Bath Spa University.

Widdowson, H. G (1978*), Teaching Language as Communication*. London: Oxford University Press.

Wilkins, D. A. (1976), National Syllabuses. Oxford: Oxford University Press.

Wilkinson, A. (1975), *Language and Education*. Oxford and New York: Oxford University Press.

Woffinden, B. (1978), 'Review of "The Kick Inside" by Kate Bush', *NME*. 25 February 1978, 39.

Yager, S., Johnson, D and Johnson, R. (1985), 'Oral Discussion, Group to Individual Transfer, and Achievement in Co-operative Learning Groups', *Journal of Educational Psychology* 77 (1): 60–6.

Zatorre, R. J. and Salimpoor, V. N. (2013), 'Why Music Makes Our Brain Sing', *New York Times*. 7 June 2013, SR12.

Zollo, P. (2003), *Songwriters on Songwriting (Fourth Edition)*. Boston, MA: Da Capo Press.

Interviews

Aldred, S. (2013) *Masterclass with Simon Aldred on 2 October 2013*. Leeds.

Archer, I. (2012) *Interview with Iain Archer at the Leeds International Songwriting Festival on 8 March 2012*. Leeds.

Archer, I. (2014) *Interview and Masterclass with Iain Archer on 10 November 2014*. Leeds.

Ashurst, J. (2014) *Interview with Jez Ashurst on 4 June 2014*. London.

Bourne, M. (2015) *Interview with Matthew Bourne on 7 May 2015*. Leeds.

Brammer, M (2014) *Interview with Martin Brammer on 4 June 2014*. London.

Chrisanthou, S. (2015) *Interview with Steve Chrisanthou on 9 March 2015*. Leeds.

Cottrell, B. (2015) *Interview with Ben Cottrell on 30 March 2015*. Manchester.

Devine, S. (2015) *Interview with Sean Devine on 8 January 2015*. Leeds.

Difford, C. (2009) *Public Interview with Chris Difford on 20 August 2009*. Bath.

Hicks, W. (2014) *Postgraduate Question and Answer Session with Will Hicks on 16 October 2014*. Leeds.

Hook, P. (2012) *Public Interview with Peter Hook on 9 March 2012*. Leeds.

Lascelles, J. (2014) *Interview with Jeremy Lascelles on 19 August 2014*. London.

Myhr, D. (2014) *Interview with David Myhr on 25 November 2014*. Stockholm.

Murphy, R. (2007) *Murphy's Law Of Songwriting Seminar on 12 September 2007*. Bath.

Olney, D. (2002) *Interview with David Olney on 2 March 2002*. Nashville.

Oniyama, J. (2014) *Interview with Josephine Oniyama on 15 September 2014*. Manchester.

Rutter, P. (2015) *Email Correspondence on 15 August 2015*.

Shapiro, S. (2014) *Postgraduate Question and Answer Session with Shain Shapiro on 11 December 2014*. Leeds.

Statham, P. (2015) *Interview with Paul Statham on 9 February 2015*. Leeds.

Turpin, C. and Ward, S. (2015) *Masterclass with Chris Turpin and Stephanie Ward on 26 February 2015*. Leeds.

Website sources

Billboard (2013), 'Review of "Yeesus" Kanye West'. Billboard (online). *Rolling Stone*. June 14 2013. Accessed September 1 2015.

Dolan, J. (2013), 'Review of "Yeesus" by Kanye West'. Jon Dolan. *Rolling Stone* (online). June 14 2013. Accessed September 1 2015.

Dombal, R (2013), 'Review of "Yeesus" by Kanye West'. Ryan Dombel. *Pitchfork* (online). June 18 2013. Accessed September 1 2015.

Feeney, N. (2013), *Why Is Sweden So Good At Pop Music?* Nolan Feeney. *The Atlantic* (online) accessed 13 May 2015.

Meacham, S. (2007), *The Best Bob Dylan Covers*. Steve Meacham. *The Sydney Morning Herald* (online). August 15 2007. Accessed 15 May 2015.

Moore, A. (2004), *Principles For Teaching And Assessing Songwriting In Higher Education*. *Palatine* (online). Accessed 15 May 2015.

Mulligan, M. (2013), 'Streaming Artist Subscriptions: A Product Strategy Proposal. Excerpt from forthcoming book provisionally titled "Meltdown"'. Posted 24 June 2013. Accessed 22 April 2015.

Pappas, S. (2103), 'Songs That Reward The Brain'. Stephanie Pappas. *Live Science* (online). 11 April 2013. Accessed 17 May 2015.

Schwartz, M. (2012), 'Interview with Lucinda Williams by Madeleine Schwartz'. *The Believer* (online). July/August 2012.

Reddington, H. (2006) 'Origins Of The Songbook Module'. *Palatine* (online). Acccessed 15 May 2015.

Reed, L. (2013), 'Review of "Yeesus" by Kanye West'. Erin Coulehan. *Rolling Stone* (online). July 2 2013. Accessed 1 September 2015.

Sounds International (1980), 'Interview with David Tretow'. Accessed 19 April 2015.

Time Magazine (2015), 'Adele is Music's Past, Present and Future'. Sam Lansky. *Time* (online). December 21 2015. Accessed 7 Jan 2016.

Ultimate Classic Rock (2012), '32 Years Ago: Bruce Springsteen Records *Nebraska*'. Accessed 15 May 2015.

Audio sources

ABBA (1974), *Waterloo* (Vinyl) Epic.

ABBA (1976), *Dancing Queen* (Vinyl) Epic.

Adele (2010), *Make You Feel My Love* (CD) XL Recordings.

Adele (2010), *Rolling In The Deep* (CD) XL Recordings.

Adele (2010), *Someone Like You* (CD) XL Recordings.

Albarn, Damon (2014), *Everyday Robots* (CD) Parlophone.

Allen, Lily (2006), *Smile* (CD) Regal.

Allen, Lily (2008), *The Fear* (CD) Regal.

Arcade Fire (2004), *Funeral* (CD) Merge.

Arcade Fire (2007), *Neon Bible* (CD) Merge.

Arcade Fire (2010), *The Suburbs* (CD) Merge.

Arcade Fire (2013), *Reflektor* (CD) Merge.

Arctic Monkeys (2006), *Whatever People Say I Am, That's What I'm Not* (CD) Domino.

Arctic Monkeys (2007), *Flourescent Adolescent* (CD) Domino.

Baker, Chet (1956), *My Funny Valentine* (Vinyl) Pacific Jazz.

Band, The (1969), *The Night They Drove Old Dixie Down* (Vinyl) Capitol.

Beach Boys, The (1968), *Meant For You* (Vinyl) Capitol.

Beatles, The (1963), *Please Please Me* (Vinyl LP) Parlophone.

Beatles, The (1963), *With The Beatles* (Vinyl LP) Parlophone.

Beatles, The (1964), *A Hard Day's Night* (Vinyl LP) Parlophone.

Beatles, The (1965), *Help!* (Vinyl LP) Parlophone.

Beatles, The (1965), *Rubber Soul* (Vinyl LP) Parlophone.

Beatles, The (1966), *Revolver* (Vinyl LP) Parlophone.

Beatles, The (1967), *Sgt. Pepper's Lonely Hearts Club Band* (Vinyl LP) Parlophone.

Beatles, The (1967), *Magical Mystery Tour* (Vinyl LP) Parlophone.

Beatles, The (1968), *Lady Madonna* (Vinyl) Parlophone.

Beatles, The (1968), *The Beatles White Album* (Vinyl LP) Apple.

Beatles, The (1969), *Yellow Submarine* (Vinyl LP) Apple.

Beatles, The (1969), *Abbey Road* (Vinyl LP) Apple.

Beatles, The (1969), *Hey Jude* (Vinyl) Apple.

Beatles, The (1969), *Here Comes The Sun* (Vinyl) Apple.

Beatles, The (1970), *Let It Be* (Vinyl LP) Apple.

Beatles, The (1994), *Live At The BBC* (CD) Apple.

Bee Gees, The (1977), *How Deep Is Your Love* (Vinyl) RSO.

Bee Gees, The (2001), *Heartbreaker* (CD) Polydor/Universal.

Beirut (2011), *Santa Fe* (CD) Pompeii Records.

Bennett, Tony (1957), *Let's Face The Music And Dance* (Vinyl) Columbia Recordings.

Bennett, Tony (1963), *I Wanna Be Around* (Vinyl) Columbia Recordings.

Bennett, Tony (1994), *The Girl I Love* (CD) Columbia Recordings.

Beyonce (2003), *Crazy In Love* (CD) Columbia Recordings.

Birdy (2011), *People Help The People* (Download) Warner Music.

Bjork (1995), *Oh So Quiet* (CD) One Little Indian.

Bourne, Matt (2013), *Montauk Variations* (CD) Leaf.

Bowie, David (1970), *The Man Who Sold The World* (Vinyl) RCA.

Bowie, David (1972), *Star Man* (Vinyl) RCA.

Bowie, David (1973), *Life On Mars* (Vinyl) RCA.

Bowie, David (1973), *Aladdin Sane* (Vinyl LP) RCA.

Bowie, David (1974), *Rebel Rebel* (Vinyl) RCA.

Bowie, David (1977), *Low* (Vinyl LP) RCA.

Bowie, David (1979), *Fantastic Voyage* (Vinyl) RCA.

Brooks, Elkie (1978), *Lilac Wine* (Vinyl) A&M Records.

Bush, Kate (1978), *The Kick Inside* (Vinyl LP) EMI.

Bush, Kate (1980), *Babooshka* (Vinyl) EMI.

Bush, Kate (2011), *50 Words For Snow* (CD) Fish People/EMI.

Callahan, Bill (2011), *One Fine Morning* (CD) Drag City.

Callahan, Bill (2013), *The Sing* (CD) Drag City.

Calloway, Cab (1931), *The Devil And The Deep Blue Sea* (Single) Classics.

Clark, Guy (1975), *Texas, 1947* (Vinyl) RCA.

Clash, The (1977), *Police And Thieves* (Vinyl) CBS.

Clash, The (1979), *London Calling* (Vinyl) CBS.

Coltrane, John and Hartman, Johnny (1963), *Lush Life* (Vinyl) Impulse!

Costello, Elvis and the Attractions (1977), *My Aim Is True* (Vinyl LP) Stiff Records.

Costello, Elvis and the Attractions (1977), *Watching The Detectives* (Vinyl) Stiff Records.

Costello, Elvis and the Attractions (1978), *This Year's Model* (Vinyl LP) Radar.

Costello, Elvis and the Attractions (1979), *Armed Forces* (Vinyl LP) Radar.

Costello, Elvis and the Attractions (1983), *Shipbuilding* (Vinyl) F Beat.

Costello, Elvis and the Attractions (1984), *The Only Flame In Town* (Vinyl) F Beat.

Charles, Ray (1954), *I Got A Woman* (Vinyl) Atlantic.

Charles, Ray (1957), *Greenbacks* (Vinyl) Atlantic.

Charles, Ray (1957) *Halleluyah, I Love Her So* (Vinyl) Atlantic.

Charles, Ray (1959) *What'd I Say* (Vinyl) Atlantic.

Charles, Ray (1960) *Georgia On My Mind* (Vinyl) ABC.

Charles, Ray (1962), *You Don't Know Me* (Vinyl) ABC – Paramount.

Charles, Ray (1964), *Smack Dab In The Middle* (Vinyl) Artone/CBS.

Cherry Ghost (2007), *4AM* (CD) Heavenly Recordings.

Cherry Ghost (2007), *People Help The People* (CD) Heavenly Recordings.

Cherry Ghost (2014), *Clear Skies Ever Closer* (CD) Heavenly Recordings.

Chords, The (1954), *Sh Boom* (Vinyl) Cat Records.

Coldplay (2005), *X and Y* (CD) Parlophone.

Crosby, Bing (1942), *White Christmas* (Single) Decca.

Crow, Sheryl (1994), *Leaving Las Vegas* (CD) A&M Records.

Crow, Sheryl (1997), *Home* (CD) A&M Records.

Crowded House (1988), *Better Be Home Soon* (Vinyl) Capitol.

Crowded House (1988), *Into Temptation* (Vinyl) Capitol.

Crystals, The (1963), *Da Doo Ron Ron* (Vinyl) Philles Records.

Cure, The (1980), *A Forest* (Vinyl) Fiction.

Dylan, Bob (1963), *The Freewheelin' Bob Dylan* (Vinyl LP) Columbia Recordings.

Dylan, Bob (1964), *The Times They Are A Changing* (Vinyl LP) Columbia Recordings.

Dylan, Bob (1964), *Another Side Of Bob Dylan* (Vinyl LP) Columbia Recordings.

Dylan, Bob (1965), *Bringing It All Back Home* (Vinyl LP) Columbia Recordings.

Dylan, Bob (1965), *Highway 61 Revisited* (Vinyl LP) Columbia Recordings.

Dylan, Bob (1966), *Blonde On Blonde* (Vinyl LP) Columbia Recordings.

Dylan, Bob (1967), *John Wesley Harding* (Vinyl LP) Columbia Recordings.

Dylan, Bob (1968), *Nashville Skyline* (Vinyl LP) Columbia Recordings.

Dylan, Bob (1974), *Planet Waves* (Vinyl LP) Asylum Recordings.

Dylan, Bob (1975), *Desire* (Vinyl LP) Columbia Recordings.

Dylan, Bob (1980), *Slow Train Coming* (Vinyl) Columbia Recordings.

Dylan, Bob (1983), *Infidels* (Vinyl LP) Columbia Recordings.

Dylan, Bob (1989), *Oh Mercy* (CD) Columbia Recordings.

Dylan, Bob (1997), *Time Out Of Mind* (CD) Columbia Recordings.

Dury, Ian (1979), *Reasons To Be Cheerful Pt. 3* (Vinyl) Stiff Records.

Dury, Ian (1979), *There Aint Half Been Some Clever Bastards* (Vinyl) Stiff Records.

Earle, Steve (1995), *Tom Ames' Prayer* (CD) Warner Bros.

Elbow (2008), *Starlings* (CD) Fiction/Polydor.

Ellington, Duke and his Orchestra (1944), *Do Nothing Til You Hear From Me* (Single) Victor.

Everly Brothers, The (1958), *All I Have To Do Is Dream* (Vinyl) Cadence Records.

Fall, The (1985), *Cruisers Creek* (Vinyl) Beggars Banquet.

Fall, The (1999), *Touch Sensitive* (Vinyl) Artful.

Fitzgerald, Ella (1956), *Sings The Cole Porter Songbook* (Vinyl LP) Verve.

Fitzgerald, Ella (1958), *Sings The Irving Berlin Songbook* (Vinyl LP) Verve.

Fitzgerald, Ella (1959), *Sings The George And Ira Gershwin Songbook* (Vinyl LP) Verve.

Fitzgerald, Ella and Basie, Count (1963), *Ella and Basie!* (Vinyl) Verve.

Four Tops, The (1966), *Loving You Is Sweeter Than Ever* (Vinyl) Motown.

Franklin, Aretha (1967), *(You Make Me Feel Like) A Natural Woman* (Vinyl) Atlantic.

Gaye, Marvin (1966), *How Sweet It Is (To Be Loved By You)* (Vinyl) Tamla.

Gaye, Marvin (1968), *Heard It Through The Grapevine* (Vinyl) Tamla.

Gaye, Marvin (1971), *What's Going On* (Vinyl LP) Tamla.

Holiday, Billie (1937), *They Can't Take That Away From Me* (Single) Columbia Recordings.

Holiday, Billie (1939), *Strange Fruit* (Single) Commodore.

Holly, Buddy (1957), *Everyday* (Vinyl) Coral.

Holly, Buddy (1958), *That'll Be The Day* (Vinyl) Coral.

Holly, Buddy (1958), *Wishing* (Vinyl) Coral.

Holly, Buddy (1959), *Raining In My Heart* (Vinyl) Coral.

Howlin Wolf (1960), *Spoonful* (Vinyl) Chess Records.

Jam, The (1978), *All Mod Cons* (Vinyl LP) Polydor.

Jam, The (1980), *That's Entertainment* (Vinyl) Polydor.

John, Elton (1971), *Tiny Dancer* (Vinyl) DJM.

John, Elton (1972), *Rocket Man* (Vinyl) DJM.

Johnson, Robert (1937), *Kind Hearted Woman Blues* (Single) Vocalion.

Joy Division (1979), *Transmission* (Vinyl) Factory.

Jones, George (1960), *George Jones Salutes Hank Williams* (Vinyl LP) Mercury.

Jones, Norah (2002), *Don't Know Why* (CD) Blue Note.

Katrina and the Waves (1985), *Walking On Sunshine* (Vinyl) Attic/Capitol.

Kill It Kid (2009), *Kill It Kid* (CD) One Little Indian.

Kill It Kid (2011), *Feet Fall Heavy* (CD) One Little Indian.

Kill It Kid (2014), *You Owe Nothing* (CD) Sire/Warner Music.

Kinks, The (1964), *All Day And All Of The Night* (Vinyl) Pye Records.

Kinks, The (1964), *You Really Got Me* (Vinyl) Pye Records.

Kinks, The (1965), *Tired Of Waiting For You* (Vinyl) Pye Records.

Kinks, The (1967), *Waterloo Sunset* (Vinyl) Pye Records.

Kiwanuka, Michael (2011), *Tell Me A Tale* (CD) Communion.

Kristofferson, Kris (1970), *Help Me Make It Through The Night* (Vinyl) Monument.

Lennon, John (1971), *Jealous Guy* (Vinyl) Parlophone.

Lorde (2013), *Royals* (CD) Lava/Virgin.

Lowe, Nick (2006), *People Change* (CD) Proper/Yep Roc.

Madonna (1984), *Material Girl* (CD) Sire/Warner Bros.

Minogue, Kylie (2001), *Can't Get You Out Of My Head* (CD) Parlophone.

Mockasin, Connan (2010), *Quadropuss Island* (CD) Phantasy Sound.

Morrison, Van (1968), *Madame George* (Vinyl) Warner Bros.

Morrison, Van (1970), *Moondance* (Vinyl) Warner Bros.

Morrison, Van (1972), *Jackie Wilson Said (I'm In Heaven When You Smile)* (Vinyl) Warner Bros.

Morrison, Van and the Chieftains (1988), *Raglan Road* (CD) Mercury.

Napalm Death (1989), *You Suffer* (CD) Earache.

Nelson, Willie (1975), *Red Headed Stranger* (Vinyl LP) Columbia Recordings.

New Order (1983), *Blue Monday* (Vinyl) Factory.

Newman, Randy (1970), *12 Songs* (Vinyl LP) Reprise.

Newman, Randy (1974), *Good Old Boys* (Vinyl LP) Reprise.

Orbison, Roy (1963), *In Dreams* (Vinyl) Monument.

Orbison, Roy (1964), *Oh Pretty Woman* (Vinyl) Monument.

Outkast (2003), *The Way You Move* (CD) Arista Records.

Palmer, Robert (1980), *Johnny And Mary* (Vinyl) Island.

Palmer, Robert (1986), *Addicted To Love* (CD) Island.

Perry, Katy (2013), *Roar* (CD) Capitol.

Petty, Tom (1994), *Honey Bee* (CD) Warner Bros.

Police, The (1983), *Every Breath You Take* (Vinyl) A&M Records.

Presley, Elvis (1955), *That's All Right Mama* (Vinyl) RCA Victor.

Presley, Elvis (1956), *Heartbreak Hotel* (Vinyl) RCA Victor.

Presley, Elvis (1956), *I Got A Woman* (Vinyl) RCA Victor.

Presley, Elvis (1956), *One Sided Love Affair* (Vinyl) RCA Victor.

Presley, Elvis (1972) *Always On My Mind* (Vinyl) RCA.

Prince (1983), *Little Red Corvette* (Vinyl) Warner Bros.

Prince (1986), *Kiss* (CD) Warner Bros.

Prince (1987), *Sign O' The Times* (CD) Warner Bros.

Prince (1994), *The Most Beautiful Girl In The World* (CD) NPG.

Prine, John (1971), *Angel From Montgomery* (Vinyl) Atlantic.

Prine, John (1971), *Hello In There* (Vinyl) Atlantic.
Prine, John (1995), *Aint Hurtin Nobody* (CD) Oh Boy!
Queen (1975), *Bohemian Rhapsody* (Vinyl) EMI.
Radiohead (1992), *Creep* (CD) Parlophone.
Radiohead (1995), *Black Star* (CD) Parlophone.
Radiohead (1995), *High And Dry* (CD) Parlophone.
Radiohead (1997), *Paranoid Android* (CD) Parlophone.
Ramones, The (1979), *I Wanna Be Sedated* (Vinyl) Sire.
Redding, Otis (1968), *Sitting On The Dock Of The Bay* (Vinyl) Volt/Atco.
Reed, Lou (1972), *Perfect Day* (Vinyl) RCA.
REM (1989), *Get Up* (CD) Warner Bros.
REM (1991), *Losing My Religeon* (CD) Warner Bros.
Rogers, Kenny and Parton, Dolly (1983), *Islands In The Stream* (Vinyl) RCA.
Rihanna (2010), *The Only Girl In The World* (CD) Def Jam.
Rolling Stones, The (1968), *Jumpin Jack Flash* (Vinyl) Decca.
Ruffin, Jimmy (1966), *What Becomes Of The Broken Hearted* (Vinyl) Soul.
Sexsmith, Ron (1995), *Secret Heart* (CD) Interscope.
Sexsmith, Ron (1995), *The Words We Never Use* (CD) Interscope.
Sheeran, Ed (2014), *Don't* (CD) Asylum/Atlantic.
Shirelles, The (1960), *Will You Love Me Tomorrow* (Vinyl) Scepter.
Simone, Nina (1966), *Lilac Wine* (Vinyl) Philips.
Sledge, Percy (1966), *It Tears Me Up* (Vinyl) Atlantic.
Small Faces (1968), *Lazy Sunday Afternoon* (Vinyl) Immediate.
Smith, Patti (1978), *Because The Night* (Vinyl) Arista.
Smiths, The (1984), *The Smiths* (CD) Rough Trade.
Smiths, The (1984), *Hatful Of Hollow* (CD) Rough Trade.
Smiths, The (1985), *Meat Is Murder* (CD) Rough Trade.
Smiths, The (1986), *The Queen Is Dead* (CD) Rough Trade.
Smiths, The (1987), *Strangeways Here We Come* (CD) Rough Trade.
Smiths, The (1987), *Louder Than Bombs* (CD) Sire/Warner Bros.
Smog (2000), *Dress Sexy At My Funeral* (CD) Drag City.
Springsteen, Bruce (1975), *Born To Run* (Vinyl) Columbia Recordings.
Springsteen, Bruce (1982), *Nebraska* (Vinyl) Columbia Recordings.
Springsteen, Bruce (1984), *Born In The USA* (Vinyl) Columbia Recordings.

Stranglers, The (1979), *Genetix* (Vinyl) UA.

Stranglers, The (1981), *The Man They Love To Hate* (Vinyl) Liberty.

Stranglers, The (1982), *Golden Brown* (Vinyl) Liberty.

Stravinsky, Igor (1913), *Rite Of Spring*. Boosey and Hawkes.

Streets, The (2002), *The Irony Of It All* (CD), Locked On/679 Recordings.

Supremes, The (1964), *Where Did Our Love Go* (Vinyl) Motown.

Supremes, The (1965), *Stop! In The Name Of Love* (Vinyl) Motown.

Supremes, The (1967), *You Can't Hurry Love* (Vinyl) Motown.

Talking Heads (1977), *Psycho Killer* (Vinyl) Sire.

Television (1977), *Marquee Moon* (Vinyl) Elektra.

Temptations, The (1964), *My Girl* (Vinyl) Gordy.

Thompson, Richard (1992), *Vincent Black Lightning 1952* (CD) Capitol.

U2 (1987), *With Or Without You* (CD) Island.

Undertones, The (1979), *Teenage Kicks* (Vinyl) Good Vibrations.

Verdi, Giuseppe (1853), *La Traviata*. Milan: G.Ricordi and C.

Waits, Tom (1973), *Closing Time* (Vinyl LP) Asylum.

Waits, Tom (1974), *The Heart Of Saturday Night* (Vinyl LP) Asylum.

Waits, Tom (1977), *Foreign Affairs* (Vinyl LP) Elektra.

Waits, Tom (1978), *Blue Valentines* (Vinyl LP) Asylum.

Waits, Tom (1980), *Heartattack And Vine* (Vinyl LP) Asylum.

Waits, Tom (1983), *Swordfishtrombones* (CD) Island.

Waits, Tom (1985), *Rain Dogs* (CD) Island.

Waits, Tom (1987), *Frank's Wild Years* (CD) Island.

Waits, Tom (1992), *Bone Machine* (CD) Island.

Waits, Tom (1993), *Black Rider* (CD) Island.

Waits, Tom (1999), *Mule Variations* (CD) Anti.

Waits, Tom (2002), *Blood Money* (CD) Anti.

Waits, Tom (2004), *Real Gone* (CD) Anti.

Waits, Tom (2011), *Bad As Me* (CD) Anti.

Warwick, Dionne (1964), *Walk On By* (Vinyl) Scepter.

Warwick, Dionne (1969), *I'll Never Fall In Love Again* (Vinyl) Scepter.

Webb, Jimmy (1996), *By The Time I Get To Phoenix* (CD) Guardian.

Welch, Gillian (1996), *Revival* (CD) Almo Sounds.

Welch, Gillian (1998), *Hell Among The Yearlings* (CD) Acony.

Welch, Gillian (2001), *Time (The Revelator)* (CD) Acony.

Weller, Paul (2010), *Trees* (CD) Island.

West, Kanye featuring Jay Z. (2005), *Diamonds From Sierra Leone (Remix)* (CD) Roc A Fella/Def Jam.

West, Kanye (2013), *Yeesus* (CD) Def Jam Recordings.

Wilco (2001), *Yankee Hotel Foxtrot* (CD) Nonesuch.

Wilco (2004), *A Ghost Is Born* (CD) Nonesuch.

Williams, Hank (1949), *My Bucket's Got A Hole In It* (Single) MGM.

Williams, Hank (1950), *Mansion On The Hill* (Single) MGM.

Williams, Hank (1953), *I'm So Lonesome I Could Cry* (Single) MGM.

Williams, Lucinda (1992), *Sweet Old World* (CD) Chameleon Records.

Williams, Lucinda (1998), *Car Wheels On A Gravel Road* (CD) Mercury.

Williams, Lucinda (2011), *Blessed* (CD) Mercury.

Williams, Pharrell (2013), *Happy* (CD) Back Lot/Columbia.

Winehouse, Amy (2006), *Back To Black* (CD) Island.

Wire (1977), *Pink Flag* (Vinyl LP) Harvest Records.

Wonder, Stevie (1985), *Overjoyed* (Vinyl), Tamla Motown.

Wyatt, Robert (1982), *Shipbuilding* (Vinyl) Rough Trade.

Film sources

CMT Crossroads Featuring Lucinda Williams and Elvis Costello (2002), CMT. Friday 13 January 2002.

Rockpalast Featuring Elvis Costello and the Attractions (1978), Germany. Thursday 15 June 1978.

The Clash: Westway To The World (2000), directed by Don Letts (DVD) UK: 3DD Entertainment.

The Joy Of Abba (2013), BBC4. Friday 27 December 2013.

Wings Of Desire (1987), directed by Wim Wenders (DVD) Germany: Road Movies Filmproduktion.

INDEX